PAMPHLET WARS

PAMPHLET WARS
Prose in the
English Revolution

Edited by
JAMES HOLSTUN
*State University of New York,
Buffalo*

FRANK CASS

First published in 1992 in Great Britain by
FRANK CASS & CO. LTD.
Gainsborough House, Gainsborough Road,
London E11 1RS, England

and in the United States of America by
FRANK CASS
c/o International Specialized Book Services, Inc.
5602 N.E. Hassalo Street, Portland, Oregon 97213

British Library Cataloguing in Publication Data

Pamphlet wars: prose in the English Revolution.
I. Holstun, James
828.40809372

ISBN 0 7146 3458 1

Library of Congress Cataloging-in-Publication Data

Pamphlet wars: prose in the English Revolution/edited by James Holstun
    p. cm.
    ISBN 0–7146–3458–1
    1. English prose literature—Early modern, 1500–1700—History and criti-
cism. 2. Great Britain—History—Puritan Revolution, 1642–1660—Literature
and the revolution. 3. Great Britain—History—Puritan Revolution,
1642–1660—Pamphlets. 4. Revolutionary literature, English—History and
criticism. 5. Politics and literature—England—History —17th century. 6.
Puritans in literature. I. Holstun, James.
PR769.P36 1992
828'.40809—dc20   91–32710
                                                                          CIP

This group of studies first appeared in a special issue on "Pamphlet Wars: Prose
in the English Revolution" of *Prose Studies*, Vol. 14, No. 3, published by Frank
Cass & Co. Ltd.

Printed in Great Britain by Antony Rowe Ltd.

For Olivier Lutaud

Contents

Notes on Contributors

Sharon Achinstein is Assistant Professor of English at Northwestern University. She has written articles on Bacon, Milton, and popular literature of the Renaissance and is currently working on a book on the idea of the public in the English Revolution.

Joan E. Hartman is Professor of English at the College of Staten Island, City University of New York. She has written on Clarendon, Milton, women's studies and professional issues, and is secretary-treasurer of the (New York) Society for the Study of Women in the Renaissance. She is an editor of *The Norton Reader* and has also edited (with Ellen Messer-Davidow) three collections of essays: *Women in Print I* and *II* (1982) and *(En)Gendering Knowledge: Feminists in Academe* (1991).

James Holstun is a graduate of the University of California at Irvine and Associate Professor of English at SUNY Buffalo. He is the author of *A Rational Millennium: Puritan Utopias of Seventeenth-Century England and America* (1987) and is now at work on a study of tyrannicide and sectarianism in the seventeenth century and socialist humanism in the twentieth.

Peter J. Kitson has lectured in English at Edge Hill College of Higher Education and the University of Exeter. He now teaches at the University of Wales, Bangor. He has published articles in *Prose Studies, The Yearbook of English Studies*, and *The Wordsworth Circle*, and is the editor of *Romantic Criticism 1800–25* and (with T.N. Corns) *Coleridge and the Armoury of the Human Mind: Essays on His Prose Writings*. He is currently working on a study of religious radicalism from Milton to Coleridge.

Ann Marie McEntee holds a Ph.D. in Theatre from UCLA, where she has guest lectured. She currently teaches at Antioch University, Los Angeles, and the Stella Adler Conservatory for Acting.

Byron Nelson is Associate Professor of English at West Virginia University. His main research interests are the Ranters, opera, and modern drama; he is at work on a book on the Ranters.

Keith Stavely is a librarian and independent scholar. He is the author of *The Politics of Milton's Prose Style* (1975) and *Puritan Legacies:* Paradise Lost *and the New England Tradition, 1630–1890* (1987).

Rachel Trubowitz is an Assistant Professor of English at the University of New Hampshire. Her main research interests are in the construction of gender and the interplay between competing utopian paradigms in seventeenth-century England.

Susan Wiseman teaches English and American Literature at the University of Kent at Canterbury.

Introduction

JAMES HOLSTUN

> Our focus, then, is upon high culture and principally upon poetry, not because they embrace all our concerns but because here the most innovative work is currently in progress which may elucidate those broader concerns.
>
> <div align="right">Kevin Sharpe and Steven N. Zwicker,
Introduction to <i>Politics of Discourse</i>: <i>The Literature
and History of Seventeenth-Century England</i> (1987)</div>

> The Cavaliers are foes, stand up now, stand up now,
> The Cavaliers are foes, stand up now;
> The Cavaliers are foes, themselves they do disclose
> By verses, not in prose, to please the singing boys.
> Stand up now, Diggers all!
>
> <div align="center">Gerrard Winstanley, <i>A Digger Song</i> (1649)</div>

Winstanley's song is amusingly paradoxical. Certainly, the Cavaliers were not reluctant to disclose themselves in prose as well as verse. And their radical opponents (including Milton, Wither and, here, Winstanley himself) availed themselves of verse. But for the most part, the pamphlet wars of 1640–60 were prose wars. With the *de facto* breakdown of censorship, the period saw a staggering output of more than 20,000 books, pamphlets, broadsides and newspapers: sermons and scriptural commentaries mixed with satires and fictions, political theory and manifestos – a polyglot Babel of print (at least from a conservative perspective, as Sharon Achinstein shows below), and almost all of it prose.[1] None the less, critics of seventeenth-century English literature have usually allowed the singing boys to drown out the prose imagination of mid-century. Sharpe and Zwicker's decision to embrace a top-down hermeneutic focusing on high-culture poetry is all too common. But if we focus on the poetry of dominant culture alone (or worse, say that its study will "elucidate" everything else), we not only consign to oblivion the remarkable prose works of radicals like Winstanley, we also risk ignoring or misunderstanding the polemical responses (in prose and poetry) of their opponents. We even risk losing sight of the Revolution itself. Sharpe and Zwicker, for instance, move easily from focusing on high culture and poetry to calling the Revolution "the finest demonstration"

1

of the "early Stuart vision or ideal of a unified polity"; indeed, they use "seventeenth-century England" and "Stuart England" interchangeably.[2]

The period from 1640 to 1660 has always been one of the most contested eras of English social and political history and, if anything, it now looms larger than ever – despite and even because of revisionist attacks on the very idea of an English Revolution, and an emerging counterattack.[3] None the less, the period continues to be one of the great lacunae in British literary history. It tends to appear in prospect (through a study of prescient political rumblings in Caroline masques) or retrospect (through a study of Milton's major poems), but seldom in the contemporary voices of the men and women who made it. The revolutionary era disappears from anthologies, literary histories and critical studies of the period with an alarming regularity. The Oxford *Literature of Renaissance England* acknowledges it through a few lyrics from Lovelace, Marvell and Milton, and excerpts from *Leviathan* and *Areopagitica*. The *Norton Anthology* adds a selection from the diary of Lady Anne Halkett, a whimsically presented excerpt from Lilburne, and a bit of Clarendon – that eminent stylist whose learning and formality of method "save him from many of the failings of partisanship." In their historical introduction to the seventeenth century, the editors remark that the Revolution was "In more senses than one . . . the central event of the century." But all in all, the image of the century's middle years is one of "hoarse and incoherent warfare" – in other words, Babel.[4]

This critical neglect of literature in the English Revolution is not altogether a plot concocted by formalist Tory editors. For more than 40 years, Christopher Hill has been building an astonishingly detailed Marxist account of the Revolution, and he is likely to remain the most influential historian of the period for some time to come. But in a recent essay entitled "Literature and the English Revolution," even he has some trouble in writing about his ostensible subject. For Hill, "literature" includes almost exclusively works printed before 1642 and after 1660, and his express goal is to see how pre-revolutionary literature can help to explain the outbreak of the Revolution, not to examine the concrete role literature may have had in it. In *Dragons Teeth: Literature in the English Revolution*, Michael Wilding follows a similar course, concentrating on pre-revolutionary works by Browne (*Religio Medici*) and Milton ("Nativity Ode," "Lycidas," *Comus*), and on post-revolutionary works by Milton (the major poems) and Butler (*Hudibras*). The only revolutionary-era works he focuses on are Marvell's "An Horatian Ode" and "Upon Appleton House."[5] And indeed, along with Milton's prose works, Marvell's poems (particularly "An Horatian Ode") are the exceptions that prove the rule of general neglect.

One might concede more readily that the revolutionary era did not really produce much "literary" prose of note if this led us not to ignore its remarkable writing but to examine more carefully our concept of "literature." The very term – always a bit dissonant when applied to writing before the nineteenth century – becomes very problematic indeed when applied to the prose of the English Revolution. To begin with, the pamphlets are diffuse, scattered and rather difficult to anthologize. It is not very surprising that Marvell's "An Horatian Ode" and Milton's "Avenge, O Lord, thy slaughtered saints" are better known than, say, Edwards's *Gangraena* and Harrington's *Oceana*. The authors of pamphlets tend to be obscure, anonymous, or corporate – perhaps the worst sin of all, given our habitually subject-centred way of defining "literature."

And the pamphlets – which frequently proclaim on their surfaces their overtly practical ends – do not immediately give themselves up to formalist techniques for the literary analysis of non-fictional prose. The literary study of Renaissance prose has typically appeared under the heading of prose stylistics – an attempt to study prose works as autobiography; or as classical, anti-classical, or Ramist rhetoric; or as imagistically-rich, well-wrought prose poems or self-consuming artifacts. These approaches work rather well with a canon of (usually Anglican and high cultural) prose by Donne, Bacon, Andrewes, Hooker, Browne, Burton, and even Milton and Bunyan,[6] but they have not been notably successful with the pamphlet literature of the revolutionary era. For instance, the antinomian stylistic excesses in the anonymous Ranter pamphlet, *A Justification of the Mad Crew*, do not immediately call out for the ministrations of prose stylistics, whether autobiographical (who is the I being fashioned here?), rhetorical (Ciceronian or Attic periods?), or formalist (what is the unifying structure of imagery?). Historically speaking, the study of these pamphlets seems almost inevitably to veer away from prose stylistics – not into the high theory of semiotics, hermeneutics and deconstruction, but into what we might call the study of language in culture, or (in its more modern forms) cultural materialism. The true imaginative vision of these pamphlets lies in their dogged but brilliant attempts to stake out new subject positions in a politically unsettled time – new models of writerly authority, new modes of collective life in the present, new languages for a New Jerusalem or a new/old court.

But this brings us to another surprising omission. If it is not premature to do so, we might characterize the 1980s as the decade of politicized post-structuralism, when Renaissance critics (or at least a brilliant and prolific avant-garde among them) argued for the essentially political nature of all writing, including literature. We might have expected such an era to produce a great resurgence of interest in the politically-saturated writings of the English Revolution. Strangely enough, though, the English Revolution has barely registered in the first decade of the new historicism and cultural materialism, which have focused on the exploration narratives, public and private drama, court culture, and coterie literature of pre-revolutionary England. I think this is partly because these criticisms tend to view "politics" as something done *to* human subjects, whereas the revolutionary years suggest rather strongly that politics is also something done *by* them – a complex array of elective practices by which human beings sometimes quite consciously make and remake themselves and their own history. The idea of revolution, counter-revolution and an engaged textual praxis associated with them sits uneasily inside the post-structuralist model of contained subversion, subjectification and theatrical display. New historicists and cultural materialists sometimes seem inclined to depict early Stuart England as a closed, deferential economy of discourse, power and patronage. Whatever the merits of this model, it is difficult to envision a similar economy that would contain the conflicts of the revolutionary era: the two Civil Wars, the rise of the New Model Army and the Putney Debates, the regicide and its aftermath, the formation of a Royalist counter-culture in exile, the Leveller Rising of 1649, the appearance of female prophets, the proliferation of political theory (patriarchalist, Hobbist, casuist, democratic, socialist, republican) and religious sects (Independents, Separatists, Baptists, Ranters, Quakers, Muggletonians, and millenarians of various stripes) – all articulated in an explosion of presses, pamphlets and newsbooks. Something more than a philosophically rigorous debunking of the liberal humanist subject seems to be called for.[7]

We might also trace this neglect of the revolutionary era to the dialectically polemical approach of the new historicism and cultural materialism: if one can still raise a few formalist hackles by claiming that Shakespeare, Donne and Herbert are political to the bone, a similar claim made for Marchamont Nedham, Anna Trapnel and Edward Sexby would produce either an immediate puzzled consent, or (more likely) a puzzled query as to the identity of these obscure figures. Anti-formalist critics of Renaissance literature still turn instinctively to the figure of the identifiable canonical author, even if they proceed to problematize that figure ruthlessly. They are still much more likely to engage their formalist predecessors on their own poetic and dramatic terrain than to view them from the perspective of the mid-century pamphlet wars. Strangely enough, in the midst of fast and furious attacks on canonical authors, the writers of revolutionary-era prose (Milton always excepted) continue to languish in the shadows of Sidney, Spenser, Shakespeare, Donne, Jonson, Herbert and Marvell.[8]

Still, this chronicle of gross neglect has been somewhat disingenuous, for just as interest in revolutionary-era prose fails to turn up where it ought to, so it turns up where it ought not to. A theoretically adventurous criticism determined to demonstrate its ruptural break with all existent criticism might well characterize the period of 1935–75 as the benighted epoch of high formalism, when the New Critic's fixation on lyric poetry and insistence on the independence of literature *qua* literature from its historical and political context should have made revolutionary-era pamphlets quite invisible. Yet it is during this period that we see the most substantial literary critical work on the English Revolution, including excellent editions of the Army Debates, the Levellers, the Diggers, Hobbes, Harrington, and that prodigious corporate achievement, the Yale *Complete Prose Works of John Milton*.[9] This period also saw the work of a number of brilliant writers on Puritanism and the revolutionary era who were by no means given to glib formalist denunciations of historicism and the heresy of paraphrase: William Haller, Perry Miller, Don M. Wolfe, Geoffrey Nuttall, Joseph Frank, Christopher Hill, Olivier Lutaud, J.G.A. Pocock and Sacvan Bercovitch. Many of these writers practise a mix of textual history, the history of ideas and literary history which is perhaps some distance from the post-structuralist and neo-Marxist emphases of the newer literary historicisms. None the less, they offer a concrete study of language in culture and a philologically detailed account of the English Revolution which have not yet been thoroughly integrated into the cultural materialist study of the seventeenth century.[10]

Most encouraging of all, there are signs of increasing critical attention to the pamphlet wars of the Revolution. To begin with, there is a continuing interest in Milton's prose works, and an increasing interest in seeing them in their polemical context.[11] Some new historicists have begun to display a certain uneasiness about the methodological implications of eliding the Revolution; as David Norbrook warns, "a cultural theory ought not to lead to the logical deduction that the English Revolution cannot have happened."[12] Furthermore, recent years have seen the appearance of several new anthologies of revolutionary-era prose, collections of essays on literature and the English Revolution (though not always literature *of* the English Revolution), and book-length studies of revolutionary-era writers.[13] Many others are in progress or soon to appear.

The essays in this volume are another sign of this increasing interest. All nine authors pursue studies of language in revolutionary culture, and they cover an unusually broad range of writers: Clarendon and royalist prose satirists, female prophets and Levellers, Roger Williams and radical republicans, Diggers and Ranters, and a later generation of writers reinterpreting the Revolution in a new revolutionary context. The emphasis is, perhaps, on the radical side of the spectrum, but not out of any desire simply to invert Sharpe and Zwicker's "top-down" model of culture. Rather, all nine essays work from what we might call (after Bakhtin) a dialogical model, focusing on the dynamic conversations, arguments and polemical conflicts between the various social sites (classes, genres, creeds, genders, political theories, physical places) that define the landscape of the revolutionary era.[14]

As Sharon Achinstein argues in "The Politics of Babel," one key concept for understanding the pamphlet wars of the English Revolution is Jürgen Habermas's idea of the public sphere: a space for publication, discourse and debate distinct from the sphere of the state. Habermas tends to associate this public sphere with the Enlightenment, but we might want to see one prototype in the Florentine republican ideal of the civil conversation, and another in the extraordinary civic culture of print and polemic that developed during the *de facto* breakdown of censorship in revolutionary England. This revolutionary public sphere is fundamentally a site of debate and controversy – not the hermetic closure of an Elizabethan world picture or a Foucauldian episteme, but a new public theatre of vigorous polyphonic controversy. Achinstein examines the opening-up of this public sphere and the anxious attempts by conservative satirists to master it by characterizing it as a mere Babel of voices – attempts which merely added other voices. She also constructs a dialogical analysis of one seventeenth-century dialogue, showing how the "low" genres of pamphlets and polemical controversy about untrammelled sectarian publication interact with the "high" genres of political theory and linguistic philosophy searching for a universal language during the Revolution and after.

In "Restyling the King: Clarendon Writes Charles I," Joan E. Hartman shows that these new voices were not the monopoly of the revolutionaries. Analysing what Clarendon called the pre-war "paper skirmishes" between King and Parliament before the outbreak of armed conflict, she argues that Clarendon, writing for Charles, tried to appropriate both the implied audience and the arguments of the parliamentarians. Clarendon presented the King's case against Parliament by opening up his state cabinet and sharing the *arcana imperii* with the English people – or at least claiming to do so. Clarendon appropriated Parliament's very arguments about the sanctity of property, the rights of the subject, the ancient constitution, and the necessity of parliamentary consultation with the King in making law. Hartman's article underlines one of the most important facts about the languages of controversy throughout the revolutionary era: they are always politically charged, but we cannot neatly read off polemical positions from them. In June 1642, Charles's propagandists issued *His Majesty's Answer to the Nineteen Propositions of Both Houses of Parliament*, which invokes the republican and potentially radical model of England as a mixed polity of king, lords and commons.[15] One month later, we can hear the two Houses appropriating a deferential rhetoric in their vote "that an army shall be forthwith raised for the safety of the king's person" – the outbreak of the Revolution.[16] We see parliamentarians like George Wither and even (as I argue below) sectarians like Gerrard Winstanley appropriating the powerful royalist rhetoric of the body politic. We see John Gauden drawing on the radical tradition of the Marian martyrs in *Eikonoklastes*, and radical Fifth Monarchists employing a strange rhetoric of kingly deference in their struggles against Cromwell and Charles II. The point here is not that these languages are radically indeterminate, but that (as Achinstein argues) they are the objects as well as the media of political conflict.

The Ranters were, perhaps, the most notoriously theatrical inhabitants of the new revolutionary public sphere, and they have become a *cause célèbre* in the wake of J.C. Davis's revisionist attempt to characterize them as a fictive projection of twentieth-century radical historians. In "The Ranters and the Limits of Language," Byron Nelson begins with a critique of Davis, arguing that the best possible evidence for the Ranters' seventeenth-century existence is the remarkable tracts they left behind them, and the accounts of their performances. Nelson sees the Ranters moving beyond a search for representational or natural language to a theory of language as pure performance and play. Ranter Abiezer Coppe, for instance, eschews the formal construction of a coherent self and disperses himself into multiple theatrical personalities, and he adapts the Cavalier practices of blasphemy, bawdy and festivity to a new antinomian street theatre. But while Nelson's theory of Ranter play challenges an emphasis (by Christopher Hill and others) on their social radicalism, he also argues that Ranter play was finally not the masterly and self-sufficient play of Huizinga's *homo ludens*. With their apparent exhaustion of the possibilities of religious language, and their inability to move from street theatre to a more permanent social practice, the Ranters' sense of playfulness was always mixed with despair and an awareness of its own inadequacy.

Keith Stavely examines a different sort of despair in "Roger Williams: Bible Politics and Bible Art." If the Ranters and their radical spiritist allies in England and New England insisted on connecting religion and politics, Williams insisted on distinguishing them. In Stavely's analysis, Williams becomes an agent of secularization precisely by insisting on the integrity and independence of these spheres. Specifically, Williams resisted incursions into the political sphere by a religious sphere marching under the banner of the elect nation – that radical but oppressive notion that led in England and New England to (among other things) imperialism, genocide and the stifling of dissent. The paradox here is that, in his effort to prevent the corrupt human imagination from presenting itself as the immutable will of God, Williams began to frown on human imagination itself, and all its efforts to realize itself through aesthetic and collective practice. Despite some early inclination to the sorts of radical spiritism that flourished among his contemporaries (including Milton, Bunyan and the Quakers), Williams found himself more and more dominated by a "relentless negativity" that denounced as idolatrous all the products of the human imagination. As a result, Stavely says, Williams becomes "a prototypical liberal, on the one hand advocating freedom, and on the other denying the legitimacy of most forms of its exercise."

One of the primary fictions of order for the early Stuart state was the patriarchalist analogy articulated in courtly literature and in the political writings of James Stuart and Robert Filmer. In this analogy, the king is to subjects as the father is to wife and children: a natural and unchallengeable lord. During the Revolution, Stuart patriarchalism came under explicit attack by radical theorists of revocable contract, civil and marital. It also came under implicit attack by women entering the public sphere – women whose "clamorous" voices caused the conservative satirists particular anxieties. Three of the essays focus on questions of gender identity in the revolutionary era – as women constructed it for themselves, as it was constructed for them, and as female gender identity became a factor in homosocial conflicts between conflicting male authorities. In "'The [Un]Civill-Sisterhood of Oranges and Lemons': Female Petitioners and Demonstrators, 1642–53," Ann Marie McEntee focuses on the discourse and practice of radical women. The wives and other women allies of the male Levellers claimed a public voice by invoking scriptural precedents and legends of female Worthies, by underlining their economic and familial contributions to the war effort, and by insisting on their own power as rational political agents. Here, too, we see a certain conservative resistance to the emergence of a specifically political public sphere, for satirists attempted to recode the Leveller women's public political language and practice as a sort of libidinal pathology caused by housewives improperly venturing out of doors.

The image of female crowds asserting their political rights in public – an event inconceivable in the pre-revolutionary world – certainly presents us with one example of what Rachel Trubowitz calls a "loosening of gender categories" in revolutionary England. In "Female Preachers and Male Wives: Gender and Authority in Civil War England," she examines another: the publishing and public preaching of women prophets. Not only did the association of women and inspired prophecy make possible a new role in the public sphere for women prophets such as Elizabeth Poole, Anna Trapnel and Katherine Chidley, it also made possible a feminized public identity for radical males (such as Cromwell), who could help to overturn the severely hierarchical implications of the Jacobean model of patriarchy by depicting themselves as the "nursing fathers" of their diverse commonwealth. Yet Trubowitz also examines the emergence of a new, non-patriarchal mode of male domination among the radical sectarians, particularly utopian writers such as Bacon, Harrington and Winstanley, and Milton in *Paradise Lost*. If McEntee reveals the way in which the revolutionary years made possible an emancipatory practice in which women could articulate a new collective identity for themselves as rational political actors, then Trubowitz shows the susceptibility of a similar practice to partial appropriation and mastery by new strategies of male domination.

In "'Adam, the Father of all Flesh': Porno-Political Rhetoric and Political Theory in and After the English Civil War," Susan Wiseman provides a historical context for understanding one of the most curious aspects of revolutionary-era political polemic: its habitual recourse to sexual raillery. A bawdy attack on a libertine republican like Henry Marten, Wiseman argues, is both a displaced version of a political attack on his republican principles, and a political attack in itself. Conservative patriarchalists relied on women as the silent and unproblematic but absolutely essential media of social exchange. When radical republicans like Marten destabilized this exchange, patriarchalists resorted to sexual raillery out of a sort of conceptual vertigo. Reconstructing another dialogue between high and low genres, Wiseman also examines Henry Neville's Restoration proto-robinsonade, *The Isle of Pines*, as a republican critique of Filmer's patriarchalist theory. By showing the degeneration of George Pine's fecund shipwrecked descendants, Neville argues that social chaos results from relying on the natural authority of fathers apart from artificial and contractual civil law.

In "Rational Hunger: Gerrard Winstanley's *Hortus Inconclusus*," I examine the recent renaissance of "local studies" from the point of view of the Diggers' utopian communism. Revisionists and new historicists

have criticized as over-theorized and anachronistic the liberal and
Marxist focus on such large and totalizing categories as seventeenth-
century revolution, ideology and class. Instead, they say we should
focus on the hard facts of local history, local knowledge, deference,
festivity and the experience of the body. Suggesting that this is a false
binary, I argue that a particular sort of localized bodily experience
(the hunger of dispossessed rural tenants) provides the Diggers with
the occasion for a full-scale, class-based critique of English society,
and a theory for a communist alternative which will overcome the
class domination inherent in both nostalgic paternalism and utopian
proposals for agricultural enclosure and improvement. The Diggers'
utopian georgic remains out of step with its contemporary dominant
culture, embodied in the aristocratic pastoral of the country-house
poem. Its alternative temporality reaches out to a future of oppositional
agrarian socialism, stretching as far as the present-day struggles of the
Amazonian forest people.

The English Revolution was and is rich with utopian futurity – a
fact that we can read in the recurrent attempts to master it, contain it,
periodize it, declare it completed, corrected, outgrown, derailed, null
and void. These attempts stretch from the crushing of the Levellers
at Burford in 1649, to the Cromwellian settlement of 1653, to the
Restoration, to the Glorious Revolution, to the attempts by Whig
historians to present the Revolution as a chapter in the rise of parliamentary democracy, to contemporary attempts by revisionist historians to
present it as a neo-medieval war of religion or a "rebellion" rather
than a modern revolution. But we can also read this utopian futurity
in the recurrent attempts to revivify and reappropriate the Revolution,
to view contemporary events from its perspective, and vice versa. In
"'Sages and patriots that being dead do yet speak to us': Readings of
the English Revolution in the Late Eighteenth Century," Peter Kitson
examines one episode in this Utopian afterlife. After critiquing the
implicit (sometimes explicit) new historicist prohibition against turning
from synchronic to diachronic cultural analysis, he turns to a group of
English and Anglo-Irish political writers who juxtaposed the English
and the French Revolutions. Kitson examines the diverse attempts
to emplot the earlier revolution as an eruption of antinomian and
libertarian energies that threaten to erupt again (Burke), or as a series
of tragic backslidings to Cromwellian and Stuart tyranny that might
be averted (Burg), or as a premature revolution without adequate
popular support whose failings can be corrected in the Jacobin era
of mass enlightenment (Thelwall). Most striking of all, he reveals a
radical republican Coleridge – one who moves towards a Christian

socialist position like Gerrard Winstanley's (whom he did not know) by thinking his way through the bourgeois republicanism of James Harrington.

NOTES

1. Joseph Frank has estimated that prose works account for more than 94 per cent of the titles published between 1640 and 1660 in England, and for more than 99 per cent of the total output of print. *Hobbled Pegasus: A Descriptive Bibliography of Minor English Poetry, 1641–1660* (Alburquerque: University of New Mexico Press, 1968), 5.
2. Kevin Sharpe and Steven N. Zwicker, eds., *Politics of Discourse: The Literature and History of Seventeenth-Century England* (Berkeley: University of California Press, 1987), vii, 3. Fortunately, all of Sharpe and Zwicker's contributors to this stimulating volume do not follow suit. For a full-scale development of Sharpe and Zwicker's monolithic, top-down model of culture, see Sharpe's "A Commonwealth of Meanings" in his *Politics and Ideas in Early Stuart England* (London: Pinter, 1989). Sharpe's decision to use "commonwealth" to indicate a happy hierarchy of epistemological consensus is, to say the least, bold and colourful, and it would no doubt be of some interest to both the commonwealthsmen who went to the scaffold in the 1660s and their royalist executioners.
3. For a critical review of historical revisionism and powerful models of an alternative historical practice, see Richard Cust and Ann Hughes, eds., *Conflict in Early Stuart England: Studies in Religion and Politics 1613–1642* (London: Longman, 1989); and Geoff Eley and William S. Hunt, eds., *Reviving the English Revolution: Reflections and Elaborations on the Work of Christopher Hill* (London: Verso, 1988).
4. John Hollander and Frank Kermode, eds., *The Literature of Renaissance England* (New York: Oxford University Press, 1973); M.H. Abrams *et al.*, eds., *The Norton Anthology of English Literature*, Vol. 1 (New York: Norton, 1986), 1733, 1049, 1056.
5. Christopher Hill, "Literature and the English Revolution" in *A Nation of Change and Novelty: Radical Politics, Religion and Literature in Seventeenth-Century England* (London and New York: Routledge, 1990), 195–217. For Hill's forays into literary criticism, see his *Milton and the English Revolution* (New York: Viking, 1977), and his "Radical Prose in 17th Century England: From Marprelate to the Levellers," *Essays in Criticism*, 32:2 (1982), 95–118. It seems to me that Hill's main weaknesses as a literary critic are his tendencies to read off ideological positions too quickly from literary texts, and to veer off from formal/historical analysis into allegorical readings. But such a critique should perhaps begin by acknowledging the ineradicable presence of a mimetic or allegorical moment in all criticism and all literature. Michael Wilding, *Dragons Teeth: Literature in the English Revolution* (Oxford: Clarendon, 1987).
6. For an excellent collection of critical essays in this tradition, see Stanley Fish, ed., *Seventeenth-Century Prose: Modern Essays in Criticism* (New York: Oxford University Press, 1971). These essays and the generally formalist methods they embody have by no means been rendered altogether obsolete by post-structuralist analysis. And Jackson Cope's contribution, "Seventeenth-Century Quaker Style" (200–35), is suggestive for an understanding of radical sectarian style more generally.
7. For a critique of the new historicism and its elision of the English Revolution, see my "Ranting at the New Historicism," *English Literary Renaissance*, 19:2 (1989), 189–225. See also David Norbrook's "The Life and Death of Renaissance Man," *Raritan*, 8:4 (1989), 89–110.

8. It seems to me no accident that the new historicism has raised the biggest controversy in fields dominated by magisterial authors (the English Renaissance, English Romanticism and the American Renaissance), and that its impact has proved less overwhelming in fields that have traditionally emphasized cross-generic studies of language in culture (medieval studies, eighteenth-century British, Colonial American and area studies of various sorts). Here, the study of Puritan New England provides a particularly strong contrast to the study of revolutionary England, given its contemporaneity and the strong ideological analogies and linkages. The general lack of overwhelming authors in seventeenth-century America (despite the considerable stature of Ann Bradstreet, Cotton Mather and Edward Taylor, they did not establish schools and literary traditions or define the nature of American literary authority in the manner of Shakespeare, Jonson, Donne and Milton) has proved a blessing in disguise, leading Colonial Americanists almost by default towards a sort of culture criticism which, if not precisely new historicist, at least tends not to begin with the debilitating question of "literary or non-literary?" But British and American critics of seventeenth-century English literature still pay relatively little attention to Colonial American studies. For a notable exception, see Keith Stavely's *Puritan Legacies: Paradise Lost and the New England Tradition, 1630–1890* (Ithaca: Cornell University Press, 1987). The study of seventeenth-century England still lacks a cross-generic anthology comparable to Perry Miller and Thomas H. Johnson's *The Puritans*, 2 vols. (1938; reprinted New York: Harper Torchbooks, 1963), which contains not only poetry, but exploration narratives, sermons, political theory, scientific disquisitions, journal entries, literary theory, theology, and a denunciation of mixed dancing – a new historicist's dream come true.

9. William Haller, *Tracts on Liberty in the Puritan Revolution, 1638–1647*, 3 vols. (New York: Columbia University Press, 1934); William Haller and Godfrey Davies, eds., *The Leveller Tracts, 1647–1653* (New York: Columbia University Press, 1944); George H. Sabine, ed., *The Works of Gerrard Winstanley* (Ithaca: Cornell University Press, 1944); Don M. Wolfe, ed., *Leveller Manifestoes of the Puritan Revolution* (1944; reprinted New York: Humanities Press, 1967); A.S.P. Woodhouse, ed., *Puritanism and Liberty: Being the Army Debates (1647) from the Clarke Manuscripts, with Supplementary Documents* (Chicago: University of Chicago Press, 1951); A. L. Morton, *Freedom in Arms: A Selection of Leveller Writings* (New York: International Publishers, 1971); G.E. Aylmer, *The Levellers in the English Revolution* (Ithaca: Cornell University Press, 1975); J.G.A. Pocock, *The Political Writings of James Harrington* (Cambridge: Cambridge University Press, 1977); Michael Oakeshott, ed., Thomas Hobbes, *Leviathan, Or the Matter, Forme and Power of a Commonwealth Ecclesiastical and Civil* (Oxford: Blackwell, 1960); Don M. Wolfe, gen. ed., *The Complete Prose Works of John Milton*, 8 vols. (New Haven: Yale University Press, 1953–1983).

10. William Haller, *Liberty and Reformation in the Puritan Revolution* (New York: Columbia University Press, 1955); Perry Miller, *The New England Mind: The Seventeenth Century* (Cambridge: Belknap–Harvard University Press, 1939); Don M. Wolfe, *Milton in the Puritan Revolution* (1941; reprinted New York: Humanities Press, 1963); Geoffrey F. Nuttall, *The Holy Spirit in Puritan Faith and Experience* (Oxford: Blackwell, 1946); Joseph Frank, *The Levellers: A History of the Writings of Three Seventeenth-Century Social Democrats: John Lilburne, Richard Overton, William Walwyn* (Cambridge: Harvard University Press, 1955); Olivier Lutaud, *Des Révolutions D'Angleterre à la Révolution Française* (The Hague: Martinus Nijhoff, 1973); and *Winstanley: Socialisme et Christianisme sous Cromwell* (Paris: Didier, 1976); J.G.A. Pocock, *The Machiavellian Moment: Florentine Political Thought and the Atlantic Republican Tradition* (Princeton: Princeton University Press, 1975); Sacvan Bercovitch, *The Puritan Origins of the American Self* (New Haven: Yale University Press, 1975). Anglophone scholars regularly ignore the work of Lutaud, one of the foremost literary scholars of the English Revolution. The case of Pocock is even more perplexing. His study of the English Revolution (in his various writings on

James Harrington, and in the central chapters of *The Machiavellian Moment*) and his argument that the history of politics is the history of the languages in which it can be conducted (one might call his approach a linguistic and political version of Kuhn's paradigmatic history of scientific practice) should be of enormous interest to literary critics. Yet his work seems more frequently invoked than read or used. Mainstream revisionist historians, with sensibilities too empirical and fine-grained to be easily waylaid by Pocock's theoretical adventurousness, also seem to be immune.

11. David Loewenstein and James Grantham Turner, eds., *Politics, Poetics, and Hermeneutics in Milton's Prose* (Cambridge: Cambridge University Press, 1990).

12. David Norbrook, "The Life and Death of Renaissance Man," 108.

13. Howard Erskine-Hill and Graham Storey, *Revolutionary Prose of the English Civil War* (Cambridge: Cambridge University Press, 1983); David Wootton, *Divine Right and Democracy: An Anthology of Political Writing in Stuart England* (Harmondsworth: Penguin, 1986); Jack R. McMichael and Barbara Taft, eds., *The Writings of William Walwyn* (Athens: University of Georgia Press, 1989). Nigel Smith's *A Collection of Ranter Writings from the 17th Century* (London: Junction Books, 1983) is now out of print, but Andrew Hopton has recently edited *Abiezer Coppe: Selected Writings* (London: Aporia Press, 1987). Elspeth Graham *et al.*, eds., *Her Own Life: Autobiographical Writings of Seventeenth-Century Englishwomen* (London and New York: Routledge, 1989); Germaine Greer *et al.*, eds., *Kissing the Rod: An Anthology of Seventeenth-Century Women's Verse* (New York: Farrar Strauss, 1989); Francis Barker *et al.*, eds., *1642: Literature and Power in the Seventeenth Century*, Proceedings of the Essex Conference on the Sociology of Literature, July 1980 (Colchester: University of Essex, 1981); R.C. Richardson and G.M. Ridden, eds., *Freedom in the English Revolution: Essays in History and Literature* (Manchester: Manchester University Press, 1986); Thomas N. Corns, ed., *The Literature of Polemical Strategy from Milton to Junius* (London: Frank Cass, 1987); Thomas Healy and Jonathan Sawday, eds., *Literature and the English Civil War* (Cambridge: Cambridge University Press, 1990); Nigel Smith, *Perfection Proclaimed: Language and Literature in English Radical Religion, 1640–1660* (Oxford: Clarendon, 1989).

14. Mikhail Bakhtin, *The Dialogic Imagination: Four Essays*, Michael Holquist, ed., trans. Caryl Emerson and Michael Holquist (Austin: University of Texas Press, 1981); for another study of the dialogue of high and low, which is very suggestive for a study of radical sectarianism in the English Revolution, see Carlo Ginzburg, *The Cheese and the Worms: The Cosmos of a Sixteenth-Century Miller*, trans. John and Anne Tedeschi (Harmondsworth: Penguin, 1984).

15. Pocock, *The Machiavellian Moment*, 361–6.

16. Samuel Rawson Gardiner, *The Constitutional Documents of the Puritan Revolution, 1625–1660*, third edn. (Oxford: Clarendon, 1906), 261.

The Politics of Babel
in the English Revolution

SHARON ACHINSTEIN

In 1668, in the final stage of his career as an advocate of the new science, preacher of natural theology, sometime Master of Wadham College, Oxford, widower of Cromwell's sister, and now Bishop of Chester, John Wilkins published his last work, *An Essay Towards a Real Character, and a Philosophical Language*. In it, Wilkins expressed his lifelong Baconian hope of improving man's estate by reforming language. The *Essay*, dedicated to the Royal Society of which Wilkins was a founding member, aimed to improve international trade, geographical exploration and, most important, clarify scientific endeavour by replacing the Latin tongue with a "Real universal Character that should not signify words, but things and notions, and consequently might be legible by any Nation in their own Tongue."[1] A new language was needed to express the truths of a new science, and Wilkins hoped that "such a thing as is here proposed, could be well established, [and] it would be the surest remedy that could be against the Curse of the Confusion, by rendering all other Languages and Characters useless" (13).

The *Essay* was Wilkins' last contribution to a stream of books comprising what historians of science now call the Universal Language Movement. In the years 1640–70, many works were published which sought to resolve the diversity of Earthly languages into a common tongue. Wilkins himself had framed this plan as early as 1641 in terms of the biblical story of Babel: "the confusion at *Babel* might this way have been remedied, if every one could have expressed his own meaning by the same kind of Character."[2] The prevailing motif of the Universal Language Movement was the hope of resolving Babel's linguistic consequences, and language projectors repeatedly referred to the biblical story as a prologue to their enterprises; "Babel revers'd," as one put it.[3] Seventeenth-century language projectors pursued topics of creating effective shorthand, constructing mathematical models for organizing language and introducing scientific vocabularies, as well as seeking new methods for teaching languages, correcting orthography, fixing pronunciation, bridging the gaps between words and things, and creating a universal grammar. Books such as Comenius's *Light to Grammar and All other Arts and Sciences* (1641), Cave Beck's *The Universal Character* (1657), John Wallis's *Grammatica Linguae*

Anglicanae (1653), George Dalgarno's *Ars Signorum* (1661), and Francis Lodwick's *A Common Writing* (1646), among many others, considered subjects such as secret communication, the correlation between sound and sense, codes, Egyptian and Chinese hieroglyphics, sign languages for the deaf, and finding the Adamic language that had been lost at Babel.[4]

The chief aims of this movement were scientific and commercial, but universal language and true grammar would also help to resolve international disagreements about religion. As Wilkins put it: "it would likewise very much conduce to the spreading of the knowledge of Religion" and promote the "diffusion of it, through all nations" (*Essay*, B_1). Wilkins continues, stressing the religious aspects of his plan for linguistic reform:

> This design will likewise contribute much to the clearing of some of our Modern differences in Religion, by unmasking many wild errors, that shelter themselves under the disguise of affected phrases; which being philosophically unfolded, and rendered according to the genuine and natural importance of Words, will appear to be inconsistencies and contradictions. And several of those pretended, mysterious, profound notions, expressed in great swelling words, whereby some men set up for reputation, being this way examined, will appear to be, either nonsense, or very flat and jejune.
>
> And though it should be of no other use but this, yet were it in these days well worth a man's pains and study, considering the Common mischief that is done, and the many impostures and cheats that are put upon men, under the disguise of affected insignificant Phrases. (B_1-B_{1v})

Wilkins explains that he was prompted by the fact of religious dispute in his day, and the Universal Language Movement has been rightly placed in histories of millenarian thought.[5] The language in need of remedy was not safe for true discussion of such matters; rather than conveying clearly the truths of religion, in its present state, language committed "mischiefs," "impostures and cheats," and "disguises" against sense. Aside from being inaccurate, language could be dangerously deceptive.

Wilkins' project, along with the many universal language schemes produced in England between 1640 and 1670, has been claimed by historians as a story of knowledge-as-order, a history of knowledge which stretches from the seventeenth century forward from Descartes, Wilkins and Locke, through to late eighteenth-century empiricism.[6] I wish to revise this story by accounting for the preconditions of this universalist discourse about language in the pamphlet literature of the English Revolution. The aim here is not to sweep away studies in the history of ideas which concern the movements for language reform, but to encourage a dialogical approach to the history of ideas, one which seeks to recover the contemporary meanings against which new ideas were posited.

Historians of ideas might gain by looking into the political meanings of, and political motivations for, a "science" of language; and those concerned with the pamphlet literature and other "low" matters of cultural detritus might better explore how "high" linguistic and philosophical traditions reflect, interact with, and give us guides for interpreting the "low" literature. The "high" and the "low" are in dialogue here.[7] I am supposing as a matter of course that those concerned with "high" and "low" might have something to learn from one another, and also that we, as teachers, should find ways of working both sides of the fence in our teaching and research. Certainly, no idea arises without a context, and my presentation here aims to expand the kinds of contexts and preconditions we might allow to inform our studies of cultural artifacts.[8] Rather than place universal language schemes such as Wilkins' at a starting point in this teleological narrative of ideas, or seek out the "politics" of the movement itself, my essay looks, instead, at Wilkins' project in relation to contemporary manifestations of concern about language. I see the universal language schemes as one response to and outcome of the pamphlet wars of the English Revolution. Put simply, to many, the English Revolution *was* Babel.

In part, I am talking about Babel as Civil War writers did, where ideological disagreements were represented as a war merely about words: "Hard words, jealousies and fears, / Set folks together by the ears," wrote Samuel Butler as he looked back on the Civil War years in *Hudibras*. For the writers and fighters of the English Revolution, the conditions of partisan conflict resembled the diversity of tongues at Babel, with over 22,000 pamphlets, sermons, newsbooks, speeches, broadside ballads and other ephemera published between 1640 and 1661 – surpassing even the output of the continental presses over 100 years later during the French Revolution.[9] The English Revolution was a wordy feat, and it was described by contemporaries as a modern-day Babel.

This essay examines how ideological disputes were represented as clashes among languages, and asks why language became the figure for such disputes. I argue that concerns about language at this time were implicated in a great historical shift, for which the dispute over the use of language is one sign: the rise of the public sphere. The contests over political and social authority were represented by figures for clashes in language because public expression was becoming the means by which political and social differences were made known. At a time when alternate languages permeated public discourse, Babel was a figure used by those who were coming to see that language was no transparent medium, and that definitions had serious political consequences.

In the first half of the essay, I explore the relation between the variety of languages in the press and the fact of political difference, drawing upon pamphlet texts from the English Revolutionary period which were critical of the press. The metaphor of Babel was used in Royalist Civil War pamphlets to register horror at the fact of political disagreement, and yet the metaphor also served to reflect that such disagreements were not only expressible *in* language, "hard words," but that they were fundamentally *about* language, about who was speaking language and to what uses language was being put.[10] This is especially visible in the satiric prose of John Cleveland, who is the sample case for study. Cleveland argued that the press was a herald of unacceptable political positions, and he expressed his fears through linguistic metaphors which suggested an analogy between anarchy in language and anarchy in politics. Cleveland was not the only one who believed that once linguistic errors were corrected, authority would return to the hands of those who rightly deserved to rule, and that political and linguistic authority would be one again. Radical sectarians, like the Ranters, also hoped for a singular linguistic and political system – but the Ranters located the authority for that structure with God;[11] Cleveland, and his fellow Royalists, with their King. Theories which expressed political difference as linguistic difference during the English Revolution could only go so far without divine aid, however; Cleveland's nostalgia for a single voice of truth and, perhaps, Wilkins' project of a universal language both failed to make the epistemological or theological moves necessary for language and politics to become one. Thomas Hobbes goes the full distance in his *Leviathan*, where the sovereign, as lexarch, resolves the epistemological and political difficulties of the belief in a universal language.

My essay ends with Hobbes, but does not seek to end as a contribution to a monological history of language. In some ways, my perspective takes issue with current literary approaches to the history of language and of ideas. One might propose the post-structuralist axiom that there is always a crisis in language. Yet the kind of crisis about language I consider here is not the epistemological black hole of the self-referentiality of language that was "discovered" in the Renaissance. The pamphlets which used the figure of Babel during the English

Revolution were really arguments about historically specific uses of language in seventeenth-century England, where Babel served both as a representation of the war of words in the press and as a figure for ideological difference.

1. BABEL AND THE OPENING UP OF THE PUBLIC SPHERE

During the English Revolution, Babel was often a metaphor for the press. Conservative writers used the image of Babel to describe the press, and they aimed their pens at a new phenomenon, which the lapse of state-sponsored censorship of the press in 1641 had allowed to occur: the participation of many different voices in political debate.[12] The writers of the English Revolution were transforming their arguments about the people's rights and duties into actual practice by reaching out to an audience of the people, and by presenting political matters which were previously forbidden.[13] The argument here exemplifies in some ways Jürgen Habermas's analysis of the structural transformation of the public sphere, where power is constructed not out of adherence to the authority of special persons, but is constituted by the conditions of public discussion.[14] This essay directs itself at those cultural materials which seem to reflect on the condition of publicity, and which disparaged it. The images of Babel were a critical response to the opening up of the public sphere, an attempt to unify and repress all the private voices making themselves public, and the revolutionary press became itself the focus of worries about the condition of linguistic diversity. The image of Babel was used strategically by a specifically Royalist and conservative group as part of an effort to master, and then to silence, the oppositional and radical voices.

The situation of the press in the mid-seventeenth century was anomalous, however: it was largely in the hands of those who resisted monarchical authority, of those who constituted the opposition.[15] The state as manifested by kingly prerogative was not imposing discipline on its subjects by means of this organ; rather, the press was the medium through which revolutionary ideas were spread. Christopher Hill has shown that the radical literature of the English Revolution can help to tell the story of popular resistance as a history from below, but it is important to remember that during this strange moment in English history "resistance" literature was the dominant mode.[16] In *Areopagitica*, John Milton was convinced that din was a sign of general reformation: "the people, or the greater part, more then at other times [are] wholly tak'n up with the study of the highest and most important matters to be reform'd, should be disputing, reasoning, reading, inventing, discoursing, ev'n to a rarity, and admiration, things not before discourst or writt'n of."[17] The relative freedom of the press in the early 1640s produced a relatively new situation in the history of political discourse: disputes began to take place in public.

A freer press allowed a wider variety of political opinions, and this variety was unprecedented in English history. John Lilburne, who coupled the idea of a free press with a free public, argued that those who would restrict the press sought to "suppress every thing which hath any true Declaration of the just Rights and Liberties of the free-born people of this Nation, and to brand and traduce all such Writers and Writings with the odious terms of Sedition, Conspiracy and Treason."[18] By his terms, "brand" and "traduce," Lilburne suggested that his enemies' very language was unreliable: either those who defended the rights and liberties of the people were true defenders of the people's freedom, or they were traitors. Lilburne's sense that there were indeed competing languages for describing the same activities is an example of a mode of Civil War pamphleteering that redefined political relations through new uses of language. Idiosyncratic uses of language marked and in some manner constituted ideological differences. Lilburne's writing attempted to present the people in heroic terms, and to make the press the battlefield on which that heroism was achieved. But he was aware there was another way of putting things.

To some Civil War writers, the fact of public disagreement seemed diabolical in the first place. For example, *Mercurius Pacificus* (1648) offered his "lectures of Concord" to eliminate the strife between those who were living in what sounds like Hobbes's state of nature: "Divided as far as Hounds and Hares in antipathizing disaffection: Heads divided in opinions, like those of the Serpent Amphibena, one fighting with another, hearts divided, like fire and water, tongues divided, as still in Babel's confusion, hands divided." The metaphor of Babel was used to represent discord as global, but at the same time most private: "Cities divided . . . Families divided . . . Bloods divided . . . yea houses divided, father against son, brother against sister, mother against daughter; yea beds divided, like oil and water, which cannot mix; husbands and wives snarling in couples."[19] The list of divisions proceeds from the most metaphorical (hounds and hares) to the most intimate (husbands and wives in bed), to illustrate how completely society was riven by discord. This discord was as irreconcilable as the oil and water which cannot mix.

The author conceived of the conflict as a problem in communication, "tongues divided as in Babel's confusion" because the differences derived from verbal acts:

> sinister constructions and mis-interpretations, one not rightly
> understanding another, (as the Orator once complained) that
> being heard with a left ear, which was spoke with a right tongue,
> and that which was clear in the fountain's head, being muddied
> and troubled through the foul pipes and channels of mis-relating
> mouths, or misconstraining minds. (7)

In this seventeenth-century version of our children's party-game, "Tele-
phone," all the trouble seemed to come from garbled messages, a
Wilkinsite conclusion. The author of *Mercurius Pacificus* thought it
possible to achieve peace between the opposing sides if only the parties
could speak clearly to one another.

In this account of strife is the view that language can function as a
transparent vehicle for thoughts – if we remove the blockages in the
"foul pipes and channels" of language, the prefix "mis," for example, we
might have true "interpretations," "relations" and "constructions." The
author's recommendations were rather like those of Oliver Cromwell
at the Putney debates in 1647: "Certainly God is not the author of
contradictions. The contradictions are not so much in the end as in
the way. I cannot see but that we all speak to the same end, and the
mistakes are only in the way."[20] The idea that "the mistakes are only in
the way" expresses a form of linguistic universalism which scientists like
John Wilkins hoped to promote, the belief that beneath the diversity of
tongues were actually common thoughts which could be expressed in
a common language. If this were true, then differences in ideologies
might not be true differences, but rather tricks of language, "cheats
of words." As we recall, Wilkins' hope in the *Essay*: "by unmasking
many wild errors, that shelter themselves under the disguise of affected
phrases; which being philosophically unfolded, and rendered according
to the genuine and natural importance of Words, will appear to be
inconsistencies and contradictions" (B_1) through a universal language.
Yet, the question remained, whose language was it to be?

2. BABEL AS A POLITICAL STORY

The illustration below, *The World is Ruled and Governed by Opinion*
(1641), represents the consequences of the clash of new voices, and it
belongs to a strain of pamphleteering which blamed the press for all the
trouble. In this broadside, a female figure rules; her gender signifies the
familiar trope of political inversion, a woman on top.[21]

The woman is blindfolded, a parody of Justice, and she addresses the
gentleman who approaches her: "'Tis true I cannot as clear judgments

THE WORLD IS RVLED & GOVERNED by OPINION.

Viator Who art thou Ladie that aloft art set
In state Maiestique this faire spreddin̄
Vpon thine head a Towre-like Coronet.
The Worldes whole Compasse resting on thy knee

Opinie I am OPINION who the world do swaie
Wherefore I beare it on my head that Towr
Is BABELS meaning my confused waie
The Tree so shaken my vnsetled Bowre

Viator What meaneth that Chameleon on thy fist
That can assume all Cullors saving white

Opinio OPINION thus can' everie waie shee list
Transforme her self save into TRVTH the right

Viator And Ladie what's the Fruite which from thy Tree
Is shaken of with everie little wind
Like Bookes and papers this amuseth mee
Beside thou seemest veiled to bee blind

Opinio Tis true I cannot as cleare IVDGMENTS see
Through self CONCEIT and haughtie PRIDE
The fruite those idle bookes and libells bee
In everie streete, on everie stall you find

Viator Cannot OPINION remedie the same

Opinio Ah no then should I perish in the throng
O th giddie Vulgar, without feare=shame
Who censure all thinges bee they right ＝ ＝wrong

Viator But Ladie deare whence came at first this fruite
Or why doth WISEDOME suffer it to grow
And what's the reason its farre reaching roote

Opinio Because that FOLLIE giveth life to these
I but retaile the fruites of idle Aire
Sith now all Humors vtter what they please
Toth loathing loading of each Mart and Faire

Viator And why those saplings from the roote that rise
In such abundance of OPINIONS tree

Opinio Cause one Opinion many doth devise
And propagate till infinite they bee

Viator Adieu sweete Ladie till againe wee meete

Opinio But when shall that againe bee ｜ iator Ladie late

Opinio Opinions found in everie house and streete
And going ever never in her waie

VIRO CLA: D: FRANCISCO PRVIEANO D: MEDICO OMNIVM BONARVM AR
tium et Elegantiarum Fautori et Admiratori summo. D. D. D. Henricus Peachamus.

Henry Peacham, "The World is Ruled and Governed by Opinion," 1641 (reproduced by permission of Folger Shakespeare Library) see,/ Through self-conceit and haughty pride of mind." This does not cause her dismay, since she is happy to see her fruit are growing everywhere: "The fruit those idle books and libels be/ In every street, on every stall you find." Her seat of power is in fact a tree bursting with its fruit, pamphlets. The titles of several of these are visible: "Taylor's Physicke," "Brown's Conventicle," "Taylor's Reply," "Hellish Parliament," "News from Elesium". Many are real titles of actual pamphlets, or are, at least, believable fictions. These pamphlets drop to the ground like ripe fruit. On her left arm lies a chameleon, then as today, a symbol for ever-changingness, and on her lap sits a globe of the earth in the place of her womb. The womb-as-earth suggests an alternate, and specifically a *female* creation story – as if she, rather than God, has given birth to the world, in an almost blasphemous parody of the catechism's first question, "who made thee?" A fool waters the tree below, performing a kind of artificial insemination: "Folly giveth life to thee." The tree of Opinion is a healthy tree, and saplings flourish in its shade. Opinion explains, "Cause one Opinion many doth devise/ And propagate 'til infinite they be." Her imperial designs are explicit; the pointer is like a sceptre, and the globe on her lap is a symbol of royal power: "I am Opinion who the world do sway," she boasts.

A final symbol rests upon her head, a "tower-like coronet" which represents the tower of Babel. Opinion explains that the tower shows her "confused way." This sign of Opinion's power is an allegorical reminder that the consequence of rebellion was the profusion of different languages. "The fruit those idle books and libels be/ In every street, on every stall you find": the pamphlets are common street-literature, catering to the lower elements of society, the "giddie vulgar," and present everywhere. Like other pamphlets which opposed pamphlet debate, this broadside used a story about language to criticize the presence of public debate: too many opinions signalled chaos, and the participation of the lower and middling sorts in the political life of the nation would lead to anarchy.

More often than not, the story of Babel was cited in order to restore authority to the King's language. Babel was a story often cited in the early modern period explaining and condemning the origins of political difference. According to the seventeenth-century political theorist Robert Filmer, power was given naturally to Adam, which "continued monarchical to the Flood, and after the Flood to the confusion of Babel: when Kingdoms were first erected, planted, or scattered over the face of the world."[22] Babel represented a state of different and incompatible languages which was God's punishment for political ambition.

Yet, a radical trope interpreted Babel differently, associating Babel with the archetypical tyrant, Nimrod. In this reading, which was Milton's, Babel's confusion was the result of tyrannical processes. In *Paradise Lost*, for example, Milton associates Nimrod with the suffocating grip of prelatical power and Babel with the pageantry and luxury of kings. As the angel Raphael in Book XII of *Paradise Lost* recounts to the fallen Adam the history of man that is to come, he points out the first tyrant, Nimrod, one "Of proud ambitious heart, who not content/ With fair equality, fraternal state," who "Will arrogate Dominion undeserv'd/ Over his brethren, and quite dispossess/ Concord and law of Nature from the Earth" (XII, 24–9). A tyrant here disrupts the fraternity, the "brethren" of humans, and constructs a hierarchy. The consequence is a breach in the law of Nature, the dispossessing of concord, as if concord is a kind of property of the earth that is banished or vanquished. Milton sees Nimrod's tyranny as a "rebellion" from God and, in punishment for that rebellious tyranny, God sets men's tongues apart, "to sow a jangling noise of words unknown" (XII, 55).[23] But the tyranny has already created discord, even before God's punishment. Milton's story agreed with the Royalists that confusion in speech was a consequence of a political sin, yet in Milton's case confused speech was a consequence of tyranny, not of a pluralistic language situation.

Milton also saw Babel in the light of Babylon, where the Catholic Church enslaved the people by a "spiritual Babel" (598). Babel was often associated with Babylon, and the zealous Protestant readers in seventeenth-century England who abhorred Popery found analogies between the Babel of their own day and the evils of Catholicism. Thomas Blount's 1656 dictionary equates the biblical city of Babel with Babylon, explaining in his definition of Babel: "'tis we use *Babelish* for confused; and *Babylonical* for magnificent and costly, and to *Babel* [sic] or *babble*, to twattle, or speak confusedly."[24] If Royalists emphasized the condition of Babel as God's punishment, then anti-Royalists emphasized the causes of Babel – ambition and tyranny – associating Babel with Popery. For them, Babel was the metaphor that expressed these ideas.

The competing interpreters of Babel agreed on one thing: there was a plethora of voices to be heard. Whether one argued that Babel was a sign of unlawful resistance to a king, and that God would "suffer those men long to prosper in their Babel who build it with the bones and cement it with the blood of their kings," as was argued in King Charles' defence, *Eikon Basilike*; or that Babel was a sign of tyranny, as Milton wrote in his response to the *Eikon Basilike*, where Babel was "*Nimrods* work, the first King, *and the beginning of his Kingdom was Babel*,"[25] the fact of Babel was acknowledged by all. The search for explanations of the conditions of Babel and the search for its cure shared an assessment of the contemporary political theatre.

3. THE ATTACK ON BABEL

Babel represented competition among different languages for political legitimacy.[26] William Prynne's pamphlet, *New Babel's Confusion* (1647) compared the biblical story to the political situation in England in 1647, when Parliament was divided over the petition called *An Agreement of the People*, which asserted that the supreme power resided in the people. Prynne's title makes an analogy between mob rule and Babel.

According to the Royalist reading, the actions of Parliament in the 1640s re-enacted the blasphemous rebellion against right authority that had taken place at Babel. The Royalist attacks on the press may be seen as criticisms of the entry of new voices into the political arena, and the likening of the press's activity to Babel was a way of opposing the notion that the people were an audience fit to participate in public debate at all. The example of Babel was cited to enlist support for a conservative antidote to the anarchy of both language and government.

Writers were recognizing the fact that ideological division was represented by verbal action, and that differences might be impossible to reconcile. The public conflict of ideas would lead not to resolution but only to more strife. In an anti-Puritan satire, *Sampsons Foxes Agreed to Fire a Kingdom* (1644), the author compares Puritans to their opposite, Papists, and concludes:

> See, two rude waves, by storms together thrown,
> Roar at each other, fight, and then grow one.
> Religion is a circle, men contend
> And run the round, disputing without end.[27]

Strife is portrayed in terms of a violent storm, and the clashes take place in language. The noise of disagreement had spurred Milton in 1644 to hope that this might be a sign of reformation. But to others (and, later, even to Milton), noise was not such a good thing. Babble and Babel (even Babylon) were identical. To Royalist John Doughty, the battle cry of the enemy religious zealot was "Bibble, Bubble, Babel."[28]

These were clashes *in* language – verbal disputes – but they were also clashes *about* language – about the proper use of words. In 1643,

Sir Thomas Browne, apologist for Charles I, wrote against the spate of newsbooks in which "the name of his Majesty [is] defamed, the honour of Parliament depraved, the writings of both depravedly, anticipatively, counterfeitly imprinted."[29] To Browne, printing the King's speech without authorization constituted treason.

In many cases during the pamphlet wars of the English Revolution those who were represented as threatening natural order were the unruly populace. Thomas Jordan's poem, "The Rebellion," presents a vision of anarchy in the many voices of the people. Anarchy in "The Rebellion" is signified by a linguistic condition where the multiplicity of voices, specifically from the lower ranks, created utter confusion:

> Come Clowns, and come Boys, come Hoberdehoys,
> Come Females of each degree,
> Stretch out your Throats, bring in your Votes,
> And make good the Anarchy;

Each voice contradicts the others:

> Then thus it shall be, says *Alse*,
> Nay, thus it shall be, says *Amie*,
> Nay, thus it shall go, says *Taffie*, I trow,
> Nay, thus it shall go, says *Jenny*.

Disagreement is the only observable feature; we do not even know what the matter is.

> Speak *Abraham*, speak *Hester*,
> Speak *Judith*, speak *Kester*,
> Speak tag and rag, short coat and long:
> Truth is the spell that made us rebel,
> And murder and plunder ding dong;
> Sure I have the truth, says *Numphs*,
> Nay, I have the truth, says *Clem*,
> Nay, I have the truth, says reverend *Ruth*,
> Nay, I have the truth, says *Nem*.

The song mixes "common" materials, "tag and rag," and the ballad refrain, "ding dong," to make light of the serious threat of popular rule, and by the names of Abraham, Judith and Ruth we see that at least some of these giddy anarchists are Puritans. The poem points to the language in which such rebellion is expressed: "tag and rag" are *not* the acceptable language of politics found among educated men. These voices are also predominantly female ones – Judith, Amie, Taffie, etc. – another instance of the slur of "women on top." The moral of the piece – "Thus from the Rout who can expect/ Ought but confusion?" – is exemplified by making the popular voices express a variety of political opinions, with no apparent reasons:

> Then let's have King *Charles*, says *George*,
> Nay we'll have his Son, says *Hugh*;
> Nay, then let's have none, says gabbering *Joan*,
> Nay, we'll be all Kings, says *Prue*.[30]

The group cannot agree on anything, on a programme, on the truth, or on the matter of who shall be king: Babel has come again. The polemical method of this poem is to caricature and distort the opposite side's disastrous disagreement in order to argue implicitly for a political point of view that is stable, one-voiced, and not confused. At a more sophisticated level, this is the argument of Hobbes's *Leviathan*, as we shall see later.

This poem reiterates political chaos as a function of class, and, indeed, Babel was often the trope assigned to low literature in the schism between "high" and "low" cultures familiar to scholars of early modern culture.[31] The forces at work beneath the distinctions in taste were explicitly political during the English Revolution, as can be seen from poems by Thomas Jordan and others.[32] Printed pamphlets were opposed not just for their sins against taste but, more importantly, because the content of the printed pamphlets posed definite threats to the social and political order.[33] As Gabriel Plattes wrote in 1641, "the art of Printing will so spread knowledge that the common people, knowing their own rights and liberties, will not be governed by way of oppression."[34] The multitude now seemed to rule all. Babel was a sign that the many were gaining access to previously inaccessible political energy.

It is not hard to see that the elite attitude was a reaction to pressures from popular literature itself. Writers at this time were aware of a new audience, and some had nothing but scorn for it. According to opponents of the press, there were too many pamphlets clamouring for authority, too many disparate assertions of truth. The public's contribution to politics seemed to be the Babel of a multitude of voices, no longer the King's single voice of truth. As the sermonizer in *A Remedy Against Dissention* warned his audience in 1644, "have a special eye to them who cause offenses; abettors, barraters, authors of libels, and seditious pamphlets, causers of quarrels, men of unclean tongues." Puritans also feared the unruliness of a popular audience.[35]

Fear of the mob was not a new phenomenon; Shakespeare's crowds in *Coriolanus* or *Julius Caesar* showed the worst effects of a republican system. Similarly, the mobs in Spenser's *Faerie Queene* evoked the political memory of mob rebellions like Jack Cade's or Wat Tyler's, and this served to provoke fear among elites.[36] But the conservatives during the seventeenth century had a specific kind of public to fear, one which could express its wants in a language of its own. This was no gullible mass, but rather an entity which was choosing sides, the object of address of a pamphlet literature in which powerful political ideas were being expressed. Sir George Wharton, a Royalist astrologer, commented on this new audience by accusing his rival, John Booker, of catering to the vulgar: "you have done very wisely in directing [your pamphlet] to the *People*: none but your seduced Many-headed-Monster *Multitude* will credit you."[37] The Stationer's comment in his introductory epistle to the reader in the 1645 edition of *The Poems of John Milton*, "the slightest Pamphlet is nowadays more vendible than the works of learnedest men," is a sign that pamphlets were circulating widely.[38] One result of this new subject matter was that the readers and writers of these pamphlets began to share a competence in political language.

4. JOHN CLEVELAND AND THE DIVINE RIGHT OF LANGUAGE

The Royalist pamphleteer John Cleveland made wide use of the conflicting languages in his day to parody those he considered politically illegitimate, and his pieces attacked the language of his enemies as a way of attacking their politics. Cleveland drew an equation between bankrupt language and bankrupt politics, and his three short prose pieces published in 1644, "Character of a Country Committee-man," "The Character of a Diurnal-Maker" and "The Character of a London Diurnal," were satiric attacks on the parliamentary newspapers. During the English Revolution, Cleveland was paid to write as an official spokesman for the King's garrison at Newark.[39] In "The Character of a London Diurnal," for instance, Cleveland mocks Parliament by presenting its actions in its own language. Not surprisingly, Parliament is made to appear ridiculous by its misappropriation of language. In this case, Parliament has misread signs, with disastrous results:

> Suppose a corn-cutter being to give little Isaac a cast of his office should fall to paring his brows (mistaking one end for the other, because he branches at both), this would be a plot, and the next diurnal would furnish you with this scale of votes: –

> *Resolved* upon the question, That this act of the corn-cutter was an absolute invasion of the city's charter in the representative forehead of Isaac.
>
> *Resolved*, That the evil counsellors about the corn-cutter are popishly affected and enemies to the State.
>
> *Resolved*, That there be a public thanksgiving for the great deliverance of Isaac's brow-antlers; and a solemn covenant drawn up to defy the corn-cutter and all his works.[40]

Because he is a cuckold, Isaac sprouts antlers (*corni*) on his head as well as having corns on his feet. Since Isaac looks the same at both ends, the corn-cutter makes an error, and trims his forehead rather than his feet. Cleveland is not only shaming Isaac (a Puritan by his name) for cuckoldry, but he is also attacking the Puritans' indecorous reversals of natural order: the world is turned upside down. The accusation of cuckoldry is another instance of the woman-on-top theme; just as there has been an illegitimate usurpation in Isaac's domestic hierarchy, there has been usurpation in language. The woman-on-top image was not merely a literary trope, since women in a very real way were participtating in public discourse as they had not before. There is evidence that women's voices were being heard in the political and public arena, as sectarian preachers and in petitions to Parliament.[41]

In the Puritan reading of this incident, the corn-cutter's mistake is treasonous, and the signs take on a wholly different meaning in the frenzied brains of Puritan divines. Isaac's forehead becomes a site representing the city charter, and surgery on this is judged a treachery. Cleveland's parody takes the political metaphor of the "body politic" literally, and shows the Puritan zeal for interpretation gone haywire. Those responsible for the "invasion," of course, were "popishly affected," with the corn-cutter acting not in isolation but as the instrument of a party. The resolutions call for a response to the "plot," including a "public thanksgiving for the great deliverance" – ridiculous considering the inanity of the cause. Parliament responds to this situation by passing resolutions; the second resolution contains a reference to the attack on evil counsellors in the "Root and Branch Petition" (1640), put forward to initiate a more "godly, thorough, Reformation," and the third, to the *Solemn League and Covenant* (1643). The language used is Puritan, with the full solemnity of their diction mockingly misapplied in a parody.

Not merely attacking his enemies in Parliament by a parody of their language, Cleveland was concerned with the disturbing social consequences of the revolutionary press. Though it is probable that Cleveland himself wrote for the Mercuries of his day,[42] his opposition to parliamentary journals takes advantage of the opportunities for public discussion – only to shut it down. His opposition to the parliamentary press used the metaphor of linguistic order to stand for political order, and we might speculate that Cleveland would have dreamed of the day when there was no public discussion. The "Character of a London Diurnal" directs fire at the news-weeklies which reported on the activities of Parliament, and it opens with an attack on the language used to describe the genre of the newsbook: "The country-carrier . . . miscalls it the urinal" (307). By calling its very name into question, Cleveland makes an issue of its legitimacy. Cleveland connects the newsbook to excrement, since they are both waste products.[43]

Naming is also contested in "The Character of a London Diurnal-Maker," where Cleveland refuses to call the producers of these diurnals "authors" so as not to dishonour the art of true authors: "List him a writer and you smother Geoffrey [Chaucer] in swabber-slops." Even to name the diurnal-maker is to pose a problem for language.[44] From the very opening, the "Character" attempts to define its subject:

> A diurnal-maker is the sub-almoner of history, Queen Mab's register, one whom, by the same figure that a north country pedlar is a merchantman, you may style an author. It is like an overreach of language, when every thin tinder-cloaked quack must be called a doctor; when a clumsy cobbler usurps the attribute of our English peers, and is vamped a translator. (303)

The diurnal-maker taking the name of writer, the peddler taking the title of merchant, or the quack of doctor are unmerited usurpations of language. The diurnal-maker is certainly not a historian, since "to call him a historian is to knight a mandrake; 'tis to view him through a perspective, and by that gross hyperbole to give the reputation of engineer to a maker of mousetraps." Again there is the topos of aberrant sexuality, with the "mandrake" a common symbol for sexual licence. To knight a mandrake is to reward the undeserving. Cleveland's definitions serve to put the upstarts in their places.

Although Cleveland fires on his enemy as if the issue were solely verbal illegitimacy, the real issue is political illegitimacy. His account provides an allegory to the House of Commons, filled with "clumsy cobblers," then ruling over the House of Lords. The cobbler "usurps" the privileges of the noble class through an act of "translation," that is, substitution of one language for another. Translation is the term drawn from the very language of Puritan theology, where the activity of any Bible reader can make a cobbler equal to a peer.[45] The prospect of equal opportunities for "translation" horrifies Cleveland, who would like to keep the lower sorts of people at a distance. According to Cleveland, the translation is fraudulent, moreover, since the two languages involved are *not* equivalent to one another: the high may not be exchanged fairly for the low.

Like Wilkins and the Universal Language Movement theorists, Cleveland is concerned with the right and true uses of language, and the similarities between Cleveland's interests and the concerns of the language reformers are even more striking when we consider Cleveland's obsessions with correct definition and proper grammar. Cleveland uses definition as a specific device to challenge the politics of his opponents, as a way to assign a thing a true meaning and to regain control over it.[46] The opening salvo of "The Character of a Country Committee-Man" is a discussion of the term "committee-man," which is shown to pose a grammatical paradox in its application of a mass noun for a singular entity. This verbal paradox presents an ideological issue: can political authority be divided among a number of men, including the multitude, and among a number of branches of the government, as the Parliamentarians would have it? Thomas Hobbes expressed horror at the divided authority of such a "mixed government" in *Leviathan*: "For what is it to divide the Power of a Commonwealth, but to Dissolve it; for Powers divided mutually destroy each other."[47] Cleveland spins his puns in analysis of the problem of number, analysing his opponent's violation of syntax to illustrate his political point:

> A committee-man by his name should be one that is possessed, there is number enough in it to make an epithet for legion. He is *persona in concreto* (to borrow the solecism of a modern statesman) . . . It is a well-trussed title that contains both the number and the beast; for a committee-man is a noun of the multitude, he must be spelled with figures. (299)

This string of phrases, clustered loosely around the term "committee-man," plays on the theme of grammatical misconstruction. According to Cleveland, such a warping of true grammar counts as a political act: "as monstrous as the man, a complex notion; of the same lineage with accumulative treason" (298–9). It is unnatural, "monstrous," and it also constitutes unacceptable political action, "treason." Both bad grammar and political treachery are betrayals of a natural trust. The idea of correct grammar implies a "natural" order in the world, which has been disrupted.

Cleveland points to the examples of ruptured etymology and syntax in the hope of pointing out analogous flaws in the politics of these committee-men. In criticizing their diction, Cleveland plays upon the greatest of their evils, the fact that they divide authority. Collectively, the committee-men are dangerous: "Look upon them severally, and you cannot but fumble for some threads of clarity. But oh, they are termagents in conjunction!" (301). He then goes on to portray a few committee-men, concluding, "these are the simples of this precious compound; a kind of Dutch hotch-potch, the Hogan-Mogan committee-man" (302). The "Dutch" were associated with republicanism, and here Cleveland has only derision for their political arrangement.

Cleveland attacks the committee-man by repeatedly expressing outrage at instances of violated grammar, as when he claims "there is no syntax between a cap of maintenance and a helmet" (300), between labourers and soldiers, and he disparages a time "when so tame a pigeon may converse with vultures" (299). Cleveland believes that there exists a proper hierachy which determines a proper way of talking about matters. The Parliamentarians have usurped this true language by imposing their own fallacious language, just as they have usurped the true, correct politics.

Cleveland's acts of definition express a definite politics: only the King has the authority to validate language. In both "The Character of a Diurnal-Maker" and "The Character of a London Diurnal" Cleveland evaluates the names which the Parliamentarians have assigned to things, and he denies meaning to these new names by an appeal to natural linguistic order, using metaphors of birth and pedigree. According to Cleveland's definition, a parliamentary "Ordinance" was: "A law still-born, dropped before quickened by the royal assent. 'Tis one of the parliament's by-blows, acts only being legitimate, and hath no more sire than a Spanish jennet that is begotten by the wind"(307). For a law to be "still-born," it comes into the world dead, here lacking the "quickening" of kingly or patriarchal potency. The Ordinance was a "by-blow," a child born out of wedlock, illegitimate by law. In these metaphors taken from patriarchal political theory, true paternal legitimacy here would mean royal approval.[48] The next paragraph in the pamphlet draws out the same metaphor, where Parliament's army is like a fatherless offspring: "Thus their militia, like its Patron Mars, is the issue only of the mother, without the concourse of royal Jupiter" (307). The failure of true royalty to provide authority was described as a failure of proper lineage in the genealogical sense.[49]

Genealogy, and the patriarchal political theory it expresses, finds its way into Cleveland's linguistic critique through the device of definition.[50] As in the description of the parliamentary Ordinance, Cleveland uses a metaphor of disturbed sexual generation to deny the authenticity of his opponents' politics. Cleveland's wildly creative definitions are not all linguistic play, though they are a good deal of that. They are analogous to the searches for political legitimacy that activists sought from the past, where genealogy gave natural precedent and justification for present actions, as well as justifying claims to inheritance.[51]

What began as an exercise in definition – what is a Diurnal? or even, what is an Ordinance? – has turned into an exposure of his enemy's politics through a study of that enemy's language. Cleveland's use of catachresis is an appropriation of the many languages coexisting in the contemporary political arena, and the "Characters" exemplify the possibilities of exposing illegitimate languages for political uses. The "Characters" rewrite enemy figures so they appear not in the enemy's language but in Cleveland's own. Framed by his own true language, Cleveland presses for them to be disqualified, both on natural and political grounds.

If exposure by framing is possible, then truth is a question of linguistic practices and the kind of seriousness with which they are observed. But Cleveland backs away from the radicalism of this general position. One claim, his own, is better than all others. In order to battle with the enemy ideologies, he wars against their languages, revealing his belief that there exists a true language, a real, royal syntax. The other languages are ungrammatical. Mikhail Bakhtin argues that "polyglossia" may be a feature inherent in any prose work, defining "polyglossia" as the "simultaneous presence of two or more national languages interacting within a single cultural system."[52] This concept of polyglossia is useful in understanding how Civil War writers coped with changing conditions in the language of their time. In some sense, it is precisely polyglossia that the conservative seventeenth-century writers wanted to keep out. Bakhtin argues that the "unitary norms of language" are imposed to defend "an already formed language from the pressure of growing heteroglossia" (271), as the two forces play off against each other in a centripetal/centrifugal battle. This interplay is dramatized in the Civil War question of authority over language. Bakhtin himself uses the image of Babel to talk about the function of multiple languages in the world: "the prose writer witnesses . . . the unfolding of social heteroglossia *surrounding* the object, the Tower-of-Babel mixing of languages that goes on around any object" (278). For Bakhtin, the Tower of Babel has the positive, liberating resonances of the "open" form of the novel, and is an inevitable consequence of recording spoken language.

But Cleveland, like many Civil War writers, would have been worried about the possibility of such a condition. Cleveland attempted to rein in the waywardness of language by an appeal to order and authority. To Cleveland, the condition of Babel was to be eradicated by using proper grammar. Correct grammar and true definition were over-arching natural metaphors for political order, and it is here that the movements for linguistic reform during the Civil War years do connect with the pamphlet wars. Cleveland's definitions are attempts to regain control of a language that has gone astray. Naming is an issue of power, since whoever controls the language can order the world as he wants it to be ordered. Cleveland sees a necessary connection between language and power, and in this Cleveland resembles Hobbes. But unlike Hobbes, Cleveland does not accept the artificiality of any language; his metaphors above all assert the idea that there is a proper use of language: his own, the King's English.

5. THOMAS HOBBES'S LEXARCHY

Thomas Hobbes agrees with Cleveland that there ought to be only one model for right grammar, and that model must be authorized by a single authority, yet Hobbes adds that this is not a natural arrangement but a necessarily artificial one. Cleveland runs the risks of a relativistic position with respect to political (and linguistic) authority in his deconstruction of his enemies' language, since he lacks a coherent explanation of how his language is any truer than that of his enemies. Cleveland would not allow that the rhetorical critique of his enemies' language might also be applied to his own; that language may be, as Hobbes would argue, conventional. Though Cleveland's extravagant and memorable use of catachresis does call into question the propriety of his own language, he does not draw the conclusion that Hobbes will, that the relation of any language to truth is always vulnerable. Cleveland asks the reader to be wary of every language except Cleveland's own, even though he also takes advantage of the situation of writing released by the competition among languages.

Thomas Hobbes supplies a few missing steps between such a critique of language as offered by the Civil War pamphleteers' sense of a transparent or true language and the universal language reformers of the late seventeenth century. *Leviathan* makes explicit the links between the need for authorized speech practices and the public conflict of opinions, between the condition of the multiplicity of languages and the condition of Babel in the press. The first sections of *Leviathan* build up a science of society, and Hobbes makes an account of language germane to his project. Only after explaining that language is conventional does Hobbes argue in *Leviathan* that a sovereign is needed to police linguistic as well as political practice. Hobbes counts on a uniform linguistic practice to counteract the phenomenon of differing public opinions.

Hobbes's version of the story of Babel is set out in Chapter Four of

Leviathan, "Of Speech." In this account, God instructed Adam how to name, a power that proved Adam's sovereignty and original dominion over the Earthly creatures. But, Hobbes continues, "all this language gotten, and augmented by *Adam* and his posterity, was again lost at the tower of *Babel*, when by the hand of God, every man was stricken for his rebellion, with an oblivion of his former language" (101). As it was for Filmer, linguistic difference for Hobbes was thus a political fact, incurred not at the Fall but as a result of the human drive for power. Because language *after* Babel was conventional, however, sovereign authority was needed to control it. According to Hobbes, human creatures learned language again after the multiplication of languages at Babel, and this time not according to God's plan but by their own need and convention: "in such manner, as need (the mother of all inventions) taught them; and in tract of time grew everywhere more copious" (101).[53] The account of the origin of languages is somewhat different in *De Corpore*, where Hobbes argues that we must *assume* language is arbitrary: "it is for brevity's sake that I suppose the original of names to be arbitrary, judging it a thing that may be assumed unquestionable." Hobbes asks,

> How can any man imagine that the names of things were imposed from their nature? For though some names of living creatures and other things, which our first parents used, were taught by God himself; yet they were by him arbitrarily imposed, and afterwards, both at the Tower of Babel, and since, in process of time, growing every where out of use, are quite forgotten, and in their room have succeeded others.[54]

In this story, even God made an arbitrary "imposition" of words on things to "teach" Adam and Eve their language. The passage of time shows not linguistic chaos, but rather a continuous process of the re-invention and forgetting of language, languages constructed by humans.

Hobbes's story of the loss of Adamic language at Babel warrants the sovereign to be chief lexarch. The condition of linguistic arbitrariness requires that the play of language be reined in by publicly accepted rules of speech. Communication through language forges a kind of social order: "names have their constitution, not from the species of things, but from the will and consent of men" (*De Corpore*, 56), like the originating government made from a covenant. Hobbes's theory of language underscores the importance of public utterances for an orderly state, since it is by utterances alone that right and wrong are decided, given the arbitrariness of language to begin with. Since "True and False are attributes of Speech, not of Things" (105), an arbitrator is needed to name right and wrong. That sovereign must set the limits on interpretation: "though it be naturally reasonable; yet it is by the Sovereign Power that it is Law" (323), since "all Laws, written and unwritten, have their Authority, and force, from the Will of the Common-wealth; that is to say, from the Will of the Representative" (315–16). The sovereign oversees the institution of language through the law, that special class of language that determines "the distinction of right and wrong" (312).[55]

According to Hobbes, without sovereign authority, opinions would inevitably create factions – to which the multitude is especially susceptible, being "distracted in opinions concerning the best use and application of their strength, they do not help, but hinder one another" (224–5). Faction arises out of private opinions expressed in public, as we saw in the "World is Ruled and Governed by Opinion" broadside. When "a number of men, part of the Assembly, without authority, consult a part, to contrive the guidance of the rest; This is a Faction, or Conspiracy – unlawful, as being a fraudulent seducing of the Assembly for their particular interest" (286). Like Jordan's "Rebellion," Hobbes's *Leviathan* considers the dangerous consequence of private opinions becoming public without a sovereign to guide human actions:

> For in the condition of men that have no other Law but their own Appetites, there can be no general Rule of Good, and Evil Actions. But in a commonwealth this measure is false: Not the Appetite of Private men, but the Law, which is the Will and Appetite of the State is the measure. (697)

In a state of nature, humans are driven by the laws of their own appetites, but in a commonwealth, the sovereign's laws must constrain them. Only in the state of nature does private judgment operate, *as expressed in verbal acts*, "calling things Good or evil":

> And yet is this doctrine still practised; and men judge the Goodness, or Wickedness of their own, and other men's actions, and the actions of the Common-wealth itself by their own Passions; and no man calleth Good or Evil, but that which is so in his own eyes, without any regard at all to the Public Laws. . . . And this private measure of Good, is a Doctrine, not only Vain, but also Pernicious to the Public State. (697)

Public manifestations of private judgments can operate only in the state of nature, and not in a civil society. Unruly expression of "private measure" leads ultimately to anarchy (185), dividing humans to make wars:

> And that such as have a great, and false opinion of their own
> Wisdom, take it upon them to reprehend the actions, and call in
> question the Authority of them that govern, and so to unsettle
> the laws with their public discourse, as that nothing shall be a
> Crime but that what with their own designs require should be so
> . . . These I say are effects of a false presumption of their own
> Wisdom. (341–2)

When private judgments are made public through "public discourse,"
they pose a threat to the peacefulness of the state. This fear of the public
sphere is a response to the growing prominence of public discourse.
Hobbes belongs to the strain of thought which sets up law as the only
possible public expression.[56]

In Chapter 29 of *Leviathan*, one "Of those Things that Weaken,
or tend to the Dissolution of the Commonwealth" is faction, which
derives from men's tendency to "debate with themselves, and dispute
the commands of the Commonwealth; and afterwards to obey, or
disobey them, as in their private judgment they shall think fit" (365).
This is a "false doctrine," a chief "poison" responsible for the dissolution
of a commonwealth: "*That every private man is Judge of Good and Evil
actions*" (365). Though this is the human condition in a state of nature, it
will not do for a commonwealth: direct links between private judgment
and the public realm must be severed. It is up to the sovereign to
prevent private judgment of good and evil from becoming public without
supervision and authority. The risks of public opinion are too great for
it to appear without such authorization. Ideological difference, just as
linguistic difference, cannot be tolerated in an orderly state.

Hobbes's account of the subject's surrender to the sovereign oblit-
erates all signs of verbal difference. In the erection of a commonwealth,

> [Men] confer all their power and strength upon one Man, or upon
> one Assembly of men, that may reduce all their Wills, by plurality
> of voices, unto one Will . . . and therein to submit their Wills,
> every one to his Will, and their Judgments, to his Judgment. This
> is more than Consent, or Concord; it is real Unity of them all, in
> one and the same Person, made by Covenant of every man with
> every man. (227)

Hobbes's refusal to equate "Unity" with "consent" or "concord" is
crucial. Unity is not a "con-sentire," an "agreeing-together" or a "concord," an agreement in combination of hearts. The many are not joined
to make a *concordia discors*, or even allied into a consensus. Instead,
the "plurality" is by force "reduced" (literally, led back) to a singleness.[57]

This is a different conception from the charged coexistence of a variety of voices in Milton's *Areopagitica*, or even the kind of consensus that was the aim of the 1640s Parliaments. It subordinates the voices of the many in deference to the one.[58] In Hobbes, difference of opinions correlates to linguistic disorder in a profound way: the sovereign is needed to prohibit both. Unlike Cleveland's insistence that language be natural and unified like patriarchal kingship, Hobbes's response to Babel is to acknowledge the arbitrary basis for both language and politics, and to construct laws and a social order to prevent their dangers.

6.

The point of bringing Hobbes into the discussion about language theories and the story of Babel in the seventeenth century is that Hobbes gives a solution to the relations between linguistic and political order, a most vivid heuristic example of the annulment of political disagreement by linguistic means. The story of Babel in the English Revolution is a complicated one, as writers used the metaphor to express their fears about the appearance of ideological difference in the press. The Royal Society's plan after the Revolution, with its motto *nullius in verba* (nothing in words), sought to reform language to make a plain English the only fit medium for expression, and thus to reduce the number of possibilities of interpretation to one.[59] In part, we may say this is a response to the linguistic situation of the English Revolution. The representation of the fear of popular anarchy as a fear of linguistic chaos reflects the actual nature of the Civil War disagreements, where each party seemed to speak in a particular dialect, with words carrying specific meanings which differed according to their use. These individual dialects were easy to identify, and in some way were mutually intelligible, but the existence of a pluralistic language situation had real consequences for traditional royalism. Whether they liked it or not, Babel had become a fact of life.

During the Revolution, the biblical story of Babel supplied a critique of the phenomenon of political difference as expressed in the public sphere. The story supplied a Providential explanation of Babel, as the many languages in public debate were thought to be evidence of divine punishment for rebellion. For a writer like Cleveland, the story of Babel was a conservative story, written in resistance to the pressures of polyglossia in the political sphere. In this reading, the authenticity of language was seen as something fundamentally *outside* politics, as if language could serve as a standard by which to measure political worth. For Cleveland, and perhaps for the universal language theorists who held that a reorganization of language would eliminate religious differences, language was a model for true order, political and otherwise. What writers who employed this metaphor did not acknowledge, however, was that their appeal to this story had profoundly unsettling implications for all political communication. If language always provided a base for authority, then word-play, jargons and manipulations of language (like the use of a metaphor such as Babel) would all be political as well as linguistic threats. Thus, in the case of John Cleveland and for the many writers who used this metaphor, the attack on Babel appears as linguistically problematic as the words of those they were criticizing, since one possible reading of the story of Babel would conclude that all language is conventional and that any language is as true as any other.

It is in this context that we should now attempt to reconsider the universal language schemes of the late seventeenth century, once we have shifted our focus from a monological history of ideas to the discussions about language and references to linguistic diversity in the pamphlet literature of the English Revolution. My presentation of the conservative motives for repressing competing languages during the English Revolution showed Babel to be an image used in response to the opening up of the public sphere, an attempt to stifle the revolutionary press and all its public voices. Linguistic diversity was a sign of deeper trouble, and this essay seeks to enliven the history of "scientific" languages in the late seventeenth century by asking that the Universal Language Movement be considered in its cultural context. In asking for dialogism in the history of ideas, I may seem to fall into the post-structuralist habit of connecting language with power, but I would like to emphasize the relation between language and power in a more specific way than post-structuralism or new historicism might. I am talking about self-referentiality in language that neither deconstructs meaning, nor merely reveals its origins in structures of power. Rather, I see the dialogics of political work in the self-referential tropes of language-clashes. The figure of Babel in the seventeenth century did not merely express the fact of linguistic difference, but it was one response writers had to a new language situation, one in which it was feared the expression of many opinions in the press would lead untimately to political anarchy. Responses to Babel were responses to a new public sphere, where debate and polyglossia were apparent. Even those who responded with fear to the new language situation also contributed to that polyglossia since they, too, presented their views in the press, paradoxically assailing public discourse in public. The paradigm provided by the texts of the English Revolution with relation to the Universal Language Movement suggests the utility of bringing together a dialogic analysis of discourse and the history of ideas.

Literary historians might consider further how the political context of the English Revolution helps to explain why in a specific period of English history a specific form of interest in language appeared. My analysis of the two axes of the metaphor of Babel – the linguistic and the political – showed that English revolutionary pamphleteers deployed this trope of linguistic strife as a figure of social and political strife, and I also argued that the very grounds of political strife were linguistic, since conflicts in the English Revolution occurred in, and over, words. The debate over linguistic authority took place in a public sphere, and Babel became the trope assigned by some writers in opposition to that public sphere. My response to the question of why the universal language schemes popped up between 1640 and 1670 is to examine how the English Revolution was conceived by its fighters as a crisis in language. Wilkins' concern with this "cheat of words" reiterates an obsession with language occasioned by the differences in religion during the English Revolution, and we can see this by setting the remedies for linguistic chaos into the context of the pamphlet wars of the English Revolution. The Universal Language Movement participated in the linguistic situation of its day not only as a project of the new science and trade, not only in the international context of the religious dispute between Catholicism and Protestantism, but also as a response to the war of words in Wilkins' own country. The pamphlet wars of the English Revolution provide commentary on the search for this linguistic philosopher's stone.

NOTES

1. John Wilkins, *An Essay Towards a Real Character, and a Philosophical Language* (London, 1668), 13. I have modernized original spelling here and throughout the essay. My thanks are to Jules Law, Richard Kroll and Kathy Maus for their helpful criticisms of earlier drafts of this essay. Jim Holstun was especially helpful in his suggestions and comments.
2. John Wilkins, *Mercury, or the Secret and Swift Messenger* (London, 1641), 106. For Wilkins' life, see Barbara Shapiro, *John Wilkins, 1641–1672: An Intellectual Biography* (Berkeley: University of California Press, 1969); Hans Aarsleff, "John Wilkins," in *From Locke to Saussure: Essays on the Study of Language and Intellectual History* (Minneapolis: University of Minnesota Press, 1982), 239–77.
3. Joseph Waite's commendatory poem to Cave Beck's *The Universal Character* (1657), A6r, in Murray Cohen, *Sensible Words: Linguistic Practice in England, 1640–1785* (Baltimore: The Johns Hopkins University Press, 1977), 2.
4. See Murray Cohen, *Sensible Words* for a survey of these aims and projects, ch. 1.

5. As does Hugh Trevor-Roper, in "Three Foreigners," in *Religion, The Reformation and Social Change* (London: Macmillan, 1967), 237–93, though Trevor-Roper is too quick to align the thinking of Dury, Comenius and Hartlib to the ideology of the purported "country party."

6. Michel Foucault, in his story of the formation of the "classical episteme" in *The Order of Things: An Archaeology of the Human Sciences* (New York: Random House, 1970), was not the only one to write this kind of teleological story; it is a practice of many historians of science and ideas, according to Cohen's critique of such teleological narratives in *Sensible Words*. There are, of course, many fascinating and excellent accounts of the rise of the universal language schemes of the late seventeenth century in the context of the continental and native philosophic traditions. See, in addition to Cohen, M.M. Slaughter, *Universal Languages and Scientific Taxonomy in the Seventeenth Century* (New York: Cambridge University Press, 1982); James Knowlton, *Universal Language Schemes in England and France, 1600–1800* (Toronto: University of Toronto Press, 1975); and Vivian Salmon, *The Study of Language in Seventeenth Century England* (Amsterdam: John Benjamins, 1979).

7. This is not just the anthropological approach of deciphering meaning out of history which still sees culture as a kind of unity of opposites, used by such "cultural historians" as Lynn Hunt, elaborated in her Introduction to the excellent collection of essays, *The New Cultural History*, Lynn Hunt, ed. (Berkeley: University of California Press, 1989); mine is rather an effort to understand the social implications of written discourse, but also to preserve the differences in meaning which make a single inscription bear several consequences.

8. I say "allow," since the business of policing contextual boundaries is still a powerful one, even within the new historicism. For comparison, see the approach taken by Kevin Sharpe and Steven Zwicker, "Politics of Discourse: Introduction," in their *Politics of Discourse: The Literature and History of Seventeenth-Century England* (Berkeley: University of California Press, 1987), 1–20.

9. *Catalogue of the Thomason Tracts in the British Museum, 1640–1661* (London: 1908), xxi. This collection is not complete for the period, but gives some idea of the volume.

10. There have been some attempts to set the projects of seventeenth-century science into the political camps of the English civil wars; Christopher Hill has argued in his *Intellectual Origins of the English Revolution* (Oxford: Oxford University Press, 1965), 106, 112, for example, that science played a "radical" role in the English Revolution because there is something inherently progressive in scientific inquiry; science was Puritan, according to Robert K. Merton, "Puritanism, Pietism, and Science," in *Science and Ideas*, A.B. Arons and A.M. Bork, eds. (New Jersey: Prentice-Hall, 1964); Trevor-Roper, too, has attempted to assign social positions to the practitioners of the new science in "Three Foreigners," in *Religion, The Reformation, and Social Change*, which allies the new science to the "country party." Charles Webster, on the other hand, has argued that the practice of science was a relief from politics in *The Great Instauration: Science, Medicine and Reform, 1626–1660* (London: Duckworth, 1975), 95–6. Yet the search for the social and political location of seventeenth-century science has too often sought ready-made categories for materials which do not suit them, and our interest here is not in the "politics" of the Universal Language Movement as much as in the ways that linguistic concerns were political in the broad sense.

    Though historians of the Universal Language Movement do assign some weight to the political situation of mid-century Britain in explaining the rise of linguistic theory, they most often do so in unhelpfully vague ways: Murray Cohen attempts to map an epistemological shift onto the sociological, referring to a "change which corresponds to an abandonment of revolutionary fervor, politically and socially," but does not elaborate, op. cit., 23; Hans Aarsleff opens his biographical account of Wilkins with an allusion to the social setting, but does not go further in elaborating how that social setting might impinge on the life itself, "John Wilkins," in op. cit., 239; Sidonie Clauss, "John Wilkins' Essay Toward a Real Character: Its Place in the Seventeenth-Century Episteme," *Journal of the History of Ideas*, 48:4 (1982), 532.

11. Nigel Smith, ed., *A Collection of Ranter Writings from the 17th Century* (London: Junction Books, 1983), 31.

12. Christopher Hill, "From Marprelate to the Levellers," in his *Writing and Revolution in Seventeenth-Century England* (Amherst: University of Massachusetts Press, 1985), 75–95; E. Eisenstein's *The Printing Press as an Agent of Change* (Cambridge: Cambridge University Press, 1985), and her seminal article, "The Advent of Printing and the Problem of the Renaissance," *Past and Present*, 45 (1969), 19–89, have engendered much debate over the deterministic path of print; T. Rabb and E. Eisenstein, "Debate: The Advent of Printing and the Problem of the Renaissance: A Comment," *Past and Present*, 52 (1971), 135–44; Anthony T. Grafton, "The Importance of Being Printed," *Journal of Interdisciplinary History*, 11:2 (1980), 265–86. For the history of the press in the English revolutionary period, see Frederick S. Siebert, *Freedom of the Press in England, 1476–1776* (Urbana: University of Illinois Press, 1952); J. Frank, *The Beginnings of the English Newspaper, 1620–1660* (Cambridge: Harvard University Press, 1961); C. Blagden, "The Stationers' Company in the Civil War Period," *The Library*, fifth series, 13:1 (1958), 1–17.

13. The larger study of which this is a part, *Milton's Public: Writers and their Audiences in the English Revolution*, tracks the workings of this shift.

14. Jurgen Habermas, *The Structural Transformation of the Public Sphere: An Inquiry into a Category of Bourgeois Society*, trans. T. Burger (Cambridge: MIT Press, 1989).

15. The term "opposition" must be taken loosely here, in light of the very great disagreement among historians of the period about exactly what, if any, concrete opposition may be said to have existed in Parliament. The debate over the question of conflict may be canvassed by the following: Conrad Russell, *Parliaments and English Politics, 1621–29* (Oxford: Oxford University Press, 1979), 1–84, and G.R. Elton, "A High Road to Civil War," in his *Studies in Tudor and Stuart Government and Politics*, Vol. II (Cambridge: Cambridge University Press, 1974), 164–82, which hold there was no formal "opposition" party, in reaction to the earlier study by Wallace Notestein, "Winning of the Initiative by the House of Commons," *British Academy Proceedings*, Vol. II (1924–25), 125–75, and, later, C. Hill, "Parliament and People in 17th Century England," *Past and Present*, 92 (1981), 100–24, and J.H. Hexter, "Historiographical Perspectives: The Early Stuarts and Parliament: Old Hat and Nouvelle Vogue," *Parliamentary History Yearbook*, I (1984), 180–205. See also Derek Hirst, "Revisionism Revisited: The Place of Principle," *Past and Present*, 92 (1981), 79–99. My meaning of "opposition" here refers to the many souls, some organized into named parties, "The Levellers" for instance, who opposed the King. Of course this lumping together is scandalous in terms of historical accuracy, but for the purposes of my argument about anti-opposition responses to the press, it is fair: those who opposed the opposition saw them as one rebellious lump.

16. Christopher Hill, "Radical Prose in 17th Century England: From Marprelate to the Levellers," *Essays in Criticism*, 32:2 (1982), 95–118.

17. John Milton, *Areopagitica*, in *The Complete Prose Works of John Milton*, Vol. II, E. Sirluck, ed. (New Haven: Yale University Press, 1959), 557.

18. John Lilburne, *England's Birth-Right* (1645).

19. *Mercurius Pacificus* (1648), 2.

20. A.S.P. Woodhouse, *Puritanism and Liberty* (London: J.M. Dent, 1951), 104. We should take care to note that Cromwell's idea about an underlying agreement was part of a political push for his own ends.

21. Henry Peacham, *The World is Ruled & Governed by Opinion* (1641), Folger P949.5. Special thanks to the Folger Shakespeare Library for their permission to publish this material. Natalie Davis, "Women on Top," *Society and Culture in Early Modern*

France (Stanford: Stanford University Press, 1985), 124–51, explains how this kind of sexual symbolism is connected with issues of power, order and hierarchy in early modern Europe.

22. Robert Filmer, *Patriarcha and Other Political Works of Sir Robert Filmer*, Peter Laslett, ed. (Oxford: Blackwell, 1949), 283. See Hans Aarsleff, *From Locke to Saussure* for discussion of various "Adamic" theories of linguistic origin, where "the relation between signifier and signified is not arbitrary," 25–6.

23. I have profited from conversation with Jim Holstun about this second meaning of Babel. David Loewenstein writes about the anti-tyrannical rhetoric as a component of Milton's myth-making in *Milton and the Drama of History: Historical Vision, Iconoclasm, and the Literary Imagination* (Cambridge: Cambridge University Press, 1990), and about Babel as it is associated with the tyrant Nimrod (109–11), yet fails to note the Royalist perspective which Milton has co-opted for his own purposes.

24. Thomas Blount, *Glossographia* (1656), F2.

25. John Gauden, *Eikon Basilike*, in *Early Modern Europe: Crisis of Authority*, University of Chicago Readings in Western Civilization, Vol. 6, Eric Cochrane, Charles M. Gray and Mark A. Kishlansky, eds. (Chicago: University of Chicago Press, 1987), 442; John Milton, *Eikonoklastes*, in *Complete Prose Works of John Milton*, Vol. III, Merritt Y. Hughes, ed. (New Haven: Yale University Press, 1962), 598.

26. My notion of a "language" here derives from J.G.A. Pocock's essays, "Languages and Their Implications," in his *Politics, Language and Time: Essays in Political Thought and History* (New York: Atheneum, 1971), 3–41; and "The Concept of a Language and the *métier d'historien*: Some Considerations of Practice," in *The Languages of Political Theory in Early-Modern Europe*, Anthony Pagden, ed. (New York: Cambridge University Press, 1987), 19–38; and also Quentin Skinner, "Language and Social Change," in *Meaning and Context: Quentin Skinner and his Critics*, James Tully, ed. (Princeton: Princeton University Press, 1988), 119–32.

27. *Sampsons Foxes Agreed to Fire a Kingdom* (1644).

28. J. Doughty, *The King's Cause Rationally, briefly, and plainly debated* (1644), 37.

29. Thomas Browne, "To the Reader," *Religio Medici*, in *Sir Thomas Browne: The Major Works*, C.A. Patrides, ed. (Harmondsworth, Middlesex: Penguin, 1977), 59.

30. "The Rebellion," *Rump: Or an Exact Collection . . . 1639 to Anno 1661*, facs. ed. (London: Henry Brome and Henry Marsh, 1874), Vol. I, 291–5.

31. According to Peter Burke, elite culture retreated from the practices of popular culture during the Renaissance in an effort towards moral reform that privileged "decency, diligence, gravity, modesty, orderliness, prudence, reason, self-control, sobriety, and thrift" over the carnival values of the populace. The "this-worldly asceticism" of high culture promoted economic power as well as cultural hegemony of the elite over the lower orders, and contributed to further schism between the two cultures. Peter Burke, *Popular Culture in Early Modern Europe* (New York: Harper, 1978), 213, 270. See also B. Capp, "Popular Literature," in *Popular Culture in Seventeenth Century England*, B. Reay, ed. (London: Longman, 1986), 198–243.

32. I share aims with Pierre Bourdieu's analysis of French cultural tastes in the 1960s, in which Bourdieu tested and confirmed the hypothesis that "good taste" is arrived at through specific social and economic paths, through learning the appropriate codes in which the language of art is encoded. See his *Distinction: A Social Critique of the Judgment of Taste*, trans. Richard Nice (Cambridge: Harvard University Press, 1985), 2, though I lay weaker emphasis on the purely economic explanation for such distinctions than Bourdieu does.

33. The issues raised by a burgeoning popular literature are also discussed by Natalie Davis in "Printing and the People," in her *Society and Culture in Early Modern France* (Stanford: Stanford University Press, 1975) and by Margaret Spufford in *Small Books and Pleasant Histories: Popular Fiction and its Readership in Seventeenth-Century England* (Athens: University of Georgia Press, 1981). Though Spufford's book

promises to be most appropriate here, her interest is more with the brute facts of literacy's spread and consumption of cheap printed matter than with the cultural impact of such circumstances on the higher orders of society.

34. *A Description of the Famous Kingdom of Macaria* (1641), quoted in F. Seibert, *Freedom of the Press in England, 1476–1776* (Urbana: University of Illinois Press, 1952), 192. Seibert attributes the utopia to Samuel Hartlib, but Charles Webster has argued more recently that it is the work of his associate Gabriel Plattes: *The Intellectual Revolution of the Seventeenth Century* (London: Routledge, 1974), 369–85.

35. *A Remedie* (1644); Margot Heinemann, *Puritanism and Theatre* (Cambridge: Cambridge University Press, 1980), 27.

36. See Eamon Duffy, "The Godly and the Multitude in Stuart England," *The Seventeenth Century*, 1:1 (1986); Annabel Patterson, "The Very Name of the Game: Theories of Order and Disorder," *South Atlantic Quarterly*, 86:4 (1987), 519–43, tracks the allusions to Cade and Tyler in the literature of the period; and the classic C. Hill's "The Many-Headed Monster," in *Change and Continuity in Seventeenth-Century England* (Cambridge: Harvard University Press, 1975), 181–204.

37. Wharton, *Mercurio-Coelico-Mastix* (1644), 2.

38. The printing history of the English Revolution may be pieced together from the following studies: Cyprian Blagden, "The Stationers' Company in the Civil War Period," *The Library*, 5th ser., 13: 1 (1958), 1–17; H.R. Plomer, "Secret Printing during the Civil War," *The Library*, n.s., 5 (1904), 374–403; Frederick S. Siebert, *Freedom of the Press in England, 1476–1776* (Urbana: University of Illinois Press, 1952), 166–76; Cyprian Blagden, "The 'Company' of Printers," *Studies in Bibliography*, 13 (1960), 3–15; William M. Clyde, "Parliament and the Press, 1643–7," *The Library*, 4th ser., 14 (1934), 399–424.

39. Cleveland's works were successful in the press, tallying 25 editions between 1647 and 1700, even though he sought a coterie audience. Concerning early editions of Cleveland's works, see John Morris, *John Cleveland: A Bibliography of his Poems* (London: Bibliographical Society, 1967) which explains the difficulty in ascertaining the Cleveland canon. The exact dates of composition, and even attribution, are still under question as literary historians attempt to settle the Cleveland canon. See Brian Morris, "The Editions of Cleveland's Poems," *The Library*, 5th ser., 14 (1964); *The Poems of John Cleveland*, J.M. Berdan, ed. (New Haven: Yale University Press, 1911), and corrected by S.V. Gapp, "Notes on John Cleveland," *PMLA* 46 (1931), 1075–86; *The Poems of John Cleveland*, B. Morris and E. Worthington, eds. (Oxford: Oxford University Press, 1967), xvii.

40. John Cleveland, "The Character of a London Diurnal," in *Character Writings of the Seventeenth Century*, Henry Morley, ed. (London: Routledge, 1891), 308.

41. Patricia Higgins, "The reactions of women, with special reference to women petitioners," in *Politics, Religion and the English Civil War*, B. Manning, ed. (London: Arnold, 1973), 179–222; K. Thomas, "Women and the Civil War Sects," in *Crisis in Europe, 1560–1660*, T. Aston, ed. (London, 1965), 317–40.

42. So speculates S.V. Gapp, "Notes on John Cleveland," *PMLA* 46 (1931), 1075–86.

43. The connection is more than a literary trope, since cheap pamphlets often served a second role in the privy.

44. Cleveland was not the first to attack the press in a "character"; Richard Brathwait's popular *Whimzies: Or, a New Cast of Characters* pokes fun at "A Corranto-Coiner," as "a state newsmonger: and his own genius is his intelligencer," as Ben Jonson had before him in *A Staple of News*. Yet these did not attack Parliament head on.

45. On "translation" as a Puritan reading activity, see William Hunt, *The Puritan Moment* (Cambridge: Harvard University Press, 1982), 113.

46. On definition as an aspect of "wit," see E. Miner, *The Metaphysical Mode from Donne to Cowley* (Princeton: Princeton University Press, 1969), 125, 151–5. But definition is also an act of power. See Foucault, *The Order of Things*, 17–42.

47. Thomas Hobbes, *Leviathan*, C.B. Macpherson, ed. (Harmondsworth, Middlesex: Penguin, 1968), 368. All references to *Leviathan* will be to this edition. Page numbers will be cited in the text.

48. See Gordon Schochet, *Patriarchalism in Political Thought* (Oxford: Blackwell, 1971).

49. Filmer's *Patriarchia* is the keystone of this theory.

50. See Derek Attridge on etymology as fiction, "Language as History/History as Language: Saussure and the Romance of Etymology," in Derek Attridge, Geoff Bennington and Robert Young, eds., *Post-structuralism and the Question of History* (New York: Cambridge University Press, 1990), 183–211.

51. J.G.A. Pocock, *The Ancient Constitution and the Feudal Law* (Cambridge: Cambridge University Press, 1957), 17.

52. *The Dialogic Imagination*, trans. Caryl Emerson and Michael Holquist (Austin: University of Texas Press, 1981), 431.

53. See Terence Cave, *The Cornucopian Text* (Oxford: Clarendon Press, 1979), on the epistemological meaning of the trope of copiousness. Terence Ball, "Hobbes' Linguistic Turn," *Polity*, 17 (1985), 739–60, writes about the construction of language from point zero (751), though Ball equates the state of nature with Babel (749), thus eliminating the possibility of natural language at all. This Wittgensteinian interpretation over-values the arbitrariness at the expense of the natural, as opposed to Howard Warrender, *The Political Philosophy of Hobbes: His Theory of Obligation* (Oxford: Clarendon, 1957) who does the opposite. My thanks to Gordon Schochet for his insatiable zest in discussing Hobbes with me.

54. Hobbes, *De Corpore*, in *The English works of Thomas Hobbes*, W. Molesworth, ed. (London: John Bohn, 1839), I, 16. Isabel C. Hungerland and George R. Vick, "Hobbes's Theory of Signification," *Journal of the History of Philosophy*, 11:4 (1973), 459–82, hold that Hobbes presumes rationality as an axiom.

55. In addition to the authority of law emanating from the sovereign, public rules of speech are also to be found in the rational method of science.

56. Habermas, *The Structural Transformation*, 53.

57. Leo Strauss, *The Political Philosophy of Hobbes: Its Basis and Its Genesis*, trans. Elsa M. Sinclair (Chicago: University of Chicago Press, 1984), argues that in Hobbes is incipient Rousseau in the sense of public opinion as *volonté générale*. I disagree, since the direction of authority in Hobbes is the opposite, from top down, though the end result might be the same.

58. See *Leviathan*, 165, on the danger of assuming communal acts are really acts of the will of the people – the susceptibility of the multitude to be led is the reason behind the need for an agreed-upon leader. Thanks to David Wootton for a vigorous discussion with me on this topic.

59. See Stanley Fish, "The Plain Style Question," in *Self-Consuming Artifacts* (Berkeley: University of California Press, 1972), who argues as a conclusion to his brilliant collection of essays, that "the triumph of the plain style, then, is a triumph of epistemology" (381): yet what I present here gives that the motive for that triumph may be more fear than hope, and that the writers themselves may not have been aware that the language issue required a new epistemology.

Restyling the King:
Clarendon Writes Charles I

JOAN E. HARTMAN

Before Charles I was forced to summon the Short and the Long Parliaments, the style in which he addressed his subjects, whether speaking to them *in propria persona* or in a textual *persona* created through writing, was synonymous with his station. In consequence, his mode of address to them – as well as theirs to him – was unproblematic. But the rifts opening among him, Parliament and his subjects that preceded his raising his standard at Nottingham in August 1642 were reflected in and created by a series of written exchanges between him and Parliament that began in November 1641. More was at stake than textual oppositions. The exchanges concerned hostile actions: among them, on Charles's side, his charging five Members of Parliament with treason, his attempt to enter Hull, and his raising forces through commissions of array; and on Parliament's side, their execution of Strafford and imprisonment of Laud and other servants of the King, their condoning (if not encouraging) the London crowds' intimidation of the King's supporters in Parliament, and their raising forces through the Militia Ordinance. The exchanges were themselves hostile actions, "paper skirmishes" (I take the metaphor from Clarendon's *History of the Rebellion*).[1] Both sides arranged to have them printed; both hoped to win the minds and hearts of (at least the literate) subjects of Charles I.

Clarendon, then Edward Hyde,[2] was chiefly responsible for the style in which Charles, his station challenged by Parliament, addressed his subjects. Hyde, a Member of Parliament, was active in and voted with the reforming party until November 1641, when he opposed both the Grand Remonstrance and its printing; he then wrote the King's answer to it and most of his subsequent messages. Writing Charles for his subjects, he restyled him. Style as he uses it (in both the King's messages and in the *History*) signifies, at times interchangeably, both title and mode of address. A title (how I am styled) prescribes two modes of address: the style I use to speak to others and the style they use to speak to me. The style proper to one styled a king expresses his royal will and, at its least peremptory, his princely and fatherly intentions. The style proper to his subjects when they address him is deferential. Hyde violated the decorum of kingly expression by writing a deferential Charles who not only defended his actions but also explained his motives.

In addition, Hyde presented a reasoned and reasonable defence of what he took to be Charles's constitutional position and a cogent analysis of Parliament's. The exchanges between them appear, at a glance, ragged, with old charges and countercharges repeated and new ones added. Parliament attacks; the King responds. Gradually, however, Hyde strengthened the King's position: if he could not choose the charges, he could at least move the debate towards what he saw as constitutional issues. He had sided with the reforming party while they legislated against the extension of the King's prerogative during the 11 years that Charles I ruled without Parliament. As Parliament extended its own prerogative, however, he was able to argue that Parliament, not Charles, was altering the established order, and to appropriate for the King many of the arguments Parliament had used against him. Both sides put themselves forward as conservative. But when Hyde began to write for the King, late in 1641, he had the stronger case to make and the rhetorical skill to make it.[3]

The importance of these exchanges between the King and Parliament has been variously estimated. Hyde thought them of considerable force in winning adherents to the Royalist cause, at least among sober and rational men. They were, of course, what he knew best when he began to write his *History*, in 1646–48, between the defeat of Charles's armies by Parliament's and his trial and execution. He included Parliament's messages as well as the King's, almost verbatim, in the 1646–48 *History*, and retained most of them when he completed it in 1668–71, even though they threaten to swamp the narrative of what became Books 4 and 5.[4] In the *History*, while he does not identify himself as the author of the King's messages, in his *persona* as historian he frames the exchanges with comments that invariably touch on their style. Royalists had accused him of inappropriately restyling the King, of writing him in too humble a style. The historian acknowledged the restyling and, on more than one occasion, the justice of the accusation: the King's style, he writes, was "not answerable to the provocation, nor princely enough for such a contest."[5] But the acknowledgment prefaces a defence of the style (and by implication of himself, its author) as proper to a king whose station was in jeopardy and strategic to his maintaining it. Parliament having engendered mistrust of the King, it was proper for him "by all gentleness and condescension to undeceive and recover men to their sobriety and understanding," and "to descend to all possible arts and means to that purpose." Among the arts to which the King must "descend" Hyde would include the art of rhetoric.[6]

Parliament's Grand Remonstrance of November 1641 initiated the paper skirmishes and Hyde's involvement with the King. In the previous spring, Parliament had voted for and Charles had assented to a bill for triennial parliaments and a bill providing that the Long Parliament could not be dissolved without its consent. He had assented to bills abolishing the several prerogative courts he had used to govern, to raise revenue, and to repress dissent. He also assented to a bill of attainder against the Earl of Strafford, and consequently to his execution. Hyde regarded these reforms as necessary and desirable.

But in the summer of 1641, while Charles was in Scotland, a project that had languished in a parliamentary committee, the Remonstrance concerning the state of the kingdom, was revived. Presented to Parliament on Charles's return, it passed the Commons by a close vote on 22 November, was presented to the King on 1 December, and ordered printed by another close vote on 15 December. Hyde actively opposed both the Remonstrance and its printing. It was, he wrote in the *History*, "a very bitter representation" of the past, inasmuch as it enumerated Charles's abuses of prerogative power from the beginning of his reign in 1625, abuses that were no longer possible because of the legislation of the previous spring.[7] Parliament acknowledged this legislation, but chiefly with respect to their own efforts to secure it. In Hyde's summary (he does not quote the Remonstrance in full in the *History*): "they left not any error or misfortune in government, or any passionate exercise of power, unmentioned and unexpressed; with the sharpest and most pathetical expressions to affect the people"; "they magnified their own services"; "they negligently and perfunctorily passed over his majesty's graces and favours, as being little more than in justice he was obliged to grant, and of inconsiderable loss and damage to himself."[8] Publishing the Remonstrance, Hyde recognized, made it "an appeal to the people, which had never been practised and might prove of dangerous consequence," for – with his characteristic perception that style and station are synonymous – "beside the matter, the dialect and expressions were so unusual, and might be thought to lessen in many particulars the reverence due his majesty, that it might be a means to alienate his majesty's heart from them, by lessening his confidence in their affection and duty."[9]

He wrote his answer to the Remonstrance, he explained (in the *Life* of himself he wrote after the Restoration), "only to give vent to his own indignation, and without the least purpose of communicating it, or that any use should be made of it."[10] It was, however, seen by Lord Digby, who secured it for the King; it was printed in January 1641, and the King's cause, Hyde noted with satisfaction, "was very much advanced by it."

This answer, Hyde's first attempt to restyle the King, is rhetorically effective. He was faced with a document of 206 (numbered) points in which Parliament surveyed past, present and future. Instead of responding point by point (a strategy all too common in controversy), he summarized what the King had done and was willing to do, first with respect to religion and then with respect to secular affairs. "Although We do not believe that Our House of Commons intended, by their Remonstrance of the State of the Kingdom, to put Us to any Apology," he had the King graciously begin,

> Notwithstanding, since they have thought it so very necessary (upon their Observation of the present Distemper) to publish the same, for the Satisfaction of all Our loving Subjects, We have thought it very suitable to the duty of Our place (with which God hath trusted Us) to do Our part to so good a Work, in which We shall not think it below our Kingly Dignity to descend to any particular, which may compose and settle the Affections of our meanest Subjects, since we are so conscious to Our Self of such Upright Intentions and Endeavours, and only of such (for which We give God thank) for the Peace and Happiness of Our Kingdom, in which the prosperity of Our Subjects must be included, that We wish from Our heart, that even Our most Secret thoughts were published to their View and Examination: though We must confess, We cannot but be very sorry in this Conjuncture of time (when the unhappiness of this Kingdom is so generally understood abroad) there should be such a necessity of publishing so many particulars, from which, We pray, no inconveniences may ensue that were not intended.[11]

In this answer, one of the earliest examples of Hyde's public prose, he carefully modulates his cadences. The sentence quoted, though long, unfolds with duly weighted logical connectives and parallelism sufficient to reinforce them: *notwithstanding, since they* – Parliament – have thought it *so very necessary* to do one thing, *we* – the King – have thought it *very suitable* to do another, *since we* are *so conscious*, *though*, we must confess, we are *very sorry*. It is further stiffened with paired nouns: "Intentions and Endeavours," "Peace and Happiness," "View and Examination." Hyde will use this style in the *History* for exhortation and reflection.[12] Perhaps in 1641, a relatively young man of 32, he was already in possession of it; perhaps he consciously developed it to make the King speak with the dignity appropriate to his station. In either case, it became a style he deployed fluently, first in writing Charles I and later in writing the history of his cause.

Answering the Remonstrance, Hyde saw both political and rhetorical advantages to putting the past behind. In substance and style he thought Parliament intended the Remonstrance "to affect the people." For the King to repeat its substance in order to rebut it point by point would, on the one hand, have him recirculate the particulars of Parliament's case and, on the other, diffuse the force of his own. Hyde chose to emphasize the King's case. He had Charles defend himself against Parliament's accusations of favouring papists by professing his attachment to the Church of England as established and, with a hyperbolic flourish that Charles would make literal, his readiness to "Seal to it by the Effusion of Our Blood, if it pleased God to call Us to that Sacrifice." He also had him express his willingness, with the advice of Parliament, to exempt "tender Consciences" from "such Ceremonies . . . held to be matters indifferent." Then he had him remind his subjects that he had not refused a single bill presented to him by the Parliament then sitting. Finally, adopting a strategy that would characterize his subsequent writing of Charles, he had him express his reverence for the law, "the Inheritance of every Subject, and the only Security he can have for his Life, Liberty, or Estate," and his resolve not only "to observe the Laws of [sic] Our Self, but maintain them against what opposition soever, though with the hazard of Our being." Doing so, he staked out for Charles a conservative position. He had him profess himself resolved to observe the law (rather than bound to obey it) – and to maintain it.

Between Hyde's writing the King's answer to the Remonstrance and its printing, the King came to Westminster to charge five members of the Commons with treason, an action that cast doubt on the benign intentions Hyde eloquently professed for him, and dissipated much of the advantage the answer might have gained. In December 1641, Charles had appointed Lucius Carey, Viscount Falkland, and Sir John Colepeper to office, asked them, in conjunction with Hyde, to manage his affairs in Parliament, and promised to consult with them – all of which led them to hope that the King intended to be the constitutionally-minded monarch seeking accommodation with Parliament that Hyde had professed him to be. Shortly thereafter, without consulting or even warning them, he charged the five members with treason, to the dismay and despair of his advisers. In the months following, he alternated between taking advice from them and from the Queen and Digby, who advocated intransigence. Hyde would be left to defend actions that he privately deplored: the King's decision not to return to London after seeing his wife and daughter leave for the Continent at the end of February 1642; his offer, in April, to settle the militia while he raised troops and went in person to Ireland to put down the rebellion there; and his attempt, the same month, to enter Hull and (probably) take possession of the magazine there. These actions exacerbated fears that he was looking to force to put an end to the quarrel between himself and Parliament, as he almost certainly was. Hyde, when he wrote the *History*, underplayed the drama of himself and his colleagues trying to manage the affairs of a king who disregarded their best advice; it takes an attentive reader of B. H. G. Wormald's study to disentangle Hyde's view of the King at the time he wrote his messages from Hyde the historian's retrospective view of him.[13]

Hyde did not undertake to write for Charles until the end of February, when they met secretly at Greenwich.[14] But on 20 January 1642, the King sent a brief and conciliatory message to Parliament that Hyde, Falkland and Colepeper, who probably did not write it, plainly approved of: he asked them to propose particular measures concerning his authority and their privilege, the revenue, and religion, and to present them to him "composed [into] one intire Body, so that His majesty and themselves may be able to make the more clear Judgment of them," that "present distractions" may be resolved "in an happy and blessed Accommodation."[15] Hyde and his colleagues expected Parliament to respond with proposals for moderate reform. The Remonstrance had passed with a narrow vote, and they did not think a majority of the Commons, including many who voted for it, favoured radical change. Hyde would allude to this conciliatory message in the messages he would write in the following months. But the measures Parliament finally proposed, in the Nineteen Propositions of 1 June 1642, were scarcely moderate. Charles (written by Hyde) observed that they would reduce him to "the Title of a King, and suffer them (according to their Discretion), to govern Us and the Kingdom."[16] Events of the spring would thwart the accommodation Hyde hoped for when he began to restyle the King.

Following Hyde's meeting with Charles at the end of February, he answered for him a declaration that Parliament presented to him at Newmarket on 9 March; this answer, the King's second to this declaration, was sent to Parliament on 21 March.[17] Parliament had announced their "Fears and Jealousies," words that would become formulaic in subsequent messages; they described papist plots to alter religion, the rebellion in Ireland, the Queen's designs to further Catholicism, another plot to raise an army in London against them, the attempt on the five members, Digby's appearance "in a Warlike manner at Kingston-upon-Thames," and news from "Rome, Venice, Paris, and other parts" that the King intended altering religion and "breaking the neck of your Parliament." They found the King's words insufficient to alleviate their fears; they pointed to the gracious words that preceded his charges against the five members. They asked for deeds, namely his return to London and his dismissal of "those wicked and mischievous Counsellors which had caused all these Dangers and Distractions." They, like Hyde, recognized gaps between the King's discourse and his practice. But while their rhetoric enlarged them, his diminished them.

Hyde, answering their declaration of 9 March, had Charles take note of "some expressions" in it "so different from the usual Language to princes." The King declined to be affronted by them: "our unalterable affection to Our People," Hyde had him explain, "prevailed with Us to suppress that passion, which might well enough become Us." Hyde had him gravely consider charges of plots based on (as Hyde characterized them) rumours and shards of evidence, exaggerated and then interpreted to his disadvantage, and respond by avowing his innocence and protesting the improbability of his acting as accused. Hyde did not ignore the particulars of the King's present transgressions as detailed in this and subsequent messages from Parliament (as he had ignored those of his past transgressions detailed in the Grand Remonstrance). But he dealt with them as briskly as possible, sometimes, as here, by appealing to the King's ethos, sometimes, as elsewhere, by ironically undercutting the evidence Parliament used to cobble together its charges. Hyde was, I think, impatiently aware that particulars clogged his larger and more telling points, such as the King's reverence for the law; "the which," he had Charles say, "we always intended shall be the Measure of our own Power, and expect it shall be the Rule of our Subjects Obedience."

Parliament anticipated receiving the King's answer of 21 March with a Humble Petition of 22 March, presented to the King at York on 26 March.[18] It was "called a petition," Hyde observed after quoting it in the *History*, to call attention to gaps between Parliament's discourse and its practice. In this petition they protested the King's refusal to accede to a previous petition (their first answer to his message of 20 January) that he should entrust the Tower of London and the militia to persons they would recommend to him. They called attention again to the abuses of his prerogative that their legislation had curbed, alluded to designs on his part to subvert that legislation, and mentioned rumours of his preparing to make war on them even as they denied believing them: "we are not apt to give Credit to Informations of this Nature; yet we cannot altogether think it fit to be neglected, but that it may justly add somewhat to the weight of our Fears and

Jealousies." They concluded by "humbly" advising and beseeching his speedy return to London "to close with the Council and desire of your Parliament."

The answer to this petition of 22 March[19] that Hyde wrote for Charles was less conciliatory than the answer to their declaration of 9 March, as well it might be: following the King's refusal to settle the militia as Parliament had asked, they had passed an ordinance giving them control of it. The Militia Ordinance raised the stakes in the contest between them, and Hyde perceived it as a constitutional issue that he could exploit for the King. Responding to Parliament's petition, he had the King profess his willingness to settle the militia in the usual parliamentary way, by a bill to which he would assent. The Militia Ordinance was unparliamentary and so not binding. Moreover, Parliament, by legislating without him, was altering the fundamental (constitutional) law of the kingdom: "and what is this," he asked them, "but to introduce an Arbitrary way of Government?" Hyde neatly reversed their scripts. Formerly, the King had extended his prerogative to rule without Parliament – and Parliament had represented itself as conserving fundamental law; now Parliament had extended its prerogative to govern without him – and Hyde could represent him as conserving fundamental law.

He also had the King insist on his own fears and jealousies, not only of the Militia Ordinance but also of seditious pamphlets and sermons and mobs and tumults in the streets of London, none of which Parliament could or would control. These, the King told them, had caused him to leave London, "driven (we say not by you, yet) from you"; until they made safe his return, he intended to stay away, content, they might be sure, were they to adjourn "to such a place, where We may be fitly and safely with you." They ought to be as sensible of his privileges as he was of theirs. He taxed them with harkening back to abuses amply remedied by legislation and, in particular, for alleging designs to subvert it: "and therefore We demand full Reparation in this point" – *demand*, after the previous messages, is strident – "that we may be cleared in the sight of all the World, and chiefly in the eyes of our Loving Subjects, from so notorious and false an imputation as this is."

In May 1643, Parliament sent the King two lengthy Remonstrances, the first in answer to his messages of 21 and 26 March, the second in answer to his message of 4 May concerning his attempt to enter Hull. All three messages were Hyde's. In April, when the King went to Hull, Sir John Hotham, a Member of Parliament as well as Hull's governor, refused to admit him, alleging that he was obeying a command of Parliament; the King charged him with treason. Parliament in turn voted Hotham's refusal no treason and declared that the King had violated their privileges because Hotham was a Member of Parliament. On 28 April, they published a declaration concerning Hull (and their votes) without sending it to the King, which was, Hyde alleged in the King's message of 4 May, "an Appeal to the People, and as if their intercourse with us, and for our satisfaction, were now to no more purpose."[20]

Not only Parliament's declaration but also the May and June exchanges between Parliament and the King, although addressed to each other, were appeals to the people. The possibilities of accommodation that Hyde, Falkland and Colepeper had worked for were diminishing; Hyde left Westminster to join Charles in May, Falkland and Colepeper in June. Both sides were raising troops, Parliament by the Militia Ordinance and the King through commissions of array – troops that both would need if the contest between them came to war. But their respective justifications for raising troops also figured in the contest, and in their May and June exchanges they debated who was acting legally and who illegally, who constitutionally and who unconstitutionally.

Hyde, in his message of 4 May concerning Hull, was left to defend an action that he privately deplored. But he made the best of a bad business. He had the King, after considering the fears and jealousies alleged by Parliament, emphasize the peaceful manner of his going to Hull and his offer, when Hotham refused to admit him, to enter with only 20 horsemen, hardly enough to seize the magazine had he intended to – which, according to Hyde, he had not. Why then, Hyde had him inquire, did Hotham not yield "that Obedience which he owed by his Oaths of Allegiance and Supremacy, and the Protestation, and which he well knew was due and warrantable by the Laws of the Land"? Was this not treason? Hyde saw the uses to which Parliament put their fears and jealousies as limitless. The "mere sitting" of Parliament appeared to "suspend all Laws, and we," His Majesty observed, "are the only Person in England, against whom Treason cannot be committed."

Hyde's constitutional argument, however, turns on Charles's right to his property – that is, the magazine at Hull, bought with his own money: if Parliament could confound his title to it, no subject was secure in his. Rhetorically (at least), Hyde reduced the King's station to that of his propertied subjects. This reduction enabled him to appropriate Parliament's script, which he did forcibly, by quoting remarks made by John Pym, the leader of the parliamentary opposition, at the trial of Strafford. On the law as the safeguard of property Pym had said (and Hyde quoted him as saying): "your Honours, your Lives, your Liberties and Estates are all in the keeping of the law; without this every man hath a right to any thing"; on the law as the safeguard of liberty: "If the Prerogative of the King overwhelm the Liberty of the People, it will be turned to Tyranny; if Liberty undermine the Prerogative, it will grow into Anarchy."

Parliament's attempts to discredit the royal ghost-writer in their May Remonstrances suggest the effectiveness with which Hyde was restyling the King. They suspected Hyde, but his authorship remained secret until he joined the King at York. In their first May Remonstrance (of 19 May), they referred for the first time, and insistently, to "him who drew his Majesty's Answer," "the Service of such a one in penning this Answer," "the penner of that Answer," "declared in his Majesty's Name"; in their second (of 26 May), there are similar locutions.[21] Did they expect the King to compose his own messages? I think not. But Parliament, professing their allegiance to him even as they acted to reduce him to an empty title, regularly diverted blame from him to his evil counsellors, to whom they added, in May, the anonymous penner of his messages who made him mis-speak. In response, in the King's answer to the first May Remonstrance, Hyde had Charles, on the one hand, speak of "this labour of Our Pen," and, on the other, specify that "our Answers and Declarations have been, and are owned by Us" – owned rather than written – and that he wished the "Contriver" of Parliament's answers "could, with as good a Conscience, call God to witness that all his Counsels and endeavours have been free from all private Aims, personal Respects or Passions whatsoever." In his answer to the second, Hyde had him refer with insistent irony to its "Contrivers" and "Framers" and "Penners."[22] Chief among them was John Pym, his particular responsibility disguised by his membership in the larger opposition to the King.[23]

Parliament's Remonstrances of 19 and 26 May are sprawling documents that contain, among familiar arguments, some new ones, chiefly rebuttals of Hyde's charge that, with respect to the Militia Ordinance, they had not only legislated without the King but also altered the fundamental law of the kingdom – what J. G. A. Pocock has called the "ancient constitution."[24] This constitution, a fiction of seventeenth-century historical thought, had been the debating property of the parliamentary opposition to the Stuarts until Hyde pushed them to square their innovations with ancient traditions. Their arguments in response were strained. In their first May Remonstrance, for example, they called into play a law of self-preservation, not of individuals but of the kingdom itself, and their (constitutional) authority to interpret it as "the supream Court and highest Council of the Kingdom":

this Law is as old as the Kingdom. That the kingdom must not be without a Means to preserve itself; which, that it may be done without Confusion, *this Nation* hath *intrusted* certain Hands with a Power to provide, in an orderly and regular way, for the Good and Safety of the whole; which Power, by the Constitution of this Kingdom, is in his Majesty and in his Parliament together: Yet . . . in cases of such Necessity, that the Kingdom may not be inforced presently to return to its first Principles, and every Man left to do what is aright in his own Eyes, without either Guide or Rule, *The Wisdom of this State* hath *intrusted* the Houses of Parliament with a Power to supply what shall be wanting on the part of the Prince . . . which Danger having been declared by the Lords and Commons in Parliament, there needs not the Authority of any Person or Court to affirm [my italics].

This ancient law warrants their legislation. Although legislative power is shared by King and Parliament, when it cannot be exercised because of divisions between them, it has been "intrusted" to Parliament by "this Nation" and by "The Wisdom of this State"; the agents implied by their abstractions – "this Nation" and "The Wisdom of this State" – are elided, as is the occasion or occasions of the entrusting.

And in their second May Remonstrance (which preceded Hyde's answer to their first), they justified their (perhaps) innovations as precedents warranted not by the particulars of the ancient constitution but rather by the reason of its fictional makers:

If we have made any Precedents this Parliament, we have made them for Posterity upon the same or better grounds of Reason and Law than those were upon which our Predecessors first made any Forms: and as some Precedents ought not to be Rules for us to follow, so none can be Limits to bound our Proceedings, which may and must vary according to the different Conditions of Times.

They also found warrant for their innovative "Precedents," if not in a historical occasion, at least in evidence of one, the King's coronation oath, confirmed "in Books of good Authority, and by the Statute of 25 of Edw. 3," which they quote (in Latin) as evidence that it obliges kings to assent to "such Laws as the people shall chuse."

Hyde, answering Parliament's Remonstrance of 19 May, already had in hand their Remonstrance of 26 May. "If We could be weary of taking Pains for the Satisfaction of Our People," he had Charles observe in his answer to the first, but it was Hyde, faced with what he describes in the *History* as "two voluminous Declarations to the people,"[25] who must have been weary. Nevertheless, he saw the advantage that Parliament's strained arguments had given him and pressed it with mordant irony and rhetorical flourishes.

Answering them, he attacked what he calls the deceptions of Parliament's language. In his answer to their first May Remonstrance he tells them they "usurp the word Parliament, and apply it to countenance any Resolution or Vote some few have a mind to make, by calling it, the Resolution of Parliament, which can never be without Our Consent." The King, he has Charles insist, is essential to the legislative process. Moreover, the King continues, "as in the usage of the word Parliament, they have left Us out of their Thoughts, so by the word Kingdom, they intend to exclude all our People, who are out of their Walls; (for that's grown another Phrase of the Time, The Vote of the major part of both Houses, and sometimes of One, is now called, the Resolution of the whole Kingdom)." Beneath their rhetoric lies

> a plain Threat, that if We refuse to join with them, they would make a Law without Us . . . which will never be justified to the most ordinary (if not partial) Understandings, by the meer averring it to be according to the Fundamental Laws of this Kingdom, without giving any direction, that the most cunning and learned Men in the Laws, may be able to find those Foundations.

Hyde continues this attack on deceptions in his answer to Parliament's second May Remonstrance. He begins with the King's commending Parliament for closing the gaps between their discourse and their practice: "like round-dealing Men, [they] tell in plain English, that they have done us no Wrong, because we are not capable of receiving any; and that they have taken nothing from us, because we have never any thing of our own to lose." Yet gaps remain, which Hyde teases out by quoting seven constitutional principles enunciated in the Remonstrance by Parliament and restating them in his own (that is, the King's) plain English.

He also teases out Parliament's high-handed interpretive strategies with respect to logic and Latin. In their May Remonstrances, they had assured the King's subjects that their titles to their property were not analogous to his: the King held property not in his own right but in their interest, of which Parliament was the true custodian. Responding to this argument, Hyde had the King ask: "Do these Men think, that as they assume a Power of declaring Law, and whatsoever contradicts that Declaration breaks their privileges; so they have a Power of declaring Sense and Reason, and imposing Logick-Syllogisms on the Schools, as well as Law upon the People?" And responding to their use of the King's coronation oath, especially to this question put by the bishop to the King – "Concedis justas Leges & Consuetidines esse tenendas, & promittis per te eas esse Protegendas, & ad Honorem Dei corroborandas, quas vulgus elegerit, secundum vires tuas?" – Hyde had the King observe:

> unless they have a Power of declaring Latin as well as Law, sure Elegerit signifyeth hath chosen, as well as will choose, and that it signifieth so here, besides the Authority of the perpetual Practice of all succeeding Ages (a better Interpreter than their Votes) is evident by the reference it hath to Customs . . . could that be a Custom which the People should chuse after This Oath taken?

Parliament's and Hyde's respective translations turn on "elegerit," the form of both the future perfect indicative and the perfect subjunctive; in classical Latin an indirect question takes the subjunctive, and Hyde's translation – the laws and customs the people have chosen – rather than Parliament's – the laws and customs the people will choose – is correct. But he rebuts Parliament not with grammar rules but with logic: while a king might promise to uphold laws his subjects will choose, he could hardly promise to uphold customs they will choose.[26]

These May and June messages are the last long ones Hyde wrote before Charles raised his standard and turned the paper skirmishes into real ones. In contrast to the earlier messages, in which Hyde made the King earnestly solicitous of accommodation, in these he made him vigorously indignant at Parliament's encroachments on his legislative function and on the ancient constitution that warranted it. He captured for Charles, at least rhetorically, the high constitutional ground that Parliament had used to curb his prerogative rule. But by the summer of 1642 the divisions between the King and Parliament had obliterated the possibility of their legislating jointly, for all that Hyde had the King assert that he and Parliament shared legislative power.

Hyde, writing Charles, attuned himself to the rhetoric of Parliament as well as to the rhetoric of the King, and to the gaps between their discourse and their practice. The *History of the Rebellion* is an account of all three: discourse, practice and gaps. But he provides different explanations for the King and for Parliament. When Charles in effect validated the constitutional position Hyde claimed for him by dying for it, Hyde, in retrospect, diminished the gaps between the discourse he invented for the King and the King's practice, though he never completely obliterated them. The gaps between Parliament's discourse and practice remained. Rather than explaining Parliament as acting, reacting, and then justifying what they had done, he presented them – or at least their leaders – as planning behind "the Mask and Vizard of their Hypocrisy" (as he put it in his answer to Parliament's Remonstrance of 26 May) to limit the King's power and aggrandize their own. The *History* afforded Hyde the opportunity to write Charles I in a different genre and to write Parliament as well.

NOTES

1. Edward Hyde, Earl of Clarendon, *The History of the Rebellion and Civil Wars in England*, W. D. Macray, ed. (Oxford: Clarendon Press, 1888), 2:13.
2. Charles I knighted Hyde in February 1644 and Charles II elevated him to the peerage at the Restoration and created him the first Earl of Clarendon at the coronation in April 1661.
3. J.H. Hexter, in *The Reign of King Pym* (Cambridge: Harvard University Press, 1941), describes Parliamentary leaders as resisting the King without thinking through their justification and groping to articulate one in their messages (175–204). See also J.W. Allen, "The War of Manifestoes," in *English Political Thought 1603–1644* (London: Methuen, 1938), 386–412, for an analysis of the exchanges between the King and Parliament.
4. I give three sources for the messages of the King: John Rushworth, *Historical Collections* (London, 1721), from which I quote; Clarendon, *History*, the most accessible; and Graham Roebuck, *Clarendon and Cultural Continuity: A Bibliographical Study* (New York: Garland, 1981), for information about the originals; and two for the messages of Parliament: Rushworth and Clarendon. I quote from Rushworth's reprint (omitting its copious italics) rather than from the *History*, because in the *History* most of the messages, the King's and Parliament's, appear in indirect rather than direct discourse; in consequence, the royal "we" that Hyde used becomes "he." In the manuscript *History* of 1646–48 (Ms. Clarendon 112, Bodleian Library, Oxford University), Hyde ordinarily left space for his secretary, William Edgeman, to copy and (presumably) transpose both the King's and Parliament's messages from direct into indirect discourse. Roebuck and I agree on Hyde's authorship of the messages I discuss here; I deny Hyde's authorship of some messages Roebuck attributes to him, and all he describes as questionable, because their author or authors have the King refer to himself as "he" rather than "we." In the speeches and declarations of the Stuart monarchs reprinted by J.P. Kenyon in *The Stuart Constitution 1603–1688*, 2nd. ed. (Cambridge: Cambridge University Press, 1986), they refer to themselves consistently within documents but randomly among them as "I," "we," and "he." I take Hyde's consistent use of "we" as an identifying characteristic of the style he created for Charles. It would, I think, help him to impersonate Charles: "he" would distance the King as other, "I" would blur distinctions between his writing the King and his writing himself. Hyde had a talent for impersonation, and three of his have been identified: *Two Speeches Made in the House of Peers, On Munday the 19. of December, For, and Against Accommodation* (London, 1642) and *A Full Answer to an Infamous and Trayterous Pamphlet* (n.p., 1648).
5. *History*, 2:6–7.
6. Hyde was ambivalent towards rhetoric. He skilfully deployed it in what he took to be a just cause, aware that it was equally available to his opponents. See my "Clarendon: History, Biography, Style" (Ph.D. diss., Radcliffe College, 1960), 216–36.
7. *History*, 1:417, written in 1668–71 rather than in 1646–48.
8. Rushworth, 1:437–51; *History*, 1:424–7.

9. *History*, 1:428n., written in 1646–48 and omitted in 1668–71.
10. Edward Hyde, Earl of Clarendon, *The Life of Edward Earl of Clarendon* (Oxford: Oxford University Press, 1857), 1:79–81. John Pym probably wrote most of the Remonstrance; he added himself to the committee for it in the summer of 1641. See Anthony Fletcher, *The Outbreak of the English Civil War* (New York: New York University Press, 1981), 81–4.
11. I quote from John Nalson, *An Impartial Collection* (London, 1682–83), 2:746–50 (the answer does not appear in Rushworth); *History*, 1:493–6; Roebuck, 11–12.
12. Hartman, "Clarendon," 172–200; Martine Watson Brownley, *Clarendon and the Rhetoric of Historical Form* (Philadelphia: University of Pennsylvania Press, 1985), 37–50.
13. B.H.G. Wormald, *Clarendon: Politics, History & Religion 1640–1660* (Cambridge: Cambridge University Press, 1951), 1–158.
14. *Life*, 1:98–103. Hyde offered to trust Secretary Nicholas with the transcription, telling Charles "he writ a very ill hand, which would give his majesty too much trouble to transcribe himself." His hand is indeed ill-writ, but Charles, recognizing the danger to Hyde, undertook the transcription himself.
15. Rushworth, 1:516; *History*, 1:529–30; Roebuck, 13–14.
16. The King's answer to the Remonstrance of 26 May; see n. 21 below.
17. For the King's first (brief) answer, sent on 15 March, see Rushworth, 1:533–4, *History*, 1:591–2, and Roebuck, 21–2; for his second (longer) answer, Hyde's, see Rushworth, 1:535–8, *History*, 2:1–6, and Roebuck, 22–4. After Parliament's declaration of 9 March was presented to the King, Hyde wrote to him; the undated copy of his letter, reprinted in *State Papers Collected by Edward, Earl of Clarendon*, Richard Scrope, ed. (Oxford, 1773), Scrope dates 9–15 March on the grounds that Hyde sent it with the King's first answer (2:138–9), which uses "he"; I think Hyde sent the letter with the second answer, which uses "we."
18. Rushworth, 1:538–9; *History*, 2:7–9.
19. Rushworth, 1:539–42; *History*, 2:10–12; Roebuck, 24–5.
20. Rushworth, 1:571–4; *History*, 2:52–6, Roebuck, 30.
21. The Remonstrance of 19 May, Rushworth, 1:691–703 and *History*, 2:95–101; the Remonstrance of 26 May, Rushworth, 1:577–87 and *History*, 2:119–34.
22. The King's answer to the Remonstrance of 19 May, Rushworth, 1:704–14, *History*, 2:135–49, and Roebuck, 33–4; his answer to the Remonstrance of 26 May, Rushworth, 1:588–99, *History*, 2:149–64, and Roebuck, 34–5.
23. Fletcher, 240.
24. J.G.A. Pocock, *The Ancient Constitution and the Feudal Law: English Historical Thought in the Seventeenth Century* (1957; reprinted New York: Norton, 1967), 45–7.
25. *History*, 2:88.
26. Hyde translated the bishop's question as follows: "Sir, will you grant to hold and keep the Laws and rightful Customs which the Commonality of this your Kingdom have, and will you defend and uphold them to the Honour of God, so much as in you lieth?"

The Ranters and the Limits of Language

BYRON NELSON

Because they were the only sect from the English Revolution to be named for their verbal habits, it should come as no surprise that the Ranters were original, inventive, playful and inflammatory in their use of written language, as they were in their notorious socially aggressive acts. Lacking the blunt egalitarian menace of the Levellers, the frightening call for communism of the Diggers, the direct political threat of the Fifth Monarchists, or the prophetic leadership of the Muggletonians, the Ranters earned their instant notoriety in the late 1640s by a series of vivid and outrageous dramatic episodes, which were both eagerly pounced upon by their critics and maliciously distorted or fabricated by opposition tract-writers. The Ranters' performance skills showed keen political awareness, and their literary styles have only begun to be seriously studied.

It is possible that the vividness of the street theatre of the Ranters, as recorded in their own writings and in the bitter anti-Ranter tracts, will ultimately be better remembered than the eloquence of their printed words. The pamphlets variously speak of the Ranters vigorously blaspheming in alehouses, as nearly every anti-Ranter tract complains; they talk of Abiezer Coppe preaching naked, then throwing apples or nutshells as he is being interrogated by a parliamentary committee;[1] they deplore the Ranter shoemaker who believed "good meat and drinke, tobacco, and merry company to be Gods";[2] they depict Thomas Tany attacking Parliament with a rusty sword, then drowning as he sets sail to Amsterdam to convert the Jews;[3] and they cite Dr Paget's maid stripping "her self naked" to join a roistering band of Ranters as "they improved their liberty."[4]

The despairing author of *The Ranters Ranting* could hardly find the words to describe a group who "delight not onely in gluttony and drunkennesse, chambering and wantonnesse, and the like, but deride the holy Scriptures, deny Christ, blaspheming, and as it were spit in the face of God himself."[5] The Ranters would be worth remembering even if their printed words were all lost and we only knew them by their alleged acts of spectacular misbehaviour from the anti-Ranter pamphlets. The tracts of the Ranter writers offer more reliable accounts of Ranter beliefs than the lively, but scurrilous and suspect, reports of Ranter misbehaviour from the anti-Ranter canon.

J.C. Davis's recent denial of the existence of the Ranters and Nigel Smith's massive study of radical prose styles, *Perfection Proclaimed*, which complements his earlier *Collection of Ranter Writings*, suggest, by the disparity of their approaches, the need for a further look at the prose style of the Ranters. In *Fear, Myth, and History*, Davis makes the mistake of denying the Ranter movement any coherence.[6] The denial of the Ranters' existence as a group complements his theory that the Ranters had only a shadowy life as a bogey to warn the pious: "There was a real phenomenon in the 1650s. It was the projection of an image inverting all that true godliness should represent" (Davis, 136); it also complements his accusation that Christopher Hill and A.L. Morton, as members of the erstwhile Communist Party Historians' Group, imposed their own frustrated political hopes on a non-existent historical political movement: "There may have had to be a group of Ranters, if the experience of defeat were not to overwhelm the English people and stifle their desire to make their own history" (137). But since Hill himself clearly states in *The World Turned Upside Down* that "there is no recognized leader or theoretician of the Ranters, and it is extremely doubtful whether there ever was a Ranter organization" (203), he scarcely earns the abuse Davis heaps on him for allegedly overstating Ranter organization.[7] Writing contemporaneously with Davis, Jerome Friedman, in *Blasphemy, Immorality, and Anarchy*, falls into the opposite trap of imposing far too tidy an organizational scheme on the Ranters. He mimics the absurdly pedantic scheme of *The Ranters Bible* (1650), which divides the Ranters into seven distinct groups with classical and biblical names like Shelomethites and Athians,[8] and he concocts such arbitrary categories as "Sexual Libertines" and "Divine Ranters."[9]

Davis's book is careless in its logic and is mean-spirited, but it has had the effect of keeping the Ranters where Hill placed them in *The World Turned Upside Down*, at the centre of the debate about the English Revolution. But as a "meagre bit of anti-history" (Thompson, 160), it fails to address the question of style, which I wish to address. The Ranter writings of Abiezer Coppe, Laurence Clarkson, George Foster, Joseph Salmon, Jacob Bauthumley and Thomas Tany reveal an extraordinary range and variety. The Ranter writers are variously associational, violent, threatening, repetitive, conversational, seductive, solipsistic, illogical and playful, and they are theatrical and artificial in their use of dialogue and role-playing, riddling and prankish wit, and jesting personae.

There are several factors that must render all critical judgments about the Ranter writers tentative. Theirs is a prophetic and populist literature, written (with the exception of Coppe and Dr John Pordage) by men of little formal education who insisted on the spontaneity of their utterance. Like all prophetic literature, their work seeks to collapse the differences between the Bible or other scriptures and the individual utterance of the latter-day prophet. The writers so deeply identify themselves with the divine voice that the writing emerges as a profound expression of popular and collective sentiments, yet the various voices remain distinctive and personal. Ranter writing is protesting and satirical; and as it seeks to make use of words as weapons, in the tradition of radical literature, it often veers close to desperation and madness; yet since "madness" is more a moral than a scientific judgment, it is often too easy to dismiss Ranter experimentation as lunacy, or to use the alleged madness as a means to evade discussion of the social goals of the Ranters. Because doubts about Ranter and sectarian sanity have usually deflected critics from their real task of observing how their words function and into pointless moral judgments, it is important to recall how convenient a brush "madness" has been with which to paint the Ranters. Coppe and Tany give signs of mental distress, but the presumption of madness does nothing to explain the power of their visionary prose. What seems most mad to us might merely be Coppe's attempt to reproduce on the printed page the widely attested power of his pulpit style.[10] One might think of Michel Foucault's implicit warning in *Madness and Civilization* that we ought not to anatomize madness until we can identify what "normal" behaviour is; or, as one of Foucault's best commentators has explained it, "Madness is not initially a fact, but a judgement – even if that judgement becomes itself a fact."[11] The Ranters had no wish to disentangle their madness from their protests or their claims to divine inspiration, because they were quite willing to accept whatever protection from prosecution madness afforded them. The madness of the Ranters cannot be defined nor separated from their total social, religious, political and stylistic experiment.[12]

Theirs is a literature indebted to the Protestant and Puritan traditions, with which it shares a predilection for biblical imagery, a belief in the sermon as a means of social change, and a sense of the urgency of the need for reform. Yet this literature also rejects and satirizes the Puritan determination to reform manners and morals, and it adheres to the religious and millenarian discourse, even as it loses confidence in its ability to achieve the transcendent. Ranter writing is a repressed literature which had to scramble its vision in the face of vigorous opposition. The harsh persecution of the Ranters quickly fragmented the movement, driving some Ranter writers into prison, emigration or recantation, as well as into deeper irony and ambiguity. Like the Quakers, the Ranters learned to adapt to harsh persecution with silence and cunning; but while silence and discretion preserved the Quakers, it extinguished the Ranter flame, which thrived on vivid verbal expression.

It is the purpose of this essay to challenge some of the classic theories about sectarian style and to propose Ludwig Wittgenstein's "tool" conception of language, in his *Philosophical Investigations*,[13] as a functional way of talking about Ranter prose styles; to suggest that the ultimate message of Ranter prose is, precisely, the limitations in language's ability to render ideas; to assert that the Ranters did exist as a style of protest, if not as a fully-organized movement, and were a palpable threat in the eyes of most of their contemporaries involved in the English Revolution; and to maintain that the best proof of the Ranters' existence is the sheer variety and vitality of their prose styles, which continue to tease and threaten readers. The Ranters are best understood as a style of protest or as an evanescent moment in the swirl of sectarian activity during the English Revolution. The Ranters deserve recognition as an informal group of religious mystics who, having embraced the prophet Jeremiah's emphasis on the Word of God written in the heart, pressed the claims for the spiritual liberty of the sons of God further than any of the other radicals of the English Revolution; that they never achieved doctrinal coherence does not threaten their existence as a vivid style.

Although the works of radicals like John Lilburne and Gerrard Winstanley have only barely begun to nudge their way into the literary anthologies, efforts to analyse radical prose styles have achieved only limited success. In one of the best studies of sectarian literary style, Jackson I. Cope argued that the "incantatory" style of the first generation of Friends is characterized by a tendency to blur the distinction between literalness and metaphor and by "an incredible repetition, a combining and recombining of a cluster of words and phrases drawn from Scripture."[14] Like the Puritan, the Quaker searches in his writing through the detritus of daily life for spiritual meaning, but since, unlike him, the Quaker rejects the identification of the individual self, he is likely to emphasize the effects rather than the experience itself (Cope, 218, 220). Unlike either the Quaker or the Puritan, the Ranter loses confidence in the power of words to evoke any transcendental reality and uses words as a creative means with which to identify himself and assert his place in the world, as a weapon with which to decry injustice, and as a desperate admission of his failure to achieve transcendent insight or political change.

John Bunyan made little effort to distinguish the Ranters from the Quakers and hated them indiscriminately, as Christopher Hill recently suggested, "because he had so nearly been convinced by them";[15] he always recognized the potential Ranter in himself. What united Bunyan and the Ranters was an un-Quaker-like concreteness of detail and a comparable love of play; the playful Bunyan who imagined Christian stalking urgently down the pathway to Heaven, beset by demons and giants, had as vigorous an imagination as Coppe or Tany. Bunyan was not the only one to conflate Quakers and Ranters. Since, to their mutual annoyance, Ranters and Quakers were routinely lumped together, it is helpful to remember Cope's suggestion that the Quakers, despite their obvious break with the past, looked backwards to the Puritan tradition and even, with their repetition and recombining of phrases, to the witty Anglican sermons of Lancelot Andrewes (Cope, 208). Similarly, Hill has reminded us of the indebtedness of the sectarians to the long tradition of the experimental prose of social protest, from the popular sermons of Latimer and the Marprelate tracts to the radical sectarians of the 1640s (Hill, "Radical Prose," 98).

To this should be added the apparently contradictory indebtedness of the Ranters to the deeply conservative tradition of popular mirth and the festive outlook. It is not so implausible to accept the charge that the Ranters' programme had affinities with Archbishop Laud's attempt to revive the festive lifestyle of "merry England." The festive view of the Ranters brought the radicals of the English Revolution full circle, back to the conservative position of the Laudians, who had evoked the festive culture of England as a means of social control, while the Ranters celebrated the same festivities for their anarchic, communitarian release of the individual, away from restraints and towards carnivalesque release. This view has recently been supported by David Underdown, who shows that some radical behaviour resulted from a clamour for the restoration of traditional festivities,[16] and by Leah Marcus, who argues that during the Revolution "there was a resurgence of the threatening side of May Day and its age-old association with the 'misrule' of public mayhem. . . . Holiday mirth shook loose from the Stuart mechanisms that had contained it and reasserted itself as class violence."[17] In this one sense the Ranters were as conservative as James I and Laud (who might not have appreciated their support), because they all sought a common worship tempered by holiday mirth. By calling for the assertion of festive customs against the Puritan plea for the reformation of manners, the Ranters provided an easy target for those social conservatives who were nervous about the dangers implicit in the Puritans' demand for liberty of conscience. In their scepticism, their desperation and their willingness to prevaricate to escape martyrdom and imprisonment, the Ranters broke sharply with the heroic Protestant and Quaker determination to suffer for the faith, in the manner celebrated by John Foxe in *The Book of Martyrs*.

The Quakers played with words as a means of bringing in the divine, whereas I want to argue that the Ranters sought to expose the limits of language, indeed the inability of words to carry divine meanings. The play, parody and prankishness became the message of the Ranters, so it is no wonder that the Quakers found them as antipathetical as did Royalist Anglicans and conservative Puritans. While the Quakers tried to bring in the divine through words, the Ranters adopted the nominalist's scepticism about the ability of words to describe ordinary reality. Examined in another way, the Ranters had more in common with the older tradition of popular protest and with Puritan prose styles than with the Quakers who, in attempting to use words as a means of actually bringing in Christ, used language in an incantational fashion which had, despite its grammatical lapses, affinities with the sermon style of High Church Anglicans like Andrewes and Jeremy Taylor. Smith argues, "The end of sectarian theology was to make human language, in its attempt to embody the divine, behave in a way entirely different both from commonly spoken and written or printed language" (*Perfection*, 341). Yet surely this is true of any of the great literary theologians, as true of more orthodox figures like Andrewes and John Henry Newman as of the sectarians. If the Quakers used language to bring in the divine, the Ranters used language up, demonstrating its exhaustion and its inability to render divine meanings.

Henry More, the Restoration philosopher who roved as widely as Montaigne's spaniel, linked the Quakers genealogically to Jakob Boehme and the Familists in their common acceptance of a "natural language" (Cope, 218). The Quakers shared with Boehme a heightened belief in the magical properties of words to describe and contain the objects they name. One would think that More's scientific inquiry into natural language would have led him to make distinctions between experiential and religious discourses. This was the same More who rowed himself into dangerous waters when he summoned up reason and described the origins of religious enthusiasm in the over-heating of internal organs, leading to a distemper of the brain, in *Enthusiasmus Triumphatus*: "Enthusiasme is nothing else but a misconceit of being inspired. . . . The Spirit then that wings the Enthusiast in such a wonderful manner, is nothing else but that Flatulency which is in the Melancholy complexion, and rises out of the Hypochondriacal humour upon some occasional heat."[18] But the natural language theory does not apply to the Ranters, because they used words in an aggressive and artificial manner, as a means of attacking social pretensions and dishonesty, and with declining confidence in their ability to render transcendental reality. That Abiezer Coppe begins *A Fiery Flying Roll* with "Thus saith the Lord, I inform you, that I overturn, overturn, overturn"[19] suggests by the repetition that the longed-for overturning is simply not happening.

Henry More's philosophical search for a natural language is related to Ludwig Wittgenstein's concerns with language, which evolved from the "picture" theory in his early *Tractatus Logico-Philosophicus* to the later "tool" theory proposed in the *Philosophical Investigations*. The "tool" theory strikes me as a particularly helpful modern instrument with which to gauge the Ranters' style; indeed, this theory provides us with a way to refute Davis's attempt to deny the Ranters their existence. I do not suggest that Wittgenstein was engaged in a nihilistic effort to deny the power of language to describe the world, although his later theory has been construed as an effort to divorce the worlds of language and facts.[20] But it can be argued that Wittgenstein's declining belief in the representational value of language is akin to the Ranters' evolving awareness that language can neither bring in nor accurately describe the divine.

In a famous passage in the *Tractatus*, Wittgenstein had argued that "The sense of the world must lie outside of the world."[21] The speaker of a language is unable to certify facts about reality, since he cannot function outside of his own linguistic understanding: "The world is *my* world: this is manifest in the fact that the limits of *language* (of that language which alone I understand) mean the limits of *my* world" (*TLP*, para. 5: 62). Such logic might have led Wittgenstein to nihilism or atheism but actually did not, and he was not pleased to hear that the *Tractatus* was read as a positivist and anti-metaphysical treatise, as it was by the Vienna Circle; instead, the philosopher maintained a lively interest in religion throughout his life, and like the sectarians of the English Revolution he kept an interest in millenarianism.[22]

When Wittgenstein returned to philosophical speculation after the long interruption that followed the publication of the *Tractatus*, he substituted the concept of "language games" within a larger "tool" or utility theory of language.[23] Beginning with the *Blue Book*, Wittgenstein studied language games, which he initially described as "the forms of language with which a child begins to make use of words."[24] He came to see language as a variety of different activities, with the emphasis on use rather than on the pictorial qualities of language – how words can describe, give orders, curse and joke, and how like children we learn to use words, as we do tools, in a playful way. In the *Philosophical Investigations* he says that "the meaning of a word is its use in the language" (*PI*, 20). Despairing of the power of language to depict reality, Wittgenstein was now content to argue that language is a series of utilitarian and playful gestures; true reality, whatever that might be, most likely had no meaningful correlation to human language, with its limited ability to describe and doubtful capacity to capture the real nature of things.

It can be argued that playful, sardonic, prophetic Ranter writers strikingly anticipate the theories of the modern Viennese philosopher in their vivid and self-consciously experimental prose. The playful literary styles of Coppe and Tany in particular help to exemplify Wittgenstein's theory of language games; the theory helps to refute the notions that words get their meanings by standing for objects in the world (as in Wittgenstein's earlier picture theory) or by evolving from an introspective process of the mind.[25] Language games have clear, immediate social use, are governed by rules, and cannot be dismissed as incoherent, and an awareness of their operation helps to shift emphasis from the meaning of words to their use.

Abiezer Coppe's conscientious use of biblical analogies in *A Fiery Flying Roll* seems at first to locate the most notorious of the Ranters squarely within the Protestant tradition, as when he carefully validates his divine order to eat the scroll (the titular "fiery flying roll") with careful reference to its precedent in the Book of Ezekiel: "Whereupon it was snatcht out of my hand, & the Roll thrust into my mouth, and I eat it up, and filled my bowels with it, (Eze. 2.8 &c. cha. 3.1, 2, 3) where it was as bitter as worm-wood" (*FFR*, 18). Coppe made obsessive use of three biblical texts in particular. The Epistle of James heads the list, and while its denunciation of the rich would have an obvious appeal to religious radicals, the emphasis on doing good works seems subversive of the Ranters' antinomian claims, insofar as practical acts of charity seem at odds with the claim that, to the pure, all things are pure. The Book of Hosea, the chronicle of the prophet who is ordered by God to marry a whore, seems understandably appealing to the man who insists that he would rather lie dead drunk with whores than oppress the poor. From Ezekiel, Coppe derived his preferred image of eating the scroll, and Ezekiel's taste for prankish behaviour (such as cutting his beard) provides a congenial precedent for Coppe's antic public behaviour.

But Coppe, who like Clarkson and Tany and the other Ranter writers was raised in the quieter Anglican or Puritan traditions of pre-revolutionary England, is doing more than imitating the Puritans' careful validation of their personal religious experiences by biblical analogy. It is not enough to explain, as Smith does, that "Coppe . . . feels that he is not only imitating Old Testament prophets. The spirit of the prophets makes him act in the strange way that he does. Thus the speech of the religious radical becomes the speech of the spirit of God" (*Perfection*, 59). Coppe, I believe, is adopting the voice of the Old Testament prophets to proclaim the superiority of his individual religious experience to theirs; his statement, not theirs, is "the last Warning Piece" (*FFR*, 21); but his constant citation of biblical texts implies too the limitation of his own vision.

Coppe can jump from the utmost debasement to divine status as witness to the inauguration of the Everlasting Gospel, in the striking Preface to *A Fiery Flying Roll*:

> First, all my strength, my forces were utterly routed, my house I dwelt in fired; my father and mother forsook me, the wife of my bosome loathed me, mine old name was rotted, perished; and I was utterly plagued, consumed, damned, rammed, and sunke into nothing, into the bowels of the still Eternity (my mothers wombe), out of which I came naked, and whetherto I returned again naked.

From this degradation, Coppe is led to "joy unspeakable," and the divine order to swallow the fiery roll, and the changing of his name, from Coppe to "Auxilium Patris" or simply the divine "I am" (*FFR*, 16–18). (It is amusing to note that after Coppe's alleged flight to quiet respectability in later life, he took up the practice of medicine in Surrey as "Dr Higham," which scarcely disguises his playful re-christening as "I am.")

Consider the complex stylistic response to his bizarre meeting with a beggar, which Coppe reports in elaborate detail in Chapter III of *The Second Fiery Flying Roll*. As is so often the case, he frames his personal experience within the context of biblical analogies, as when he suffers a violent visceral response to the words of Scripture, "and the 5. of James thundered such an alarm in mine ears, that I was fain to cast all I had into the hands of him" (*FFR*, 40). Coppe's gesture blurs social distinctions while it preserves the ritualistic gestures of an unequal social system. At one moment he speaks in the voice of "the WEL-FAVOURED HARLOT," who disguises her meanness of spirit with a series of clichés: "True love begins a home, &c. . . . Have a care of the main chance." While riding away, however, "I, as she, was struck down dead," with the coins in Coppe's pocket rising up in negative judgement (*FFR*, 39–40). Coppe returns to the beggar to empty his pockets into his hands, a gesture which fills him not with the humility a Puritan might wish for, but with a mystical intimation of his own power and transcendence: "I rode away from him, being filled with trembling, joy, and amazement, feeling the sparkles of a great glory arising up from under these ashes" (*FFR*, 40). Even less puritanical is his symbolic gesture of bowing ritualistically to the beggar in the quiet awareness of his own Christ-like status: "Whereupon I beheld this poor deformed wretch, looking earnestly after me: and upon that, was made to put off my hat, and bow to him seven times . . . yet I rode back once more to the poor wretch, saying, because I am a King, I have done this, but you need not tell any one" (*FFR*, 40–1). In an inverted ritual, Coppe's humble gesture really affirms his social superiority to the beggar.

Thus Coppe's language game playfully evokes his meeting with the beggar as if it were a fairy-tale encounter and aggressively transforms the sectarian's private divine message (with James 5 throbbing in his ears) to a demand for the urgent need for charity, which for Coppe was the chief Christian virtue. Following Wittgenstein's admonition, if we examine how Ranter prose functions, how it is used as a functional implement rather than as a smooth philosopher's cloth for polishing up coolly rational arguments, and if we ask for the use rather than the meaning, then we are in a better position to judge its power and effectiveness. In a playful farrago of voices, Coppe plays a succession of roles: the miserly "harlot" who disapproves of beggars, the St Paul-like convert who is smitten with guilt, the sensitive soul who feels "trembling, joy, and amazement," and the king-like figure who pays homage to the beggar and asks him not to reveal his gracious act of condescension. There is no consistent "Coppe" against whom we can measure these eccentric acts, and no "Coppe" outside of his own distinctive language game; this is not a clear radical call for the immediate sharing of wealth with the poor, nor a puritanical lesson on the need for personal acts of practical charity; it is a series of game-like impersonations, described in a series of abrupt, playful prose improvisations.

Coppe loves to shock his readers with startling inversions of the code of normal behaviour: "Not by sword; we (holily) scorne to fight for any thing; we had as lief be dead drunk every day of the weeke, and lye with whores i'th market place, and account these as good actions as taking the poore abused, enslaved ploughmans money from him" (*FFR*, 24) or his insistence that he "had rather hear a mighty Angell (in man) swearing a full-mouthed Oath . . . then heare a zealous Presbyterian, Independent, or spirituall Notionist, pray, preach, or exercise" (*FFR*, 27). The functional and socially aggressive nature of the Ranters' style is nowhere clearer than in their swearing, for which they were notorious. Coppe vigorously endorses "swearing i'th light, gloriously" in *A Fiery Flying Roll*, a boast that is qualified by Coppe's surprising admission, in *Copp's Return to the Wayes of Truth*, that in his puritanical youth he was careful not to offend with his tongue and did not swear for 27 years (Coppe, 73). But Coppe's reputation for swearing was such that Laurence Clarkson distanced himself from the Ranters: "Now Coppe was by himself with a company ranting and swearing, which I was seldom addicted to" (Clarkson, 181).[26]

When we add examples from Coppe's other tonal registers, it all adds up to an impressive, virtuoso performance: his direct attack on the family unit ("give over thy stinking family duties," *FFR*, 45); his fierce apocalyptic wrath, as when he promises that "the dreadful day of Judgement is stealing on thee, within these few hours" (*FFR*, 54); and his insinuating embrace of his unsuspecting reader: "My Deare One. All or None. Every one under the Sunne. Mine own" (*FFR*, 16). The Ranter writers offer experimental prose of extraordinary energy and tonal variety, unique among the many styles of the revolutionary era. The Ranters' message is about the inability of language to render ideas, and thus their prophetic message can be said to deconstruct itself. The play, parody and sheer prankishness in themselves become the message, as the Ranter writers struggle with the frightening awareness that, although the spirit of Christ has risen within them, they are unable to transcend their historical experience or the hostility and persecution that greet their message; they are aware that their identification with the divine has not succeeded in liberating them. The Ranters proclaimed in their speech and action an end to sin, but their words suggest that they could not find redemption; Christ has not returned, has not overturned. Lacking the fortitude of the Quakers and Muggletonians, the Ranter writers drifted off to new sectarian allegiances; unable to certify the divine interventions it predicted, Ranter prose testified only to its own originality. The stylistic energy and variety of the Ranters is the best proof of their brief, vivid existence. Against Davis, Smith is shrewd to argue that "if the Ranters were a fiction, they were one of their own as well as of others' making."[27]

Individual Ranters like Coppe existed and flourished, however briefly, in a provocative Ranter "moment." Ranterism as a phenomenon was a massive assault on the Puritan call for respectability and the reformation of behaviour; not King Jesus, but the spirit of playfulness rose up in the hearts of the Ranters. The Ranter experiment which began with a boisterous, noisy celebration of the liberated self, ended in the quiet surrender, under duress, of the self to silence. Whereas silence was a strategic tactic at the heart of post-revolutionary Quaker discipline, the enforced silence of the Ranters was a disastrous blow to their existence. Joseph Salmon wrote in his recantation tract, *Heights in*

Depths, "My great desire (and that wherein I most delight) is to see and to say nothing."[28] Salmon had come to understand the limits of language, and he uncannily anticipates Wittgenstein at the end of the *Tractatus*: "What we cannot speak about we must learn to pass over in silence" (*TLP*, para. 7). The Ranters were suppressed as a fledgling movement, and the Ranter writers were dispersed: Tany drowned *en route* to his proposed conversion of the Jews, Clarkson converted to a belief in the divine witness of Reeve and Muggleton, Coppe adopted his disguise as "Dr Higham," Bauthumley (his tongue bored through) fled into quiet country retirement, and Salmon adopted exile, as an emigrant to Barbados.

The Ranters' silence was imposed upon them, but it is tempting to believe that their playful, sardonic spirit lived on in the blasphemy and scurrility of the Restoration stage and in the profane vigour of British working-class movements of the next two centuries.[29] But the Ranter phenomenon in its purest form was short-lived, and its distinguishing features were, alternately, playfulness and despair. A sharp contemporary critic of the Ranters, John Tickell, grudgingly admired Abiezer Coppe for his merriness: "Mr Coppe on the Lords day before this lecture . . . his Text (as I am informed) was: There is a time to sing, and a time to dance. It seems he was very merry."[30] The spirit of playfulness rose briefly in the hearts of the Ranters and was eloquently recorded in the prophetic prose of the Ranter writers. Official persecution, such as in the parliamentary acts directed against them, certainly contributed to their quick disintegration; but the Ranter writers had already exhausted the vocabulary of religious discourse and, unlike Hobbes and Locke, were unable to propose social solutions in purely secular terms. The Ranters did not learn to withhold their speech, as the Quakers did, as a prudential political decision;[31] for the Ranter writers, the deprivation of language meant an end to their style of protest.

This essay has argued that the Ranters existed briefly as a style of protest, as a sub-station for a group of like-minded religious radicals. They have been remembered more for their creative acts of guerrilla theatre than for their prose tracts, and they became preferred bogey figures for a variety of oppositional figures, because they seemed clearly to illustrate the dangers released by revolutionary energy. Their prose style is marked by creativity, playfulness, desperation and an experimental quality. At their cheerful best, as with Coppe claiming a time for merriment or Tany brandishing his rusty sword, playfully but with clear political menace, the Ranters exemplify J. Huizinga's famous celebration of "play consecrated to the Deity" as "the highest goal of man's endeavour."[32] When their prose became incoherent and unintelligible, it was the result of their desperation and their inability to turn the dross of religious and millenarian discourse into the gold of positive social action. Unable to win more than fleeting notoriety, the Ranters became prisoners of the limits of language and lost their own distinctive language games; aware only of his own consciousness, Abiezer Coppe as the last move in his language game simply affirmed that "I am." While the second generation of Quakers chose silence as a survival strategy, the Ranters expired as a phenomenon when they understood that their words had not meaningfully described their political and millenarian hopes.[33]

NOTES

1. On Coppe's naked preaching, see "Abiezer Coppe," *DNB*; on Coppe's flinging of apples or nutshells, see *The Weekly Intelligencer*, 1–8 October 1650; *The Ranters Ranting* (London, 1650), 2; A.L. Morton, *The World of the Ranters* (London: Lawrence and Wishart, 1970), 103–4; and Hill, *The World Turned Upside Down* (Harmondsworth: Penguin, 1972), 282.
2. *The Arraignment and Tryall With a Declaration of the Ranters* (London, 1650), 2.
3. On Tany's attack on Parliament, see "Thomas Tany," *DNB*, and Andrew Hopton's Introduction to Thomas Tany, *The Nations Right in Magna Charta . . . With Other Writings* (London: Aporia Press, 1988), 5–6; on Tany's abortive mission to Amsterdam, see Lodowick Muggleton, *The Actes of the Witnesses of the Spirit* (London: 1764, originally published 1699), 44–5.
4. Laurence Clarkson, *The Lost Sheep Found* (Exeter: Rota, 1974, facsimile of 1660 edition), 28.
5. *The Ranters Ranting* (London, 1650), 2.
6. Davis's denials are frequent and shrill: "They were not so much a real religious movement, sect or group, made up of real men and women identifying themselves with particular beliefs and practices, but existed rather as a projection of the fears and anxieties of a broader society" (Cambridge: Cambridge University Press, 1986), x; "Conceding the Ranterish nature of *A Single Eye* does not admit the existence of a cohesive Ranter core, a coherent group" (63); "The Ranters did not exist either as a small group of like-minded individuals, as a sect, or as a large-scale, middle-scale or small movement"(75). Davis's thesis amounts to a negative version of Anselm's ontological argument: the Ranters were so bad, and so useful as bogeys in the seventeenth century and as models for modern radicals, that they could never have existed.
7. Hill's own response to Davis was characteristically gentle. In "The Lost Ranters? A Critique of J.C. Davis," *History Workshop* (1987), 139, Hill paraphrases the second half of Davis's main thesis more succinctly than Davis: "Conservative conspirators invented the Ranters in the seventeenth century, communist conspirators re-discovered (or re-invented) them in the twentieth."
8. Gilbert Roulston, *The Ranters Bible* (London, 1650), 3.
9. Jerome Friedman, *Blasphemy, Immorality, and Anarchy: The Ranters and the English Revolution* (Athens: Ohio University Press, 1987), xiii–xiv. Davis's reactionary debunking of Morton and Hill attracted far more critical attention than Friedman did. E.P. Thompson's review of Davis, "On the Rant" (*London Review of Books*, 9 July 1987, 9, reprinted in Geoff Eley and William Hunt, eds., *Reviving the English Revolution* (London: Verso, 1988), 153–60), blasted Davis's book as "silly and unnecessary" and "a work of anti-history" (155), distasteful for its repetitions and

offensive tone. Barry Coward, "Exaggerated Reports" (*TLS*, 6 February, 1987, 143) is more sympathetic but rebukes Davis for the ferocity of his revisionist attack on Hill. R.C. Richardson (*History*, June 1988, 318–19) credulously accepts Davis's thesis: "The notion of a Ranter movement, even a coherent core, disintegrates under close scrutiny."

10. Christopher Hill, "Radical Prose in 17th Century England: From Marprelate to the Levellers," *Essays in Criticism* (1982), 98.

11. Alan Sheridan, *Michel Foucault: The Will to Power* (London: Tavistock, 1980), 13.

12. The madness of individual Ranters is too often assumed: "At the very least the Ranters often appear as if their minds have outrun their capacity for expression" (Nigel Smith, *Perfection Proclaimed: Language and Literature in English Radical Religion* (Oxford: Clarendon Press, 1989), 336); "Some, like Coppe and Robins, were probably insane, and Tany was absolutely mad" (Friedman, xii). Alternatively, and just as unwisely, the madness is denied: "to describe [Coppe] as 'no doubt unbalanced' is to misread these actions and their context" (Davis, 49). In a sensible approach to the problem, Michael MacDonald reminds us of Richard Napier's early seventeenth-century diagnosis of "verbal pandemonium" for those of his patients who "suffered from severe mental alienation and babbled rapidly and incoherently" (*Mystical Bedlam: Madness, Anxiety, and Healing in Seventeenth-Century England* (Cambridge: Cambridge University Press, 1981), 142). Lacking hard medical evidence, Hill's explanation seems the most attractive: "Mental breakdown is a form of social protest, or at least a reaction to intolerable social conditions" (Hill, "Radical Prose," 279).

13. Ludwig Wittgenstein, *Philosophical Investigations*, trans. G.E.M. Anscombe (Oxford: Blackwell, 1963), 6 (hereafter referred to as *PI*).

14. Jackson I. Cope, "Seventeenth-Century Quaker Style," in Stanley E. Fish, ed., *Seventeenth Century Prose* (New York: Oxford University Press, 1971), 210, 208.

15. Christopher Hill, *A Tinker and a Poor Man: John Bunyan and His Church, 1628–1688* (New York: Knopf, 1989, originally published in England as *A Turbulent, Seditious and Factious People*, 1988), 75.

16. David Underdown, *Revel, Riot and Rebellion: Popular Politics and Culture in England, 1603–1660* (Oxford: Oxford University Press, 1987), 291.

17. Leah Marcus, *The Politics of Mirth: Jonson, Herrick, Milton, Marvell, and the Defense of Old Holiday Pastimes* (Chicago: University of Chicago Press, 1986), 21.

18. Henry More, *Enthusiasmus Triumphatus* (Los Angeles: Augustan Reprint Society, 1966, facsimile of 1662 edition), 2, 12.

19. Abiezer Coppe, *Selected Writings*, Andrew Hopton, ed. (London: Aporia Press, 1987), 21. (References to *A Fiery Flying Roll*, hereafter called *FFR*, are to this edition.)

20. Henry Staten is eager to cast Wittgenstein as an ancestor of deconstruction: "Wittgenstein is unique among Derrida's predecessors in having achieved, in the period beginning with the *Blue Book*, a consistently deconstructive standpoint" (*Wittgenstein and Derrida* (Lincoln: University of Nebraska Press, 1984), 1). By one account, Bertrand Russell deplored Wittgenstein's suggestion "that the world of language can be quite divorced from the world of fact" (Erich Heller, *The Importance of Nietzsche* (Chicago: University of Chicago Press, 1988), 147). It might seem a short step beyond Wittgenstein to post-structuralist indeterminacy, in which the writer flails helplessly, never in control of the meanings which he assigns to the words; but Wittgenstein sought only to warn against the mistake of assuming that there is a vantage point outside of language from which we can somehow perceive reality.

21. Ludwig Wittgenstein, *Tractatus Logico-Philosophicus*, trans. D.F. Pears and B.F. McGuinness (London: Routledge, 1961, originally published 1922), para. 6.41 (hereafter referred to as *TLP*, with number references to paragraphs rather than to pages).

22. Despite his lifelong pessimism, which linked him emotionally to German pessimistic thinkers like Schopenhauer, his most recent biographer, Ray Monk, credits him with a "Hebraic" sense of religious awe. One characteristic quotation suggests that he saw

human life itself, like the language we use, as hopelessly cut off from the transcendent: "We are in a sort of hell where we can do nothing but dream, roofed in, as it were, and cut off from heaven" (cited in *Ludwig Wittgenstein: The Duty of Genius* (New York: Free Press, 1990), 383). Monk also quotes his astonished response to the question in Malachi 3:2, "But who may abide the day of his coming and who shall stand when he appeareth?": "I think you have just said something very important. Much more important than you realize" (Monk, 540).

23. Language games have been variously defined. D.F. Pears argues that "the later term 'language-game' was first introduced as a synonym for 'calculus' and it was then developed to mean any operation with language carried out by a group of people in appropriate surroundings" (*The False Prison: A Study of the Development of Wittgenstein's Philosophy* (Oxford: Clarendon Press, 1988), 2: 279). Monk reports that by 1932–33 Wittgenstein thought of language games as "the method of inventing imaginary situations in which language is used for some tightly defined practical purpose" (330); the emphasis is on the use to which language is put. In his effort to suggest that the structure of language determines the way we perceive the world, Wittgenstein had urged a search not for the meaning of words but their use, as tools or weapons.

24. Ludwig Wittgenstein, *The Blue and Brown Books* (New York: Harper, 1958), 17.

25. John Searle, "Wittgenstein," in Bryan Magee, ed., *The Great Philosophers* (Oxford: Oxford University Press, 1988), 345.

26. George Fox, while sharing a prison cell with Ranters, argued with them about their swearing: "And the Ranters opposed me and fell a-swearing, and when I reproved them for swearing then they would bring Scripture for it, and said Abraham, and Jacob, and Joseph swore, and the priests, and Moses, and the prophets swore and the angel swore" (*The Journal of George Fox*, John L. Nickalls, ed. (London: Religious Society of Friends, 1975; originally published 1952), 181).

27. Smith falters in his uncertainty about the playfulness of the Ranters. At one point, he persists in arguing (as he had in the introduction to his *A Collection of Ranter Writings* (London: Junction Books, 1983)) that "there is no narrator figure of apparent common sense and good will, an impartial observer of events. Neither is there a satirical or jesting 'persona' which is not implicitly part of a larger prophetic stance" (*Perfection*, 62; contrast with *Collection*, 28). But by the end of his study, he has come to accept that "There is a sense of playfulness, of divine folly realized" (*Perfection*, 337); this is the point I argued in my doctoral dissertation ("Play, Ritual Inversion and Folly Among the Ranters in The English Revolution," University of Wisconsin, 1985), which Smith acknowledges as "a wider definition of satire in Ranter pamphlets" (*Perfection*, 62 n.). I feel that to miss the sense of play and folly in the Ranters is to miss their greatest and most radical contribution, to the English Revolution and to English prose.

28. Joseph Salmon, *Heights in Depths and Depths in Heights*, in Smith, *Collection*, 216.

29. Robert Markley hints provocatively at the continuity of the Restoration dramatists with the radical sectarian writers in Ch. 2, "Language and Ideology," in *Two-Edg'd Weapons: Style and Ideology in the Comedies of Etherege, Wycherley, and Congreve* (Oxford: Clarendon Press, 1988), 30–55. On the continuation of radical protest, see E.P. Thompson, *The Making of the English Working Class* (New York: Vintage, 1963), especially Ch. 2, "Christian and Apollyon," 26–54.

30. John Tickell, *The Bottomles Pit Smoaking in Familisme* (London, 1651), 64 (misprint for 80).

31. In *Let Your Words Be Few: The Symbolism of Speaking and Silence Among Seventeenth-Century Quakers* (Cambridge: Cambridge University Press, 1983), Richard Bauman discusses "the situated use of language in the conduct of social life" (5); in regard to silence, he explains, "For the Quakers, one of the most fundamental means was *silence*. Silence was very close to the centre of seventeenth-century Quaker doctrine and practice" (21).

32. Johan Huizinga, *Homo Ludens: A Study of the Play Element in Culture* (Boston: Beacon Press, 1955, originally published 1950), 27.

33. Early versions of this essay were read at the Seventeenth-Century Conference at the University of Durham in July 1989 and in Professor Esther Cope's seminar, "Preachers, Prophets, and Petitioners," at the Folger Library in June 1990. I am grateful to the participants of the Durham conference, to Professor Cope, the members of her seminar and the librarians of the Folger, and to Professor Rudy Almasy, Chair of English at West Virginia University, for helping to arrange my sabbatical leave in the fall semester of 1990.

Roger Williams: Bible Politics and Bible Art

KEITH W.F. STAVELY

I

Modern scholarship on Roger Williams has stressed his dissent from the idea of England, or New England, as the Elect Nation, the Christian era antitype to Old Testament Israel. Williams' views were based on his interpretation of the typological relation between the Old and New Testament dispensations. Israel had been "selected and separated to the *Lord* . . . from all the *people* and *Nations* of the *World* beside to be his peculiar and onely people"; but there was no evidence in the Gospel that, after the coming of Christ, God had ever intended a corresponding separation of "whole *Nations* or *Kingdomes (English, Scotch, Irish, French, Dutch*, &c.) as a peculiar people and *Antitype* of the people of *Israel*".[1] In response to the claim that some of these European nations were apt to make, that the way in which they had "wonderfully come forth of Popery" offered a striking parallel to the miraculous passage of the Chosen People from "*Aegypts bondage*" into the Promised Land, Williams brusquely advised his readers to "bring the *Nations* of *Europe* professing *Protestantisme* to the ballance of the *Sanctuary*, and ponder well whether the *body, bulke*, the generall or one hundreth part of such peoples be truly turned to *God* from *Popery*" (*BT*, 3: 325).

Israel's only genuine antitype, Williams insisted again and again, was no single nation but rather the world-wide, scarcely visible church of the regenerate, "the *New-borne Israel*, such as feare *God* in every *Nation*" and are "commanded to come forth and separate from all uncleane things or persons" (*BT*, 3: 324). A large part of what made Williams so deeply annoying to the Puritan establishment of his day, on both sides of the Atlantic, arose from his eagerness to emphasize, rather than elide, the possibility that these bearers of God's purposes for the human race, these few who had truly experienced a new birth in the orthodox Calvinist sense, were indeed to be found "in every Nation" – as often, that is, in the parts of the world that were not formally Protestant, or even Christian, as in the parts that were: "to . . . *Jewes, Turkes, Antichristians, Pagans* . . . *God* peradventure may at last give

76

repentance," and therefore "that *Soule* that is lively and sensible of *mercy* received to it selfe in former *blindnesse,* opposition and enmitie against God . . . will not onely be patient, but earnestly and constantly pray" that as many people as possible from the ranks of these hostile or marginal groups "may be called to the fellowship of *Christ Jesus*" (*BT,* 3: 93). Such an emphasis constitutes, in effect, the subtext of *A Key into the Language of America,* the work in which Williams introduced the English reading public to the one group of pagans he had come to know well.

With this particular and peculiar version of Protestant biblical typology, Williams placed himself at the cutting edge of the processes of secularization that were going forward in the seventeenth century. Michael McKeon has recently demonstrated some of the ways in which, in the course of the century, such realms of discourse and practice as politics and literature began to free themselves from their medieval subservience to religion. The very emergence of the categories "religion," "politics," and "literature" indicates religion's loss of hegemony, he argues. The need to resort, in descriptions of the seventeenth-century terrain, to such phrases as "religious politics" and "devotional poetry" arises from the fact that religion no longer subsumes politics and literature, but must instead reach out to embrace them in all their distinctness.[2]

Translated into these terms, Williams' understanding of sacred history was that only in Old Testament Israel had it been legitimate for religion and politics to be integrated. The woeful tale of their antichristian merger had commenced with "the unknowing zeal of *Constantine* and other Emperours," the result of whose efforts to function as nursing fathers to the Church had been that "*Babel* or *confusion* was usher'd in, and by degrees the *Gardens* of the *Churches* of *Saints* were turned into the *Wildernesse* of whole *Nations*" (*BT,* 3: 184). During the long ensuing period of apostasy, which the Reformation had not yet succeeded in bringing to an end, scarcely anyone had grasped the fundamental principle that "the *civil state* and *Magistrate* are meerly and *essentially civil*; and therefore cannot reach (without . . . transgressing the bounds of *civility*) to judge in matters *spiritual,* which are of another *sphere* and *nature* then *civility* is" (*The Bloody Tenent Yet More Bloody* . . . (1652), 4: 203).

But to liberate religion from politics, as Williams in arguing for liberty of conscience most strenuously sought to do, was at the same time to liberate politics from religion. Thus, not only was it true that "a *Christian Captaine,* . . . *Merchant,* . . . *Magistrate,* &c. is no more a *Captaine, Merchant,* . . . *Magistrate,* &c. then a Captaine, Marchant,

&c. of any other Conscience or Religion," it was also quite likely that most Christians, being among "the *poore* of the *World*" whom God had chosen to be "*rich* in *Faith*," would be "no wayes *qualified*" for high political office, "though otherwise excellent for the *feare* of *God*, and the *knowledge* and *Grace* of the *Lord Jesus*." Such places of civil leadership were best reserved as the exclusive domain of those very "*Wise* and *Noble*" who were the least likely to be receptive to the Gospel message (*BT*, 398–9, 414–15).[3] In a clairvoyant anticipation of the later American social landscape that would emerge from the processes to which he was himself contributing, Williams argued that from the point of view of politics, religion comprises simply one set of voluntary associations among many other such sets:

> The *Church* or *company* of *worshippers* (whether true or false) is like unto a Body or Colledge of *Physitians* in a *Citie*; like unto a *Corporation, Society*, or *Company* of *East-Indie* or *Turkie-Merchants*, or any other *Societie*, or *Company* in *London*: which Companies may hold their *Courts*, keep their *Records*, hold *disputations*; and in matters concerning their *Societie*, may dissent, divide, breake into *Schismes* and *Factions*, sue and implead each other at the *Law*, yea wholly breake up and dissolve into pieces and nothing, and yet the *peace* of the *Citie* not be in the least measure impaired or disturbed; because the *essence* or being of the *Citie*, and so the *well-being* and *peace* thereof is essentially distinct from those particular *Societies*; the *Citie-Courts, Citie-Lawes, Citie-punishments* distinct from theirs. The *Citie* was before them, and stands absolute and intire, when such a *Corporation* or *Societie* is taken down. (*BT*, 3: 73)

In this version of the argument, clearly, politics has not merely liberated itself from its medieval subordination to religion. Standing "absolute and intire" amidst the mutability prevalent in religion and all other spheres, it has become definitive and dominant.

If, as McKeon argues, early modern history was marked by the establishment of discrete, autonomous domains of secularized discourse and practice and by the consequent loss of the more comprehensively sacralized and integrated medieval world, it was also simultaneously marked by efforts to re-integrate what was being thus fragmented and dis-integrated. Perhaps the most noteworthy of these was that very same merger of religion and politics we have already seen Williams opposing, that effected by the idea of the typologically and eschatologically significant nation-state.[4] Another was the merger of religion and literature that was given distinct encouragement by the radical spiritism of the Interregnum and that helped to produce, among other things, the major works of Bunyan and Milton. Against this form of re-integration Williams also ultimately set his face, as we shall see. So suspicious was he of the coercive potential of all forms of human assertion and construction, whether political or aesthetic, that he functioned as an agent of secularization in a double sense, undermining not only traditional but also contemporary and innovative forms of sacred authority and coherence. Even his most significant legacy to us, his defence of liberty of conscience, is rendered problematic by this relentless negativity. The same reasoning that discountenanced medieval Christendom and the Elect Nation also frowned upon the imagining and building of alternative forms of human collectivity. In the end, Williams must be counted as a prototypical liberal, on the one hand advocating freedom, and on the other denying the legitimacy of most forms of its exercise.

II

Williams was perhaps even more deeply suspicious of the works of the human imagination than were the other Puritans such as John Cotton with whom he disputed. The standard Protestant opposition between the "faire and beautifull *countenance* of the pure and holy Word of *God*" and the "uncomely deformed *looke* of a meere humane invention" (*BT*, 3: 392–3) lay at the heart of his understanding of ecclesiastical history. In his eyes, the central tradition of institutional Christianity had always been nothing but a tissue of "*Idolatrous inventions*," and "*superstitions*." Idolatry was as significant a desecration of Christian truth as his more immediate polemical target of persecution, in the description of which he also had frequent recourse to the idiom of iconoclasm. The prefatory passage to *The Bloudy Tenent* just quoted continues by describing persecution as "bloudy irreligious and inhumane *oppressions* and *destructions* under the maske or vaile of the Name of *Christ*, &c." (3: 11) Most often the occasion of persecution was the refusal of "*Christs witnesses . . .* to practise *worships*, unto which the States and Times (As *Nabuchadnezzar* to his golden Image) have compelled and urged them" (*BT*, 3: 63). Williams was fully prepared to view all extant Christian groups in these terms, even (or perhaps especially) those that had emerged from the Reformation and the sectarian fecundity of Rhode Island and Interregnum London: "the many strange waies, and kindes, and formes of *Protestant* Churches, *National, Provincial, Diocesan, Parochial, Presbyterian, Independent, Separated, Half-separated, Baptized* one way, a *second*, a *third* way (as to their various Formes and Constitutions) are but *Images* and *Pictures*, and none but one of them (if any of them be yet) according to the first pattern" (*The Examiner Defended* . . . (1652), 7: 257–8).

Besides defining his central arguments, Williams' hostility to imaginative effects was often woven into his discourse on a more incidental level. He confessed to a correspondent in 1652 that the sermons he had once written had been "Paints and flowrishes" that merely revealed his own "Vanitie and soule Deceit."[5] John Cotton's central argument that a person "may lawfully be persecuted . . . for sinning against his *Conscience*" had been able to gain a measure of temporary plausibility only from its having been "painted over with the *vermilion* of *mistaken Scripture*" (*BT*, 3: 89). The perpetrators of the Spanish Inquisition had taken care to "varnish . . . and guild" their atrocities "with the painted *Title* of *Gods Glory*" (*BTYMB*, 4: 57). The New England ecclesiastical system, he explained to John Cotton's son in 1671, was no different in kind from the Church of England and other parochial/national establishments, "though sifted with a finer Sive [Sieve] and painted with finer Colours" (*Correspondence*, 2: 629).

In one of his briefer pamphlets of the 1650s, Williams nicely summarized this aspect of his intellectual temper, plumbing the depths of falsehood as he ascended the scale of imaginative elaboration: "*And Oh how many are the* Skreens, *the* Veils, *the* Hoods, *the* Vizards, *the* Curtains, *the* Hangings, *the* Cloaks, *the* Clouds, *and* Colours, *by which the* lustre *and* shining *of that which we call* Truth, *is hidden and eclipsed from us!*" (*ED*, 7: 198) The suggestion in such language that the entire realm of artifice, human construction as such, constitutes an affront to divine truth is made more explicit later on in the same work, when Williams proclaims that "all the Inhabitants of the World," including "*Gods* owne people," are guilty of such forms of "Moral *Idolatry*" as "Coveting of Gold and Silver, *House* and *Lands* . . . Oh what an object of the *Jealousie* of the most *High*, is this *Idolatrous Ball* of the Earth" (7: 239–40).

With his denial of any legitimate connection between religion and politics and his comprehensive recoil from the realm of the aesthetic, Williams developed a view of history, especially recent history, as a series of cataclysmic attempts by man to join together what God had put asunder. Self-righteous nation states coerced people into obedience to their shamelessly aestheticized religious establishments, "invented worships," and when they met with resistance, as they did again and again, the world was reduced to "heapes upon heapes in the slaugh[t]er houses and shambles of Civill Warres" (*BT*, 3: 62, 270). Williams was particularly disposed to regard the historical consequences of the Reformation in this light. In 1644, he thought he could hear "the *cry* of the *whole earth*, made *drunke* with the *bloud* of its *inhabitants*, slaughtering each other in their *blinded zeale*, for *Conscience*, for *Religion*, against the *Catholickes*, against the *Lutherans*, &c." (*BT*, 3: 60) The wars of religion of the sixteenth and seventeenth centuries were inscribed upon Williams' consciousness as indelibly as the holocausts of the twentieth century are inscribed upon our own, and he was as little inclined then as most of us are now to look upon the carnage around him as a sign of forward providential motion.

Even the English political and religious upheavals in which he had himself participated seemed to him to be for the most part merely the latest in an endless series of "so many thousand *slaughters, murders, ravishings, plunderings*" committed by "the *Pope*, the *Bishops*, the *Presbyterians*, the *Independents*," in response to such idolatrous clamours as "*Great* is the *Church* of *Rome*, . . . *Great* the *Christian Magistrate*, . . . *Great* the *swearing* and *covenant* of the people, &c." (*BTYMB*, 4: 440, 112) Williams was apt to think of providence not in linear and progressive terms, but rather in a manner that recalled the medieval wheel of fortune. Applying this conception to what historians now call the English Revolution, he found these events to be but several random circular revolutions, as one "*Power* or *Parliament*" after another was installed, "in the constant turning of the Wheeles of *Providence*" (*ED*, 7: 262). Nowhere did Williams more sharply indicate his detachment from the idea that the mid-century Civil Wars were leading the world towards the Millennium than when he declared in 1652, in the wake of Cromwell's victorious Irish campaign, that "Ireland *hath been an Akeldama, a* field *of* blood," and that this blood had been mostly "*spilt in the few* years *of our* Protestant Princes" (*The Hireling Ministry None of Christs* . . . (1652), 7: 155).[6] God had smiled on the regimes created by Parliament and the Army only insofar as those regimes had set consciences free; insofar as they had not, they were identical to what Williams was still declaring in 1679 to be the essence of the New England Way: "state policies and a mixture of goulden Images unto wch (were Your Carnal Sword So long) You would musically perswade or by ferie [fiery] torments Compell to bow downe, as many as (that great Type of Inventors and Persecutours) Nebuchadnezzar did" (*Correspondence*, 2: 769).

III

With church and state coalescing throughout history into a witch's brew of violence and illegitimate imaginative expression, the one reliable deposit of divine meaning and truth that remained available in human affairs was the Bible. Inevitably Williams espoused such platitudinous Protestant claims as that the Scriptures exhibited an "admirable consent and *Angelical Harmony*," and that a single true believer had always "been able with those plaine *smooth stones* out of the brook of holy *Scripture*, to lay groveling in their *spiritual gore*, the *stoutest Champions* (*Popes, Cardinals, Bishops, Doctors*) of the *Antichristian Philistins*" (*BTYMB*, 4: 39, 248). Yet he was forced to acknowledge that the conflicts and controversies of the Reformation in general and of mid-seventeenth-century England in particular had been so severe that they had called the integrity and credibility of the Bible itself into question. It seemed to be turning into "a stumbling *Block*, and *Rock* of offence" to multitudes of people, in view of the way in which "so many, and so wonderfully different perswasions and Consciences" had based themselves upon it: "How many are assaulted by Satan, to question . . . the *truth* of the holy Scriptures; Whether there are *no more* holy Scriptures but these; and whether the *Translations* are infallible, and which are to be *rested* or *relied* on?" (*ED*, 7: 258, 260)

The tide of secularism that Williams had himself done much to let loose appeared to be threatening to engulf his own defences against it. In order to assess Williams' response to this predicament, we must briefly consider the spectrum of "Puritan responses to the Bible" that John R. Knott has surveyed. Knott stresses the centrality in the Protestant and Puritan tradition of the doctrine that scripture "hath all its authority and credit from itself," impressing itself on attentive readers as inherently credible by means of the special force and energy the Holy Spirit had infused into it. It was further held that the peculiar animating power of the sacred writings overflowed from the text itself into the preaching of true ministers of the Word. Luther, Martin Bucer, William Perkins and many other Protestant spokesmen stressed that in a genuine sermon, "it is not so much [the preacher] that speaketh, as the Spirit of God in him and by him."[7]

As Geoffrey F. Nuttall demonstrated many years ago and as Nigel Smith has recently and massively confirmed, in the revolutionary ferment of mid-seventeenth-century England, the spiritism that Perkins and others had authorized was more widely espoused than at perhaps any other time in Christian history, and often in a manner that ripped it loose from its moorings not only in such clerical authority as that of Perkins, but even in the text of the Bible itself.[8] The 1650s were filled both with the perplexity and scepticism regarding biblical truth that Williams noted and with attempts to counteract it through forms of utterance that strayed far from the sober hermeneutics of a Perkins or a Luther, but were nevertheless believed by their lay vessels, female as

well as male, to manifest "the Spirit of God in [them] and by [them]."[9]
Knott's description of Gerrard Winstanley's approach to Scripture could
be applied to many others in the period:

> Where the orthodox Puritan divine, instructed by Perkins, pain-
> stakingly collected parallel texts and tested his interpretations by
> the analogy of faith, Winstanley followed his intuitions of the Spirit
> in rendering what he saw as the truth behind the letter, not so much
> expounding Scripture as re-creating it. . . .[He] approached the
> Bible as a poet might, alive to the power of images and the symbolic
> force of names.[10]

John Bunyan's use of the Bible approaches somewhat nearer to
the issues raised by the case of Williams, in that Bunyan reports
being assailed by exactly the sorts of doubts Williams recognized were
widespread during the Interregnum. "How can you tell but that the Turks
had as good Scriptures to prove their *Mahomet* the Saviour, as we have
to prove our *Jesus* is," he asked. "Everyone doth think his own Religion
rightest, both *Jews*, and *Moors*, and *Pagans*; and how if all our Faith,
and Christ, and Scriptures, should be but a think-so too?" But according
to Knott, the very work in which these anxieties are expressed, *Grace
Abounding*, is itself characterized by a free approach to the scriptural
text not unlike that of Winstanley, as Bunyan "conflates Old and New
Testaments and moves easily from their language to that of his everyday
experience." In the case of the orthodox Calvinist Bunyan, one way to
deal with spiritual uncertainty was evidently to respond to the Bible
in the same manner as had the heretical spiritist Winstanley, "as a
Poet might." And in *The Pilgrim's Progress*, of course, Bunyan went
on to give himself even greater latitude in adapting the Bible to his
own imaginative purposes. As Dayton Haskin observes, he offers his
readers the pleasures of "great interpretive and imaginative freedom in
the face of the forbidding text."[11]

The most obvious instance of Interregnum spiritists feeling themselves
empowered to take liberties with the forbidding biblical text is of course
that of the Quakers, and George Fox incurred the wrath of Roger
Williams and many others when he insisted that the basis of Christian
faith and truth was not the Scriptures themselves, but rather "the Holy
Spirit, by which the holy men of God gave forth the Scriptures."[12] But
the Quakers did not incur the wrath of John Milton. Knott shows how
the Holy Spirit became more significant to Milton, as he worked his way
through the hermeneutic tangle he confronted as a result of his marital
calamity. He concludes that Milton shared a "regard for the dynamism
of the Spirit" with the Quakers and other Interregnum radicals, and he

explores the imaginative results of such a regard in *Paradise Lost* and *Paradise Regained*.[13] A case in point he does not mention occurs at the outset of *Paradise Lost*, when Milton invokes the "heavenly Muse, that on the secret top / Of Oreb, or of Sinai, didst inspire / That shepherd, who first taught the chosen seed, / In the beginning how the heavens and earth / Rose out of chaos." "That shepherd," Moses, is clearly being presented in terms remarkably similar to those of George Fox, as, indeed, one of Fox's "holy men of God," giving forth the Book of Genesis at the behest of the Holy Spirit. In praying for the blessing of that same Spirit on his own re-creation of that same Book of Genesis, Milton distinctly suggests an equivalency between his poem and its scriptural source. The ways of God to doubting and sceptical man are to be justified not by retreating into the Bible as into a fortress, but rather by soaring imaginatively through and beyond it in pursuit of "things unattempted yet in prose or rhyme."[14]

IV

It is not difficult to find passages in the writings of Roger Williams that seem to suggest a full participation in the traditions of Protestant spiritism. One of the verses in *A Key into the Language of America* unambiguously affirms that "*'tis not the Word that can*; / But *'tis the* Spirit *or* Breath *of God* / *That must renew the man.*"[15] In 1652, as the claims for inspired utterance began to multiply, part of Williams' argument against the plans for an Independent establishment was that, like all other such establishments, this one would amount to a refusal to co-operate with God's determination "to work freely and in his own way, by the free *Breathings* of his most *powerful Spirit*, in the *mouths* and *hearts* of such by whom and in whom he freely pleaseth" (*The Fourth Paper Presented by Major Butler* . . . (1652), 7: 135). And Williams had no doubt that it had pleased God to work thus freely and in his own way as often in the mouths and hearts of "*Lawyers, Physitians, Souldiers, Tradesmen*, and others of higher and lower *rank*," as in the mouths and hearts of clergymen. His affirmation that such lay people, "by *Gods holy Spirit* (breathing on their *meditations* of the *holy Scriptures*, . . . have attained and much improved, an excellent *Spirit* of *knowledge*, and *Utterance* in the holy things of Jesus Christ" (*HM*, 7: 166–7) was as close as he ever came to a celebration of Interregnum spiritual radicalism.

Not only did Williams thus express agreement in principle with the orientation that helped to produce Quakerism and the imaginative biblical adaptations of Winstanley, Bunyan and Milton, he also himself put this principle into imaginative practice in his first published work. Knott describes how in *Pilgrim's Progress* Bunyan draws out all the implications and resonances of the central Christian and Protestant metaphor of life as a pilgrimage, the wayfaring of the individual soul towards and in faith, and the wayfaring of the community of the faithful through the wilderness of this world.[16] To the extent that it has one, wayfaring is also the organizing motif of Williams' *A Key into the Language of America*; it is exploited quite compellingly, for example, in the account of how Williams presented the concept of monotheism to a Narragansett audience: "*How many Gods bee there?/ Many, great many./ Friend, not so./ There is onely one God./ You are mistaken./ You are out of the way*" (195).

Williams notes that the concluding phrase "much pleaseth them, being proper for their wandering in the woods," and it also much pleases the reader, who, by the time he or she has read this far, has previously encountered such passages as this:

> *I will aske the way.*
> *I will inquire of you . . .*
> *Shew me the way . . .*
> *There is the way you must goe.*
> *There the way divides.*
> *A guide.*
> *Be my guide . . .*

they are so exquisitely skilled in all the body and bowels of the Countrey (by reason of their huntings) that I have often been guided twentie, thirtie, sometimes fortie miles through the woods, a streight course, out of any path. (147, 149)

The passage originally quoted, with its calm, inviting tone and its use of a figure of speech firmly grounded in the experience of both European and Native American cultures, is perhaps sufficient in and of itself to clear Williams' mode of evangelism of all charges of cultural imperialism except those that are irreducibly inherent in the enterprise itself. But such implications are decisively sharpened when passages such as the second one quoted are taken into account. As we realize that guidance through the wilderness has been repeatedly sought by the European and expertly given by the Native American, we begin to suspect that in Williams' hands, evangelism is being given a decisive push in the direction of mutuality. His conviction that regeneration was a phenomenon that showed no respect for established geographical and cultural hierarchies is transformed from a debating point into a distinct, experienced possibility.[17]

Unfortunately, there was little in the structure of Williams' thought to encourage such proclivities and much to discourage them. Although he warned the projectors of ecclesiastical establishments not to interfere with "the free *Breathings* of [God's] most *powerful Spirit*," he himself was all too inclined to contain such breathings within a rigid eschatological script. Fully inspired, fully imaginative Christian speech, "free proclaiming or preaching of Repentance & forgiveness of sins," could be undertaken only "by such Messengers as can prove their lawfull sending and Commission from the Lord Jesus, to make Disciples out of all nations." Since apostolic times, no one had been able to prove that he or she had been lawfully sent and commissioned to engage in such free, inspired proclaiming, and no one would be able to prove it in the foreseeable future – not, that is, until the millennial climax: "Gods great businesse between Christ Jesus the holy Son of God and Antichrist the man of sin and Sonne of perdition, must . . . be first over, and *Zion* and *Jerusalem* . . . rebuilt and re-established, before the Law and word of life [can] be sent forth to the rest to the Nations of the World, who have not heard of Christ" (*Christenings Make Not Christians* . . . (1645), 7: 39, 40). In the meantime, the most one could hope for was inspired negative utterance, that of "*Prophets* and *witnesses* against the *Beast*, . . . furnished sufficiently with *spirituall Fire* in their *mouthes*, mightily able to consume or humble their *Enemies*" (*BTYMB*, 4: 383).[18] Almost every other form of religious and human expression that might be developed during these days of the apostasy seemed to come within the scope of Williams' infinitely extendible definition of idolatry.

Williams' argument for liberty of conscience had always harboured a crippling self-contradiction, one that is inseparable from the hostility to oppressive political and aesthetic inventions that had engendered the argument in the first place. Conscience was "a *perswasion* fixed in the minde and heart of a man, which inforceth him to judge (as *Paul* said of himselfe a *persecutour*) and to doe so and so, with respect to *God*, his worship, etc." (*Correspondence*, 1: 340) Liberty of conscience was the solution, but as the example of Paul's persecuting behaviour before his conversion indicates, it was a solution to problems created by conscience itself, by energy of conscience. Williams refers repeatedly to conscientious, zealous persecutors, such as the magistrate who, "according to his *conscience*, endures not such *profanation* of *Ordinances* as he conceives" and proceeds to this or that punitive measure against "obstinate *abusers*" (*BT*, 3: 230). In addition, persecution was usually associated with another form of energy of conscience, that manifested by those sixteenth-century bishops whose "mistaken *Consciences* in matters concerning the *worship* of *God*" had led them to compose the Book of Common Prayer, "in its Time, as glorious an *Idoll*, and as much adored by *Godly persons*, as any *Invention* now extant" (*Correspondence*, 1: 341). The preponderance of the historical evidence seemed to show that the conscientious person was likely to be a either a persecutor, an idolator, or both at once. So the argument chased its own tail. Liberty of conscience was needed to protect conscience against itself; but once the conscience thus protected began to express itself, it reproduced the conditions of tyranny, violence and illegitimate human invention from which it had originally needed to be protected. And at that point, the cycle had to begin all over again.

This contradiction came to a head, I believe, in Williams' final polemical intervention, his debates with the Quakers in the 1670s. The timing of the debates is highly suggestive. The Quakers had been protected in Rhode Island while being persecuted everywhere else. And by the 1670s, this protection was bearing the fruit of highly successful evangelizing and organizing efforts. Williams thus faced the prospect that the ecclesiastical life of Rhode Island would soon be dominated by a group basing itself entirely on those idolatrous faculties of human invention he had always despised. The Quakers "had set up a Christ within them which was but an *Imagination*, an Image, a Christ in the mystical *Notion*: but in reality *Nothing*" (*George Fox Digg'd Out of His Burrowes* . . . (1676), 5: 70). Moreover, the Quakers had just won control of the Rhode Island government for the first time.[19] It must have seemed to Williams, on the basis not of empirical evidence but rather of the inner logic of his own thought, that he faced his old enemy yet again, deluded and energetic conscience in power, prepared to utilize either musical persuasion or fiery compulsion in pursuit of its goal of making all and sundry bow down before its golden images.

But this debate was different from all the others in which Williams had engaged. It was not enough this time simply to discredit the myriad versions of antichristianity. One version in particular threatened to take over his de-sacralized commonwealth, and he had to offer an alternative to it. But having discarded all forms of institutional Christianity as illegitimate, and being forbidden by his anathema on invention from projecting his own imaginative Christian vision, Williams had no recourse but to echo the proto-fundamentalism – the insistence that since the Spirit had inspired the authors of the Bible, it would henceforth inspire nobody else – that had already been formulated in response to the Quaker threat by more respectable Protestant authorities:

this Record, this Word Will or Mind of God written and pen'd
by chosen Pen-men as Pens in the hand of his holy Spirit, and
so miraculously preserved from the Rage of the Devils fiery
Instruments, *Babilonian, Assyrian, Romane* and *Popish Tyrants*
. . . is the outward and external *Light, Lanthorn, Judge, Guide,
Rule* by which God witnesseth himself and his Truth in the World
. . . it hath been most wonderfully to amazement preserved like the
Sun in the Firmament, and shines most gloriously again and again,
after the blackest and longest storm and night of *Apostacies* and
Persecution. (George Fox, 5: 141, 144–5)[20]

It seemed that in one way or another, human invention was bound
to have an impact on the ways in which seventeenth-century Anglo-
American Protestants read the Bible. It could take the freer imaginative
form developed most fully by Milton, or it could, at approximately the
same time, take the form of the bibliolatry to which, as we see, Williams
was driven in the course of his confrontation with the Quakers.[21] It is
worth reflecting for a moment on this temporal coincidence between
Williams' final, sterile discursive gesture and the major poems of Milton.
One of these two Puritan friends succeeded in synthesizing religion and
literature into a great biblical vision for the modern world. But he was
a man without a country. Patriotism "has almost *expatriated* me, as
it were," he told one of his correspondents the year before *Paradise
Lost* was published. "One's *patria* is wherever it is well with him."[22]
The other of these radical Puritans founded the only political unit in
the modern Anglo-American world that was opposed in principle to
aggressive, expansionist political power. But he was a man without a
vision. So near and yet so far. We – our public discourse dominated,
with scarcely a dissenting murmur, by the rhetoric of the Elect Nation,
by proclamations that history has reached its millennial fulfilment in an
embrace of American enterprise, freedom, and democracy world-wide –
are still living with the consequences of the seventeenth-century division
of cultural, intellectual and political labour.

NOTES

1. *The Bloudy Tenent of Persecution* . . . (1644), in *The Complete Writings of Roger
   Williams*, Perry Miller, ed., 7 vols. (New York: Russell and Russell, 1963), 3: 324.
   Except for those from *A Key into the Language of America*, all quotations from
   Williams' writings are taken from this edition; citations are identified parenthetically
   in the text. The most important discussions of this aspect of Williams' thought are Perry
   Miller, *Roger Williams: His Contribution to the American Tradition* (1953; reprinted

New York: Atheneum, 1966), 52–4; Edmund S. Morgan, *Roger Williams: The Church and the State* (New York: Harcourt, Brace and World, 1967), 6–10, 64–103, 120–6; Sacvan Bercovitch, "Typology in Puritan New England: The Williams–Cotton Controversy Reassessed," *American Quarterly*, 19 (1967), 166–91; Richard Reinitz, "The Separatist Background of Roger Williams' Argument for Religious Toleration," in *Typology in Early American Literature*, Sacvan Bercovitch, ed. (Amherst: University of Massachusetts Press, 1972), 107–37; and W. Clark Gilpin, *The Millenarian Piety of Roger Williams* (Chicago: University of Chicago Press, 1979), 39–41, 43, 75–81, 109, 122–4.

2. Michael McKeon, "Politics of Discourses and the Rise of the Aesthetic in Seventeenth-Century England," in *Politics of Discourse: The Literature and History of Seventeenth-Century England*, Kevin Sharpe and Steven N. Zwicker, eds. (Berkeley: University of California Press, 1987), 35–51.

3. These aspects of Williams' thought are noted in Morgan, *Roger Williams*, 108–14, 116.

4. I have argued this point elsewhere; see Keith W.F. Stavely, "The World All before Them: Milton and the Rising Glory of America," *Studies in Eighteenth-Century Culture*, 20 (1990), 156.

   The literature on early modern millennial nationalism in England and America is extensive. For England, see William Haller, *The Elect Nation: The Meaning and Relevance of Foxe's* Book of Martyrs (New York: Harper and Row, 1963); B.S. Capp, *The Fifth Monarchy Men: A Study in Seventeenth-Century English Millenarianism* (London: Faber, 1972), chap. 2; Capp, "The Political Dimension of Apocalyptic Thought," in *The Apocalypse in English Renaissance Thought and Literature: Patterns, Antecedents and Repercussions*, C.R. Patrides and Joseph Wittreich, eds. (Ithaca, N.Y.: Cornell University Press, 1984), 93–124; Bryan W. Ball, *A Great Expectation: Eschatological Thought in English Protestantism to 1660* (Leiden: E.J. Brill, 1975); Richard Bauckham, *Tudor Apocalypse: Sixteenth Century Apocalypticism, Millennialism and the English Reformation: From John Bale to John Foxe and Thomas Brightman* (Oxford: Sutton Courtenay Press, 1978); Paul Christianson, *Reformers and Babylon: English Apocalyptic Visions from the Reformation to the Eve of the Civil War* (Toronto: University of Toronto Press, 1978); and Katherine R. Firth, *The Apocalyptic Tradition in Reformation Britain, 1530–1645* (Oxford: Oxford University Press, 1979). The leading advocate of the idea that the founders of New England thought they were carrying the Elect Nation identity with them across the Atlantic is Sacvan Bercovitch; see the article cited in n. 1 above; *The Puritan Origins of the American Self* (New Haven, Conn.: Yale University Press, 1975), especially chaps. 2 and 3; and *The American Jeremiad* (Madison: University of Wisconsin Press, 1978). Bercovitch's position has been adversely scrutinized in recent years; see Andrew Delbanco, "The Puritan Errand Re-Viewed," *Journal of American Studies*, 18 (1984), 343–60; Delbanco, *The Puritan Ordeal* (Cambridge, Mass.: Harvard University Press, 1989), 90–117; and Theodore Dwight Bozeman, "The Puritans' 'Errand into the Wilderness' Reconsidered," *New England Quarterly*, 59 (1986), 231–51. The latter article includes a useful summary of the various positions in the debates that have arisen over the Elect Nation idea in the historiography of sixteenth- and seventeenth-century England as well as in that of early America. Whatever the outcome of these debates, one thing is certain: the idea of the Elect Nation seemed to Williams of sufficient significance to prompt him to develop a withering critique of it.

5. *The Correspondence of Roger Williams*, Glenn W. LaFantasie, ed., 2 vols. (Hanover, N.H.: University Press of New England, 1988), 1: 357. All quotations from Williams' correspondence are taken from this edition; citations are identified parenthetically in the text.

6. According to John R. Knott, Jr., Richard Baxter tended to view the mid-century wars and upheavals in a similar fashion, as signs not of God's approval of Roundhead victories, but rather of a judgment He was passing against England for its spiritual

sluggishness; see *The Sword of the Spirit: Puritan Responses to the Bible* (Chicago: University of Chicago Press, 1980), 75.

7. Knott, *Sword of the Spirit*, 34 (quoting William Whitaker, *A Disputation on Holy Scripture*, 1588), 38 (quoting Perkins, *The Arte of Prophesying*). For a discussion of comparable claims of inspired or semi-inspired status for the manifold forms of clerical discourse disseminated in seventeenth-century New England, see David D. Hall, *Worlds of Wonder, Days of Judgment: Popular Religious Belief in Early New England* (New York: Knopf, 1989), 22–43.

8. Geoffrey F. Nuttall, *The Holy Spirit in Puritan Faith and Experience* (Oxford: Blackwell, 1947), viii, 3–7, and passim; Nigel Smith, *Perfection Proclaimed: Language and Literature in English Radical Religion, 1640–1660* (Oxford: Clarendon Press, 1989), especially 26–32, 268–75.

9. Smith states that the spiritism of the Interregnum produced, often within the same group, contradictory results: on the one hand, a "rational and sceptical critique of biblical language" (since "human language cannot possibly be divine"), and on the other hand, efforts to make post-biblical language "actually become part of divine expression", see *Perfection Proclaimed*, 307.

10. Knott, *Sword of the Spirit*, 96.

11. John Bunyan, *Grace Abounding to the Chief of Sinners* (1666), Roger Sharrock, ed. (Oxford: Clarendon Press, 1962), 31 (I owe this reference to Dayton Haskin); Knott, *Sword of the Spirit*, 137, 139–40, 151; Dayton Haskin, "The Burden of Interpretation in *The Pilgrim's Progress*," *Studies in Philology*, 79 (1982), 278.

12. Quoted in Nuttall, *Holy Spirit*, 27.

13. Knott, *Sword of the Spirit*, 116, 124, 125–30.

14. *The Poems of John Milton*, John Carey and Alistair Fowler, eds. (London: Longman, 1968), 459–61 (*Paradise Lost*, Book I, ll. 6–10, 16).

15. Roger Williams, *A Key into the Language of America* (1643), John J. Teunissen and Evelyn J. Hinz, eds. (Detroit: Wayne State University Press, 1973), 162. All quotations are taken from this edition; citations are identified parenthetically in the text.

16. Knott, *Sword of the Spirit*, 140.

17. For discussions of the *Key* that emphasize its open, positive portrayal of the Narragansetts, see *Key*, Teunissen and Hinz, eds., "Introduction," 13–69; and by the same authors: "Anti-Colonial Satire in Roger Williams' *A Key into the Language of America*," *Ariel*, 7 (1976), 5–26; "Roger Williams, St Paul, and American Primitivism," *Canadian Review of American Studies*, 4 (1973), 121–36; "Roger Williams, Thomas More, and the Narragansett Utopia," *Early American Literature*, 11 (1976–77), 281–95. See also Jack L. Davis, "Roger Williams among the Narragansett Indians," *New England Quarterly*, 43 (1970), 593–604; and Gordon Brotherston, "A Controversial Guide to the Language of America, 1643," in *1642: Literature and Power in the Seventeenth Century*, Francis Barker et al., eds. (Colchester: University of Essex, 1981), 84–100.

18. For an analysis of the relations between Williams' eschatology and his interpretation of ecclesiastical history, see Morgan, *Roger Williams*, 28–61.

19. For the political context of the Williams–Quaker debates, see Arthur J. Worrall, "Persecution, Politics, and War: Roger Williams, Quakers, and King Philip's War," *Quaker History*, 66 (1977), 73–86.

20. Compare John Owen: "the whole word of God, in every letter and tittle, as given from him by inspiration, is preserved without corruption", *The Divine Original, Authority, Self-Evidencing Light, and Power of the Scriptures* (1659), in *The Works of John Owen*, William H. Goold, ed., 24 vols. (London, 1850–55; reprinted 1965), 16: 301; quoted in Dean Freiday, *The Bible: Its Criticism, Interpretation and Use in 16th and 17th Century England*, Catholic and Quaker Studies, No. 4 (Pittsburgh, 1979), 93.

21. Williams speaks more favourably of the New England ecclesiastical system in *George Fox Digg'd out of His Burrowes* than in any other of his works; see 5: 103, 246, 260–1, 343, 388, 464–5. His search for a positive alternative to Quakerism

must have been truly desperate! For an argument that the Massachusetts authorities assisted in the publication of *George Fox Digg'd out of His Burrowes* as part of a campaign to make the Quakers the scapegoats for King Philip's War, see Worrall, "Persecution, Politics, and War," 84.

22. *Complete Prose Works of John Milton*, Don M. Wolfe *et al.*, eds., 8 vols. (New Haven, Conn.: Yale University Press, 1953–82), 8: 4. The principal evidence for friendship between Williams and Milton is Williams' statement that during his stay in London in the 1650s, "The Secretarie of the Councell (Mr Milton) for my Dutch I read him read me many more languages", see Williams to John Winthrop, Jr., 12 July 1654, *Correspondence*, 2: 393.

"The [Un]Civill-Sisterhood of Oranges and Lemons": Female Petitioners and Demonstrators, 1642–53

ANN MARIE McENTEE

I

Seventeenth-century female petitioners considered themselves citizens as well as wives, mothers and widows, and so dismissed male permission in order to speak for themselves. Their public demonstrations thus contradicted a cultural stereotype of women as passive and incapable of organizing themselves as a political unit. Previously, images of female collectives focused upon women's need for male guidance and leadership. The self-representations with which these petitioners presented themselves to Parliament between 1642 and 1653 thus reveal an altered perception of womanhood.

The petitions incorporated representations of mannish women, images of biblical and historical Worthies who had displayed heroic action in defending their respective societies. Such figures suggested models of non-sexual behaviour to the petitioners. Originally used to justify Elizabeth's political power and seemingly masculine attributes, female Worthies and Amazons were temporarily discredited during the reigns of James I and Charles I. That the petitioners appropriated such female images of leadership to explain their presence before Parliament indicated, to a certain degree, the unsuccessful campaign, on the part of the Stuart writers, to discredit (or, at least, render politically ineffective) representations of the mannish woman. The petitions thus initiated the political significance of such images and extended that power to non-aristocratic women.

Patricia Higgins has argued that the female petitioners retained both an awareness of acting out of place and an acceptance of their inferior social position.[1] I would like to argue that the petitions reveal not so much a retention of cultural convention as a subtle undercutting of that convention. The women proclaim their humility and acknowledge that they have presumed a rather forward cultural position by entering the political arena, yet their demands for civil liberties supersede these demurrals. Their proclamations denote an expansion of women's roles, an expansion which simultaneously disrupted the traditionally male political arena and yielded these women freedom of personal expression. By claiming rights for themselves, not as wives, but rather as citizens, the petitioners projected a self-identity that was independent of stereotypical perceptions of wifehood. In demanding the right to define themselves politically, and hence publicly, the women called for a diminution of the male privilege of cultural inscription.

Newspaper accounts of the petitioners' activities, on the other hand, attempted to discredit women's political power by relocating them in a traditionally gendered realm. The women were likened to bold Amazons and gallant Lacedemonians. Whereas the petitioners ascribed non-sexual traits to the image of the mannish woman – self-assertion, independence and honesty – newspaper accounts used similar figures to reinforce the notion of women's power as exclusively sexual. By linking the Amazon to rampant sexual behaviour, the accounts reinforced a stereotypical, gendered polarity between masculine and feminine behaviour. Such a transference to the sexual realm thus suggests the writers' tacit acknowledgement of the women's collective, and belies the anxiety about female political power that the petitioners' presence generated. Perhaps more importantly, it implies the erosion of a sex/gender system that could no longer sustain its security with respect to female behaviour.

II

One of the first petitions delivered by women to Parliament, on 31 January 1641/1642, addressed the loss of trading and "the present distractions and distempers of state."[2] The Palace Yard filled the following day with approximately 400 women who demanded an answer to this petition. Twelve women were eventually admitted to the Lords' chamber to state their grievances, but the result of their appearance was never disclosed.[3] In all likelihood, the women's demands were not met, for the House of Lords received another petition on 4 February, entitled *Humble Petition of many hundreds of distressed women, Tradesmens wives, and Widdowes*.[4] The issue of trading was readdressed, for the women "had divers times petitioned for redresse thereof . . . which had not yet been answered" (568). This reminder of the previous dismissals of their concerns denoted a serious political campaign. Furthermore, the women directly petitioned the Upper House because the Lower House had failed to respond to their pleas.

This petition defines the women as wives and citizens:

> And whereas we, whose Hearts have joined chearfully with all
> those Petitions . . . on the Behalf of the Purity of Religion, and

> the Liberty of our Husbands, Persons, and Estates, recounting ourselves to have an interest in the common Privileges with them, do with the same Confidence assure ourselves to find the same gracious Acceptance with you, for easing of those Grievances, which, in regards of our frail Condition, do more nearly concern us, and do deeply terrify our Souls. (568)

Although they assume the same political "privileges" as men, the women do not demand an explanation for the dismissal of their earlier petitions. Their self-representation as "Persons" as opposed to "ourselves" suggests, perhaps, an identity independent of their marital status which "Husbands" denotes. Their "frail Condition" softens the tone of their demand for "common Privileges."[5] They seem undecided, perhaps even ambivalent, about their right to express themselves politically, and so rely on religious rhetoric to justify their presence before the House of Lords:

> *Christ* hath purchased us at a deare a rate as he hath done men, and therefore requireth the like obedience for the same mercy as of men . . . [I]n the free enjoying of Christ in his own Laws, and a flourishing estate of the Church and Common-wealth, consisteth the happinesse of Women as well as Men . . . Women are sharers in the common Calamities that accompany both Church and Common-wealth. (*True Copie*, 5–6)

The women claim their right to organize collectively and petition the governing body, but legitimate that claim with Puritan doctrine. "Purity of Religion" precedes "the Liberty of our Husbands, Persons, and Estates" in the first account, while "the Church" and "Common-wealth" are linked together in the second. Religious conviction justifies political conviction. Furthermore, the women state that "neither are we left without Example in the Scripture," and cite the woman of Tekoa and Esther's appearance before Haman.[6] The use of such biblical images reveals the petitioners' self-perception as intercessors for their fellow citizens. It also suggests an awareness that they had assumed a political purpose, a purpose that ignored the demand for male permission before acting.

In August 1643, the Commons addressed the Lords' peace proposals. Fearing the result of such a political settlement, London citizens summoned a common council at Guildhall on 6 August, and a petition for the continuation of war was drawn up and signed, to be submitted to the Commons the following day. Offended by rumours about pro-war broadsides being circulated in the City, the Lords convened with the Commons; the Upper House threatened to punish the authors of such petitions. Consequently, when presented with the petition by City representatives on 7 August, the Commons rejected it. Orders were then issued against unlawful assemblies and the printing and circulating of papers for that purpose.[7]

In response to Parliament's attempt to reach a peace settlement, women demonstrated and petitioned on 8 August 1643. Their blockade of Parliament's entrances met with violence: "[A] man upon the top of the stairs, drew his sword, and with the flat side stroak some of them upon the heads, which so affrighted them, that they presently made way and ran downe the stairs."[8] The women returned the following day to present another petition for peace to the Commons. Again, they were met with violence:

> About an Hundred women with white Ribbons in their hats pressed to make way through [sentinels] . . . more women came to second them, fell upon [sentinels] and beate them away, and by violence made their way into the West side of the yard, and then all of them cried out mainely, we will have Peace presently. (*CI*, 232)

Such an account stereotypes the women as illogical: they supposedly stampeded the Commons, and then demanded peace. Another account, offered by *The Parliament Scout*, states that this demonstration drew five or six thousand women "of the poorer sort," whose husbands were "in the one or other Army." It also notes that "some 500 of them were whores."[9] These descriptions, although they provide justification for the women's aggressive behaviour (their husbands had not been compensated for their military service), bias the reader to dismiss the women's political concerns. They are represented as abrasive poor folk and whores who did not know how to behave in the presence of Members of Parliament. This account increases its bias by reporting that the women "fell upon all that have shorte haire and pulled them, both Ministers and Souldiers, and others" (*PS*, 55). *Certaine Informations* claims that the women "threw brick-bars" (*CI*, 232).

Such accounts reveal that the petitioners' collective political action had yet to be taken seriously by the dominant political culture. The women wore white ribbons, a traditional symbol for peace, and claimed to be marching for peace, yet the event is reported as a riot during which several innocent bystanders were killed.[10] Ministers and soldiers are presented by the newspaper accounts as victims of this all-female mob by virtue of their religious beliefs: short hair, being the fashion of the Puritans, singled these men out as targets. Thus, according to these accounts, these female petitioners are decidedly anti-Puritan. They are not allied to the Leveller Party which, by 1642, was distinctly Puritan. The fact that this particular group of women was acting independently of any political party, and thus perhaps received little or no male guidance or leadership, may account for the biased reporting of this demonstration. Furthermore, typecasting the women as a mob justifies the authorities' dismissal of them.

After 1645, female petitioners played a central role during Leveller demonstrations. Women sympathized with John Lilburne who had been imprisoned for seditious writings during the summer of 1646. His wife, Elizabeth, had been barred from attending him during his internment at Newgate Prison. Accompanied by a group of 20 women, Elizabeth presented to the House of Commons a petition for justice, entitled *For J. Lilburne from his wife and many women*. Although the Lower House initially dismissed this request, the women continued to demonstrate at Westminster for days until a committee of the House was appointed to review Lilburne's case.[11]

Women also sympathized with the plight of Mary Overton, wife of the Leveller pamphleteer Richard Overton who was arrested and sent to Newgate in 1646 for printing several of John Lilburne's pamphlets. Mary herself was arrested, along with her brother Thomas Johnson, when they were discovered stitching the sheets of a seditious pamphlet, *Regal Tyranny Discovered*, penned by Overton and Lilburne. During her appearance before the House of Lords, she refused to co-operate and was sent to prison (Fraser, 235). In March 1647, women presented an appeal to the House of Commons, on Mary's behalf, in which she requested a speedy sentence.[12] The Lower House, however, could not overturn the Upper House's decision, and Mary was not released until July.

The House of Commons responded sternly to the appearance of these female Leveller sympathizers. On 26 August 1647, it ordered its sentries "to observantly keep all the passages, and with all to clear them from those clamorous women, which were wont to hang in clusters on the staires, and before the doores of the Parliament" (Higgins, 199). On 15 October, the Lower House went one step further by ordering the sentries to apprehend all women "who clamour about the Houses, and speake any scandalous words against the Parliament"; the women were to be detained and punished according to law (Higgins, 200).

Such measures suggest the effectiveness of the female demonstrations. Their persistence as a collective ("clamorous" and "wont to hang in clusters") caused a reaction within the dominant political culture, perhaps an undesired one, but none the less a reaction that acknowledged the petitioners' presence in the political arena. That they were unsuccessful in their attempts to secure the release of John Lilburne or Mary Overton did not, however, diminish their strength as a political collective. Quite simply, they failed to garner the necessary support among Members of Parliament for two reasons: first, they supported the cause of the Levellers whose parliamentary power-base challenged that of the Lords, and, second, their public demonstrations called into question stereotypical perceptions of women as passive and relegated to the domicile. In short, the behaviour of these female petitioners suggested political and cultural sedition.

In spite of the Lower House's enforcement of these stern measures, women continued to exercise their appropriated political freedoms as petitioning for the release of Leveller leaders increased during April and May 1649. Women assumed the roles of wardens and division leaders and were responsible for circulating copies of a petition for other women to sign during a congregational meeting held on 22 April. The petition, a plea for the release of Lilburne, was presented to the Lower House on 23 April (Higgins, 200). Newspaper accounts agree that hundreds of women petitioned the Lower House on the morning on 23 April.[13] One account reports that "brave Petitioners made a gallant reply, . . . 1000 hands to a petition."[14]

It is difficult to assess the influence of male Levellers on these women, for the execution of the latter's demonstration on 23 April parallels the canvassing activities associated with the former.[15] Newspaper accounts suggest a conspiracy in which dissident males were compelling women to act on their behalf, hoping that female frailty would sway Parliament. Such suggestions, however, reveal the anxieties generated among conservative elements of the dominant political culture by the presence of the female petitioners. Given the women's involvement with Elizabeth Lilburne and Mary Overton, their collective demonstration on the morning of 23 April denotes their willingness to act independently of men, Leveller or otherwise.

The petition itself presents the women as political intruders: "We are not able to keep in our compasse, to be bounded in the custom of our Sex . . . it is not our custome to addresse ourselves to this House in the publike behalf."[16] They approached the Commons in an attempt to plead for relief of "the poverty and famine which plague the city." Their humble introduction is, however, short-lived, for the petition shifts rather abruptly to a justification that is couched in convincing political and religious rhetoric. Such a shift may have been due, in part, to the fact that the women were addressing their own economic concerns as well as the demands of Elizabeth Lilburne and Mary Overton.

> We have a very equal share and interest with men in the Common-
> wealth, and it cannot be laid out (as now it is). . . . Considering
> that God hath wrought many deliverances for severall Nations
> from age to age by the weak hand of women, By the counsell
> and presence of Deborah . . . and by the British women this land
> was delivered from the tyranny of Danes . . . therefore we shal
> take the boldnesse to remember you, That our Husbands, selves,
> and friends have done their parts for you, and thought nothing too
> dear and precious in your behalf, our money, plate, jewels, rings,
> bodkins, and c. have bin offered at your feet. . . . Make good those
> promises of freedom and prosperity to the Nation, by which good
> men were invited to your service. (*EMM*, 2–3)

The women demand to be heard and so dismiss their gender, for
they believe that it can no longer disqualify them from appearing
before the Lower House. They believe that God supports their claims
("deliverances . . . by the weak of hand of women"). The image of
Deborah, the biblical Worthy who figured in Elizabeth I's coronation
pageant in 1558, is appropriated to legitimate the women's right to judge
and act upon Parliament's unwillingness to support its troops financially.
Delivery "from the tyranny of Danes" further legitimates their right to
petition, for non-aristocratic women had once affected political change.

The petition recalls the support of their families during the Civil War.
The women value the Lower House's ability to dismiss the Royalist
structure through legislative measures. Their donation of manpower,
money and valuable possessions confirms their commitment to society's
struggle for political freedom.

The "bodkins" call up a very particular cultural image. Both a small
sword and a piercing tool used by tailors, a bodkin was also an
ornamental hairpin. A fashion accessory and therefore of some value,
either monetary or sentimental, it became part of the donations that
non-Royalist factions received during the war. Without their bodkins,
these parliamentarian women would suggest the conventional image of
a mad woman with loose, flowing hair. The petition also refers to the
sacrificing of their wedding rings for the cause. It thus offered to the
Commons an image of these petitioners as disoriented and enraged,
and so tacitly stated that the Civil War contributed greatly to women's
loss of decorum. In giving up their bodkins and wedding rings, women
sacrificed their personal appearance for a political cause. Their rights
as English citizens supplanted cultural conventions. Their donations
were thus presented as sacrifices of tangible items that defined them
within the culture – their husbands, estates and personal appearance.

For these women, their public self-representations could no longer be predicated upon something as insignificant as the maintenance of a gendered appearance. In one sense this sacrifice made their possession of political rights a *fait accompli*.

The Commons dismissed this petition in spite of its claim that the signatories had to be heard. Their response to the women, a reminder that they were acting out of place, is no more than an attempt to redomesticate them:

> That the matter you petition about is of higher concernment then you understand, that the House gave an answer to your Husbands; and therefore that you are desired to go home, and look after your own business, and meddle with huswifery. (*EMM*, 3)

Neither logic nor religious and historical justification swayed the Lower House. The response expressed their political concern, for they chose to discuss such matters only with the husbands of the petitioners, namely the men who voted the Commons into power. Furthermore, this dismissal ("look after your own business, and meddle with huswifery") shows the extent to which perceptions of women as apolitical were espoused by Members of Parliament. This became more apparent and emphatic as female petitioners presented economic demands to the Commons.

Pro-Royalist accounts claim that the women rioted after hearing the Commons' response to their petition:

> Their tongues hail-shot against the Members as they passed to and fro, whilst the Souldiers threw in squibs under their coats . . . Noll Cromwell laies his nose out at the dore . . . and sent Philip Harbert . . . to baule them out of Westminster. . . . [The women responded by] rounding him in a Ring, til he swore for the Liberties of these people . . . they gave him a Passe, with *Papers* pinn'd at his *Back* for *Bedlam*.[17]

Another account states that the soldiers not only threw squibs, but also cocked pistols and forced the women down the Parliament stairs at gunpoint. The report goes on to say that one of the women clutched Cromwell's cloak and threatened him with violence ("Sir, we will have your life if you take away theirs!").[18] Both accounts represent the petitioners as meddlesome, outspoken and contained only with violence. The womens' demands for the release of Lilburne and compensation of the military expose sensitive issues which had plagued Parliament for several years. That the women explain in detail the economic hardships they had personally endured during the Civil War anger

Parliament even further. The newspaper accounts thus reveal not so much an accurate record of the day's events as an emotionally charged response to the presence of women within Parliament's doors.

Another account of the events of 23 April dismisses the petitioners with anxious raillery: "It is fitter to be washing your dishes, and meddle with the wheel and distaffe. . . . It can never be a good world, when women meddle in the matters of state."[19] This anxious raillery, however, can be considered the undoing of the Members of Parliament. Spinning, carding, weaving and knitting were traditionally female occupations, yet they were the very activities during which women learned collective behaviour. Presumably, these petitioners had come to understand co-operatives through such occupations and to realize how a governing body functioned.

The newspaper accounts countered the petitioners' use of biblical Worthies with representations of other mannish women to deride the petitioners and undercut female political action. The women's collectivizations, forwardness and conviction were parodied via images of both Worthies and Amazons. Such accounts disclosed a fear that the petitioners threatened the class/peerage system as well as the sex/gender system. Female petitioners were thus ridiculed as both citizens and as women. *The Man in the Moon* offered the following response to the 23 April demonstration and petition:

> But *Hannah Ienks*, *Ruth Turn-up*, *Doll Burn-it*, and sister *Wagtayle* have petition'd the *Supreame Authority* for their man *John*, and *Mr. Overton*, that they would in their great *Wisdoms* spare those Worthys for *breeders*, for the better *propagation* of the *righteous*, it seems those *Levelling* She-saints have lately had strange visions on their backs; *Holofernes Fairfax* look to thy head, for *Judeth* is a comming, the women are up in armes, and vow they will tickle your *Members*.[20]

This response dismisses the economic concerns of the petitioners in favour of Leveller-bashing. It assigns to Lilburne and Overton the roles of male Worthies, a formerly significant role with respect to monarchical self-fashioning. It then strips that role of its political significance and relocates it in the sexual realm. The reference to Judith, which displaces a female Worthy in a corresponding manner, dismisses the petitioners' activities as sexual. Thomas Fairfax, Commander in Chief of the Parliamentary Army, suffers a direct association with Holofernes, Judith's nemesis. Fairfax is threatened with decapitation and castration ("look to thy head," "Judith is a comming," and "they will tickle your *Members*"). The *double entendre* "*Members*" further reinforces this sexually charged image: the Levellers, male and female, had merely fallen prey to their libidos.

Mercurius Pragmaticus also employs sexual innuendoes in its account of the 23 April demonstration:

> The meek-hearted Congregation of *Oyster-wives*, together with the Civill-Sisterhood of *Oranges* and *Lemons*, and likewise the mealy-mouth'd Mutton-Mongers *wives* . . . presented a well-penned Petition. . . . the cryes of the oppressed Sisterhood cannot pierce the eares of the hard-hearted Fraternitie; there have been kinder complements exchanged in corners between some and some of them, but now the House stood in danger to have been beleagured, had the Amazones committed a Rape upon these Capons.[21]

The irony with which this account introduces the petitioners ("meek-hearted . . . Oyster-wives," "Civill-Sisterhood," and "mealy-mouth'd") intimates the author's ambivalent support. It acknowledges both their political significance and the disaffection of Parliament, but the word "pierce," coupled with the dichotomy Sisterhood/Fraternitie, tacitly suggests a retention (and perhaps an inversion) of the sex/gender system. Identifying the women as Amazons reveals both the newspaper's political bias and partial acceptance of the women's role as political activists, a role that unfortunately was linked to their sexuality. The women appeared powerful, but only because the Members of Parliament were supposedly castrated and thus incapable of acting forcefully. The Amazon, an image formerly employed to represent a female self-identity independent of sexual behaviour, was appropriated by this newspaper as a vehicle with which to suppress such self-identities.

The next edition of *Mercurius Pragmaticus* develops further the image of the Amazon as a sexual assailant:

> [W]hole *Troopes* of *Amazons* . . . came in their warlike posture taking hold of their *Tayle* in stead of their *Targets*, and marching with confidence to encounter *Tyrannie*, and with abundance of courage exceeding the ordinary sort of *Women* . . . and as the proverb goes of the *Female Sex*, they make use of their *Tongues* (as their best weapon), against *tyranny*, and their *Tayles* for propagation of the now Saynted Fraternity.[22]

The back-handed compliment ("marching with confidence to encounter *Tyrannie*") reveals the author's anxiety about the women's public action. Although he supports their cause, he fails to endorse their actions fully because of their unconventionality. He acknowledges their confidence and courage, but reminds the reader that these women are no ordinary women. The account thus portrays the women as cultural deviants, and this deviancy, demonstrated historically by the Amazons, was culturally unacceptable. The Amazon thus became reduced to a sexual image upon which a female stereotype was superimposed (a woman's tongue is her "best weapon"). The author thus reconfirmed the cultural prejudice that women act out of sexual desire: they approached the Lower House with their "*Tayles*," eager to propagate. Essentially, according to this author, women petitioned Parliament for sexual gratification.

Such accounts failed to dissuade women from participating in demonstrations or signing petitions. In fact, alliances with Leveller causes intensified shortly after the appearance of these editions of *Mercurius Pragmaticus*. Many women participated in the funeral of Robert Lockyer, the most public example of Leveller sympathies. Lockyer, a recognized political leader of Whalley's Regiment, stationed in London, led a Leveller rebellion on 24 April 1649. Lockyer and his followers were protesting against an aggressive colonial war in Ireland. The rebellion was crushed, and Lockyer was executed three days later in St Paul's Churchyard. As the rebellion and hasty conviction of Lockyer became known, a Leveller pamphlet was circulated in London calling on soldiers to refuse to participate in the Irish campaign and to set up a council of agitators (Morton, 66). Lockyer's funeral on 29 April thus provided the Levellers with a theatrical event in which they expressed their opposition to Parliament's Irish campaign and manifested their strength as a unified political party. The coffin was decorated with sprigs of rosemary which were dipped in blood, signifying martyrdom. The long column of mourners, possibly numbering in the thousands, wore sea-green ribbons – the Leveller party had come to be associated with this colour by 1649 – as well as black ones, and a large group of women, who also wore these colours of party preference and mourning on their breasts, brought up the rear of the procession (Fraser, 238).

On 5 May 1649, women donned green ribbons to petition the Lower House for "the Rights and Libertyes of all Petticoat Petitioners" and demanded retribution for the execution of Lockyer.[23] Much was made of the women's use of green ribbons, for another account described the women's procession to Westminster as the "bonny Besses/ In Sea green dresses . . . marching down Battalia to give the members of Westminster a second charge, with the artillery of a Petition."[24] A third account also reported the women's use of green ribbons: "On May 7 there were many women with a new Petition at the Doores of the House of Commons, they did weare on their breasts Sea-green Ribands, as they did at the funeral of Master Lockyer."[25]

The women's appearance denoted not only their affiliation with the Levellers, but also an awareness of their strength as a political collective. The accounts of their petitioning, much more sympathetic than those printed during the week of 24 April, actually supported the collective. Represented as a military force, they were expected to do battle with their petition ("artillery of a Petition"). The women's participation in Lockyer's funeral may have dismissed, or at least mitigated, public opinion about them as meddlesome gossips who understood precious little about the workings of politics. *Mercurius Pragmaticus* actually supported the petitioners: the Lower House "shall know what it is to jeer Woemen with their *Huswifery*, when their businesse is *Liberty*" (17). The women had gained acceptance, to a certain extent, as a political collective whose demands deserved to be heard. Whereas Members of Parliament were portrayed as victims in earlier accounts, it was the petitioners who received sympathy in reports of events related to the Lockyer execution.

The petition focuses on the fact that Lockyer had been tried by martial law in time of peace. Like the course of Leveller rhetoric, it shifts from religious justifications to legislative precedents:

> We are assured of our Creation in the image of God, and of an interest in Christ, equall unto men, as also a proportionable share in the Freedoms of this Commonwealth. . . . Have we not, in the liberties and securities, contained in the Petition of Right, and other the good Laws of the Land? Are any of our lives, liberties or goods to be taken from us more then from men, but by due processe of Law and conviction of twelve sworn men of the Neighbourhood?[26]

The women present themselves as citizens who are both conscious of their political freedoms and determined to see those freedoms maintained.

The petition blames the Commons for violating the civil rights of Lockyer and other political prisoners, and harangues its members for presuming that their constituents will tolerate such violations: "Can you imagine us to be so sottish or stupid, as not to perceive, or not to [be aware that we were] trod under-foot by force and arbitrary power" (*WOMEN*, n. p.). They pose these questions as angry citizens. The deference of "female frailty," found in earlier petitions, is replaced by open confrontation. The petition does not suggest a resolution, but rather explains the course of action which the women will pursue if Parliament fails to release political prisoners:

> Let it be accounted folly, presumption, madness, or whatsoever in
> us, whilst we have life and breath, we will never leave them, nor
> forsake them, nor ever cease to importune you. . . . Nor will we
> ever rest until we have prevailed, that We, our Husbands, children,
> Friends, and Servants, may not be liable to be thus abused, violated
> and butchered at mens Wills and Pleasures. (*WOMEN*, n. p.)

By using such forceful language, the women dismiss stereotypical
images of themselves as "frail females." They list themselves before
their husbands, underlining their identity as individuals, not simply
as wives. Their petition evidences both their refusal to tolerate social
injustice and a determination to express that refusal. Their pledge to
continue the demonstrations revealed to the Lower House a political
consciousness which no longer had to rely on religious justifications. This
petition thus located and confirmed women's presence in the political
arena: their self-perception as female citizens, sharing the same civil
rights as their husbands and fellow men, emerged as the fundamental
tenet upon which they could now act.

Not all newspapers were sympathetic to the female Levellers, for
Mercurius Britannicus likened the "levelling ladies" to "a company of
meddlesome gossops [who] ran up and down [Parliament's steps] and
shewed their petition to everyone."[27] It echoed the redomestication
efforts of the 24 April edition of *The Moderate Messenger*: "They
should go home and spin, it being the usual work of women, either
to spin or knit, and not to meddle with state affairs." Another account
stated that the women "have ever loved to meddle with what they should
not from the beginning; Small bait will soon catch such silly fish."[28] Such
accounts intimate an unwillingness on the part of court reporters to
respond directly to the changing demands of the petitioners. Whereas
the women's petitions soon replaced deferential pleas for attention with
economic concerns couched in legalistic rhetoric, newspaper accounts
continued to respond with misogynous harangues.

Much to the chagrin of these journalists and of Members of Parliament,
female petitioners voiced their opinions about legislation governing
economic policy in 1651 in *The Women's Petition*, which addresses
"the Right Honorable, his Excellency, the most Noble and Victorious
Lord General Cromwell" and attacks the Debtor's Law as an unfair
measure that maintained class distinctions. Harsh and inefficient, this
law placed the debtor in prison, thus removing all possibilities for
repayment, retaining him there until the day to pay his debt – which,
in essence, perpetuated this cycle of debt and imprisonment.[29] Although
Parliament had attempted to reform this law in 1641 and in 1649, the

women, dissatisfied with the measures, appealed to Cromwell directly to be their "Deliverer from Oppression and Slavery."[30]

This petition, when viewed alongside those of 1649, marks a turning point in women's self-expression. It delivers neither religious justifications for their presence before Cromwell nor deferential requests for specific considerations based on gender. Instead, it operates on the assumption that women, like men, have the right to demand legislative reforms from Parliament:

> [O]ur expectation of Freedom (the fruits of our bloud shed, and expence of our estates), is removed far away; yea the hope of our Liberty is cut off like the Weavers thrumb. We have for many years (But in especial since 1647) chattered like Cranes, and mourned like Doves; . . . because the *Head* of Tyrannie being cut off in 1648 (was expected to dy, and be dead) still liveth in and by his ordained members of Injustice and Oppression; and the Norman laws of the Oppressors still bear Dominion over us.

In contrast to earlier petitions, *The Women's Petition to Cromwell* focuses on the women themselves as opposed to husbands, friends and children. "The fruits of our bloud shed" issues a maternal/menstrual image which calls up images of family members who had suffered needlessly because of the Debtor's Law. "Weavers thrumb," the fringe or excess threads of a bolt of cloth, was usually sheared off before the cloth was sold. The "Liberty" of these petitioners had thus been treated as waste or excess fibres, cut off from the fabric of the culture by Members of Parliament. Hence, Parliament had blatantly and unconscionably discarded a basic freedom of its constituents. The bird analogy, which intimates stereotypical activities ("chattering" and "mourning"), reinforces their anger and frustrations.

This passage also echoes Digger rhetoric. Gerrard Winstanley's *An Appeal to the House of Commons* (11 July 1649) argues that Members of Parliament retained "kingly power" even after the king had been executed: "you cut off the king's head, that you might establish yourselves in his Chair of Government, and that your aym was not to throw down Tyranny, but the Tyrant."[31] He also claims that Parliament in subscribing to Normanism acted in defiance of the will of "Almighty God." Such rhetoric when used by the female petitioners denotes the alliance they shared with other politically suspect groups. The women's determination to be heard was also manifested in another way, for they now addressed Cromwell rather than the House. They chose to go directly to the one executive whose influence over Parliament could be exercised. Their petition thus isolated Cromwell from the tyrannous factions, thereby implying the women's expectations of him as the new leader. Although "the *Head* of Tyrannie" had been cut off, its power continued to reside in the "ordained members of Injustice and Oppression." The petitioners now looked to Cromwell to reform Parliament.

Higgins suggests that female petitioners were instrumental in the reform of the Debtor's Law in 1653 (207). Female Levellers had resumed their efforts to secure the release of John Lilburne, enduring yet another term in prison, in July 1653.[32] At first glance, *The humble Petition of divers afflicted WOMEN, in behalf of M. Lilburne Prisoner in Newgate* seems to dismiss the women's self-awareness as a political collective, for the tone is decidedly humble and self-effacing, as opposed to self-assertive.

> Seeing nothing is more manifest then that God is pleased often times to raise up the weakest means to work the mightiest effects, and inasmuch as the holy *Prophet* David himselfe was prevented, by the timely addresses of weak women, from a most resolved purpose of shedding of Blood. . . . [The last Parliament] was swift to shed blood, whilst their ears were deaf to Petitioners, and Prisoners, the Widdow and Fatherless were neglected by them . . . we crave leave to alude unto in your case, that if it be possible, we may prevaile with you to purpose unto your selves to be unlike them in al things. (Higgins, 207)

Biblical history reappears as the justification for the petitioners' presence before Parliament. But, rather than the example of Judith or Esther who had appeared in earlier petitions, the prophet David is employed. The petition thus casts Members of Parliament in the role of biblical Worthies who, it was believed, could be swayed by the "addresses of weak women," while the petitioners assume a role that portrays them as out of place.

The petitioners thus approached Members of Parliament in a flattering manner. Their petition juxtaposed "the last Parliament" with the present one, thereby creating an image of a paternal legislative body which would both listen to and protect the society it governed. In reality, this was the Little Parliament, also known as the Barebones Parliament, which was established after Cromwell had purged the Rump Parliament in April 1653 (Fraser, 240). The petition presented no political demands, but simply suggested that this Parliament dissociate itself completely from the previous one, as earlier petitions had suggested that Cromwell dissociate himself from Parliament.

The peremptory tone and self-determination that characterized the 1649 petition do not appear in this document. The author may have believed that a deferential approach would be more effective. Digger rhetoric, which would have portrayed Parliament as a tyrant, is not used as it had been in *The Women's Petition* of 1651. Lilburne's imprisonment was a tendentious issue, but one whose implications were not so far-reaching as those of the Debtor's Law. To address such a politically sensitive issue as Lilburne's release with self-assertiveness would perhaps have frustrated the efforts of the petitioners. Thus, this petition does not necessarily indicate a loss of political consciousness or a reassimilation of cultural stereotypes about women. If anything, it reveals a heightened awareness of self-representation through certain forms of rhetoric. Sensitive to the political climate that surrounded the Lilburne case, the women subordinated their demand for political freedom to humble entreaties in order to appeal to the Barebones Parliament.

A second petition of 1653, *The humble representation of divers afflicted Women-Petitioners to the Parliament*, followed on 27 July. *The Faithful Post*, which printed this petition in its 26 July–2 August 1653 edition, prefaces the tract with the following remark:

> In my last edition I presented you with the humble Petition of the afflicted women in behalfe of Mr. John Lilburn; the rejection whereof occasioned a second Representation to every individual member of Parliament.[33]

Although it is another plea for the release of Lilburne, this petition also asserts women's right to petition. Deference and humility had failed to sway Parliament, hence the petitioners resumed the tone found in earlier petitions.

> [W]e cannot be but much saddened to see our undoubted Right of Petitioning withheld from us, having attended several days at your House-door with an humble Petition . . . it is the known duty of Parliament to receive Petitions: and it is ours and the nations undoubted right to petition, although an Act of Parliament were made against it. (*FP*, 2004)

It was apparent to the petitioners that the Barebones Parliament would respond in the same way as the Rump, and so they shifted their main concern from Lilburne to their right to petition. The casting of Members of Parliament in the roles of biblical Worthies remains: Ahasuersus not only heard Esther's petition, "but reversed that Decree or Act gone forth against the Jewes" (*FP*, 2005). Examples from secular history also justify the petitioners' appearance: "your honours . . . may call to mind that never to-be-forgotten deliverance obtained, by the good women of England against the usurping Danes in this Nation" (*FP*, 2005). A legislative precedent appears as further justification: "the ancient laws of *England* are not contrary to the will of God: so that we claim it is our right to have our petitions heard" (*FP*, 2005). What, therefore, emerges from these statements is a well-defined political consciousness rooted in an understanding of civil liberties that transcends sex/gender divisions.

The self-assured, political tone, expressed through such phrases as "undoubted right" and "claim it is our right," was the petitioners only recourse to the responses received from Parliament. Twelve women, led by Katherine Chidley who had preached from the pulpit at Somerset House on behalf of John Lilburne earlier in July, presented this petition, which was believed to have been "subscribed by above six thousand of that sex" (Higgins, 180–1). In spite of this support in number of signatories, Parliament rebuffed the women:

> [The women] boldly knocked at the doore, and the House taking notice that they were there, sent out Praise-God Barebones to disswaude them from their enterprize, but he could not prevaile; and they persisting in their disturbance another Member came out and told them, the House could not take cognizance of their Petition, [to which the women responded] if they refused, they should know that they had husbands and friends, and they wore swords to defend the Libertys of the People, and c. and withall admonished them.[34]

As in the dismissal of earlier petitions, Parliament's response angered the women and incited them to vocalize their demands. That they admonished Parliament and threatened its members with civil war suggests they were aware that the Barebones Parliament, like the Rump Parliament, acted in its own interests, interests which were diametrically opposed to those of the petitioners. It was perhaps Parliament's failure to deal with disaffection that solidified the petitioners' self-perception as a politically powerful collective which had the right to admonish its legislative representatives.

III

It is tempting to dismiss the actions of the female petitioners as being of little consequence, for one could conceivably argue that theirs was a unique situation, occurring when English culture was in a state of post-Civil War turmoil. Such turmoil enabled the Levellers and the Diggers, two groups of individuals who existed on the fringes of the dominant political culture, to present religious and political platforms. It could be argued that the actions of these two marginal groups paved the way for the female petitioners. The women's petitions and demonstrations suggest an emergence of a political consciousness that was based on a demand for cultural emancipation (as do the Leveller tracts and the writings of Gerrard Winstanley). Their alliance with Leveller causes, in particular, reveals their insistence on a *public* definition of themselves as political actors whose roles are as significant as that of male political actors. The women thus succeeded in petitioning Parliament because of male precedents.

Female petitioning, however, went further in its demands for civil rights than its Leveller and Digger precedents. By 1649, when women began to petition fervently, perhaps even with a vengeance, the Leveller party had begun to decline (Morton, 59–70). The Digger's communal experiment at St George's Hill had begun to collapse in the autumn of 1649, and the move to Cobham did not stave off its dissolution in 1650 (Kenyon, 182–3). There may have been continued male support for women's demonstrations, but during the funeral of Robert Lockyer women assumed an identity independent of political factions controlled by men. By 1651 "we women" had replaced "we wives and widows." Furthermore, their petitions focused on their own actions ("chattering like cranes" and "mourning like doves") as opposed to those of their husbands, sons and fathers. Their use of female Worthies, Judith and Esther in particular, indicated their appropriation of a former monarchical image. They, too, commanded the right to demand justice and civil liberties as citizens of the Commonwealth. Legal precedents and the threat of civil insurrection replaced the self-effacing, humble language of the early petitions. Ironically enough, it was Parliament's continual dismissal of their demands that served as the catalyst which led to their more determined resolution to demand political rights.

The demand for political rights, in turn, proposed a reconsideration of the culture's sex/gender system which granted men the power of inscription, the power to define women as their property as opposed to their helpmates who retained civil rights of their own. The women did not consciously threaten to upend this ideological structure, but rather, through their self-presentation as citizens, exposed it as a crumbling structure which could no longer maintain its claim with respect to female behaviour.

NOTES

Special thanks to John J. Flynn and Randall S. Nakayama for their insightful readings.

1. "The Reactions of Women, with special reference to women petitioners," in *Politics, Religion and the English Civil War*, Brian Manning, ed. (London, 1973), 179–97.
2. *The True Diurnal Occurrences, Or, The Heads of the Proceedings of Both Houses* (31 January–7 February 1641/1642): A2r. All dates which fall between 1 January and 24 March are indicated by both Julian and Gregorian calendar year dates; all others are indicated by Gregorian calendar year only.
3. *Diurnal Occurrences* reported that 12 women were admitted to the Lords' chamber, but do not discuss the result of this meeting. In their accounts of the women's activities on 1 February 1641/1642, neither Wallington nor Gardiner refer to the women's appearance before the Upper House; Nehemiah Wallington, *Historical Notes of Events Occurring Chiefly in the Reign of Charles I*, R. Webb, ed., 2 vols. (London, 1869), 2:6; Samuel Gardiner, *History of England from the Accession of James I to the Outbreak of the Civil War*, 10 vols. (London, 1884), 10: 162–3.
4. London, 1642; reprinted *Harleian Miscellany*, 8 vols. (London, 1744), 7: 568.
5. Another account of the same petition, entitled *A True Copie of the Petition of Gentlewomen and Tradesmens-wives, in and about the City of London*, states that the women "fall submissively at the King's feet" in order to submit this petition. Such a claim also suggests a conscious attempt to soften the demand for "common Privileges" (London, 1642); 3.
6. *Harleian Miscellany*, 7: 568, 569.
7. Ellen A. McArthur, "Women Petitioners and the Long Parliament," *English Historical Review*, 24 (1909): 701.
8. *Certaine Informations* (7–14 August 1643): 231. Hereafter referred to as *CI*.
9. *The Parliament Scout* (3–10 August 1643): 55. Hereafter referred to as *PS*.
10. *The Kingdomes Weekly Intelligencer* (8–15 August 1643): 229.
11. Antonia Fraser, *The Weaker Vessel* (New York, 1985), 237.
12. Fraser does not state who wrote this petition, but suggests that it was written by Mary herself. D.M. Wolfe states that it was written by Richard, on behalf of Mary and other family members; see *Leveller Manifestoes* (New York, 1944), 166.
13. *A Perfect Diurnall of Some Passages in Parliament* (23–30 April 1649): 14c; *Continued Heads of Perfect Passages in Parliament* (20–27 April 1649): 11–12.
14. *Mercurius Pragmaticus* (17–24 April 1649): n. p.
15. A.L. Morton, ed., *Freedom In Arms: A Selection of Leveller Writings* (New York, 1975), 30.
16. *England's Moderate Messenger* (23–30 April 1649): 2. Hereafter referred to as *EMM*.
17. *Mercurius Pragmaticus* (24 April–1 May 1649): 10.
18. *Mercurius Militaris* (17–24 April 1649): 13–14.
19. *The Imperial Intelligencer* (25 April 1649): 62–3.
20. *The Man in the Moon, Discovering a World of Knavery under the Sunne* (16–23 April 1649): 11.
21. *Mercurius Pragmaticus* (23–30 April 1649): A2.
22. *Mercurius Pragmaticus* (24 April–1 May 1649): Qqq 3v.
23. *Mercurius Pragmaticus* (1–8 May 1649): 15.
24. *Mercurius Militarius, Or, The People's Scout* (8 May 1649): 32.
25. *The Kingdomes Weekly Intelligencer* (1–8 May 1649): 1351.
26. *The Humble Petition of divers well-affected WOMEN of the Cities of London and Westminster, the Borough of the Southwark, Hamblets, and Parts Adjacent* (London, 1649): n. p. Hereafter referred to as *WOMEN*.
27. *Mercurius Britannicus* (1–8 May 1649): 11, 16.
28. *A Modest Narrative of Intelligence* (5–12 May 1649): 42.
29. In *Social Problems and Policy during the Puritan Revolution* (London, 1930), Margaret

James explains the women's response to the Debtor's Law: "The women prayed that 'the Norman yoke of perpetual imprisonment for debt' might be abolished, and complained that the prisons were merely places of sanctuary to wilful, obstinate debtors, and 'cruel slaughter houses' to pay the poor men who were ready to pay their debts if given a chance" (328–9).

30. James, 335–6. *The Women's Petition . . . to Cromwell* (London, 1651).
31. *An Appeal to the House of Commons, Works*, 307. Cited by Timothy Kenyon, *Utopian Communism and Political Thought in Early Modern England* (London, 1989), 175.
32. Although Thomason dated this petition "June 25, 1653," the newspapers do not refer to it around this date, whereas in July two newspapers reported that "the Women have drawn up an excellent Petition in behalf of M. Lilburn," and they printed a petition identical to Thomason's (Higgins, 207).
33. *The Faithful Post* (26 July–2 August 1653): 2004. Hereafter referred to as *FP*.
34. Clarendon MSS, Vol. 46, fo. 131. Cited by Higgins, 207–8, and Fraser, 241.

Female Preachers and Male Wives: Gender and Authority in Civil War England

RACHEL TRUBOWITZ

I

On 29 December 1648, Elizabeth Poole, a widow from Abdington, came before the General Council of the parliamentary army to deliver a prophetic vision of the English nation and to plead for the life of Charles I. After many days of acting as "a sad mourner" for "the distresses of this Land," Poole had come to believe that she had learned the cure for England's "dying state" through two symbolic figures revealed to her by the divine spirit. One figure was that of a woman, "crooked, sick, weak and imperfect in body," which Poole interpreted as a "similitude" of "the weak and imperfect state of the kingdom"; the other was of a man, "a member of the Army" who "would gladly be a sacrifice" for the sickly woman that was England. Poole elaborated on the army's redemptive national role by assigning it a female part. Turning the Stuart image of the king as father and husband to his state to her own (moderately) revolutionary ends, she told the General Council that "The King is your Father and husband which you were and are to obey in the Lord and in no other way," and the army was his "wife." Like other separatist "wives," the army would be justified in repudiating and even abandoning its husband since "he forgot his Subordination to divine Faithhood and headship, thinking he had begotten you a generation to his own pleasure"; the army was not, however, entitled to execute the king.

Reinforcing her message through scriptural example, Poole offered the army a model for its spousal relation to Charles I. She encouraged it "to act the part of Abigail," who condemned Nabal for refusing to recognize and serve David but "lifted not her hand against her husband to take his life"; "no more doe yee against yours," she said, for the king's failure to recognize and serve Cromwell.[1] Just as Abigail was prevented by God from shedding her evil husband's blood and instead brought about his death at the hands of the Lord ten days after she accused Nabal of wrong-doing, so for Poole, the army, acting the part of Abigail, must respect God's mandate against shedding the blood of its ungodly husband and simply bring the king to trial, leaving his conviction a matter for divine providence.

Poole delivered her vision to an audience that included, among

112

other army grandees, Henry Ireton and Oliver Cromwell. Cromwell's appearances at Council meetings were infrequent, but he nevertheless came to hear Mistress Poole. Possibly he believed that her prophecies could work to his political advantage by helping to strengthen his and Ireton's efforts to prevent the execution of Charles. Ireton appears to have spoken both for himself and the Lord General when, after Poole finished speaking, he exhorted the General Council to accept her prophecy against regicide as "the fruites of the spiritt of God." "I thinke," he said, "the summe of that which shee offers, that wee ought to doe for God."[2]

Poole was invited back to the Council to repeat her prophecy in support of Cromwell's position on 5 January 1649, one day after the Commons passed the ordinance to set up the High Court of Justice to try the king. Ireton's and Cromwell's hopes of staving off regicide were, however, fleeting: Charles was executed on 30 January 1649. Poole was immediately repudiated by William Kiffin, a member of her Baptist church and an ardent supporter of Cromwell, and she was cast out of the congregation. Although she retaliated by prophesying that the army officers would share the same fate as the king, her charge only intensified the efforts by Kiffin and his associates to defame her, and she lapsed into obscurity.[3]

The story of Elizabeth Poole is only one of many accounts of female preaching and prophesying during the Civil Wars.[4] I have singled it out because it nicely encapsulates the complex connections between the construction of gender and the nature of religious and political authority in the 1640s and 1650s. I will begin by noting two aspects of this issue. First, the story illustrates the fluidity of gender boundaries during these revolutionary decades. The case of Elizabeth Poole provides compelling (though not unequivocal) evidence of both the serious attention given to women acting in the prototypically "male" roles of preacher and prophet, and the considerable stature and visibility that such culturally androgynous women enjoyed. Poole's depiction of the army as a wife also suggests that this kind of cultural cross-dressing worked in both directions. While women entered the public arena, from which they had hitherto been largely excluded, to gain "male" authority as preachers, prophets and pamphleteers, men were "domesticated" by their appropriation of the tropes of wife and mother as emblems for their subjugation to and rebellion against monarchical and prelatical authority as well as for their hopes of personal redemption. Second, the circumstances surrounding and following the delivery of Poole's prophecy help to outline the rather narrow sphere in which such latidutinarian perceptions of gender were tolerated. By trying behind-the-scenes to turn Poole's vision to his own political advantage, Cromwell re-establishes traditional male dominance at the very moment in which such dominance – at least in terms of gender – is challenged by Poole's "masculine" ministerial and prophetic authority. The defamation of Poole's character and identity – her easy slide from preacher/prophet to heretic – by Kiffin and his associates after the execution of the king even more fully imposes the same kind of male dominance through the discourse of religion.[5] While Poole is comprehensible to the parliamentary army in the "male" role of prophet, she also remains, for Cromwell and Kiffin, conventionally "female," the subject of "male" authority, containment and appropriation.

The emergence of women as preachers and prophets has been correctly described as "an early manifestation of feminism," and the spiritual and political posture of men as "wives" and "mothers" ascribed to feminizing tendencies in Protestant religious experience;[6] more attention, however, still needs to be paid to the ways in which the elevation of the "feminine" in Civil War England equivocally coexists with the emergence of new and more efficient methods for reasserting the supremacy of male authority and rule. Unlike earlier efforts to settle the "transvestite controversy," which dates to the 1570s, cross-dressing (both literal and figurative) in the Civil War period is increasingly checked by invisible, non-legible forms of male control rather than by sumptuary laws and other paternalistic legal and institutional measures of public record, through which the boundaries of gender categories had hitherto been protected against transvestite incursions.[7] In 1620, King James responded publicly to the growing female transvestite movement in London by ordering the clergy of the city to make scathing attacks against cross-dressing women in their sermons, as John Chamberlain records in his letter of 25 January:

> Yesterday the bishop of London called together all his Clergie about this towne, and told them he had expresse commaundment from the King to will them to inveigh vehemently and bitterly in theyre sermons, against the insolencie of our women, and their wearing of brode brimd hats, pointed dublets, theyre haire cut short or shorne, and some of them stillettaes or poinards, and other trinkets of like moment.

Should pulpit admonitions not reform the mannish tendencies of these insolent women, the king "would proceed by another course."[8] By the 1640s and 1650s, however, such efforts to restrain cross-dressing in the form of both male and female role reversal are no longer most effectively launched from the public stage; rather, not unlike Elizabeth Poole's "masculine" prophetic authority which Cromwell publicly applauds but secretly turns to his own advantage, the scandalous mixing of gender categories, while (more or less) openly accepted, is covertly restrained through the programmes for patriarchal discipline contained within Puritan Utopianism and science. It is the not-at-all easy confluence between these "off-stage" assertions of traditional male authority and the public spectacle of cultural androgyny tolerated during the Civil War period that this essay will chart.

II

The remarkable figure of the woman prophet and preacher first enters the social scene with considerable frequency in the early 1640s. Mysticism had, as Margaret George points out, "traditionally been an outlet for the most energetic, committed, forceful, articulate, and imaginative women."[9] But while the cloistered world of the convent had hitherto served as the most important arena for female prophetic activity, in Civil War England, following the collapse of censorship, the press and the pulpit – two almost exclusively male platforms – offered new forums for women who wanted to make their opinions known in public.

Of these newly visible women preachers and pamphleteers, Katherine Chidley provides an evocative exemplar.[10] Chidley sustained a career as an Independent preacher for more than 20 years, from 1630 – when she and her husband, having fled to London from religious persecution in Shrewsbury, joined with other separatists to found a new congregation – to 1653, when near the end of her life, she headed a group of 12 women who confronted the Barebones Parliament with a petition in support of Leveller John Lilburne that contained the signatures of more than 6,000 women. Her prominence as a lecturer at separatist churches around London was such that the Presbyterian divine, the Reverend Thomas Edwards, singled her out among the numerous female and "mechanical" sectarian preachers whom he repudiates in *Gangraena* as an especially pernicious heretic. For Edwards, Chidley epitomizes the scandal and threat of radical activity, both religious and political. Specifically, it is Chidley's "unnatural" vociferousness as a woman preacher that Edwards equates with sectarian disdain for custom and tradition. Just as Edwards demands that Independents "speake not against what is established by common consent nor practise to the scandall and contempt of the magistrate and church," he condemns Chidley for the fact that "she with a great deal of violence and bitterness spake against all Ministers"; she was "so talkative and clamorous" when she denounced the Established Church to William Greenhill, the orthodox minister of the congregation in Stepney where she had won some converts.[11] Sectarian dissent is for

Edwards a form of loud and unruly female discourse, and the figure of the woman preacher a symbol of the monstrous world turned upside down that the sectaries hoped to create on English soil.

Along with the pulpit (however metaphorically understood), the unlicensed printing press, which proliferated in London after the Long Parliament abolished the censorship authority of the Archbishop of Canterbury, provided women with expanded opportunities to publish and circulate their religious ideas and prophetic revelations. The genteel and sometimes insane Lady Eleanor Davies (or Douglas) published at least 37 visionary tracts between 1641 and 1652, the year of her death.[12] Like Davies, Chidley used the printing press to create a public record of herself and her vision of the world; she also turned it into an instrument by which she could correct and counter Edwards' anti-female efforts to defame her ministerial authority by systematically proving his paternalistic arguments for centralized church government to be ungodly. In the 84 pages of her first publication, *The Iustification of the Independent Churches of Christ* (1641), which was intended as "an Answer to Mr Edvvards his Booke, which hee hath written against the Government of Christs Church," Chidley argues that, in supporting the Presbyterian effort to implement new state controls over religious expression, Edwards had constrained and obscured the authority of Christ: he had "thrust Christ into a narrow corner." Edwards' efforts to systematize religious experience similarly sentenced the individual conscience to a state of confinement. "I know no true Divinities," she asserts,

> that teacheth men to be Lords over the Conscience; and I thinke it is no part godly policie to drive the king's subjects out of the land because they desire free libertie to worship God in the land according to his will; the State[s] of Holland are counted politicke, and yet they esteeme it the Strength of their Kingdome to grant free libertie of conscience.[13]

Chidley's successful efforts to wrest the authority of the press and pulpit away from men like Edwards is testimony, in part, to the considerable stature that women achieved in the various sects. It was, as Keith Thomas points out, "quite usual for women to preponderate" in separatist congregations, especially after 1640 when the sects who had exiled themselves in Holland and elsewhere on the Continent during the Laudian repression returned to England.[14] Women also played key roles in the organization and government of separatist churches. The sectarian church became an arena in which women could experience something close to parity with men and push beyond the subordination and submissiveness traditionally required of their sex towards the central and primary roles generally accorded to their male counterparts.

Unsurprisingly, the culturally threatening spectacle of women's "male" supremacy as preachers, pamphleteers, church organizers and leaders was not welcomed by those hostile to the radical sects. Indeed, it became a standard form of ridicule to mock the sectaries for their tolerance of women. One of the first tracts to attack sectarian women for their desire to preach is the anonymous pamphlet, *Discovery of Six Women Preachers*, published in 1641, which energetically deplores the scandalous sight of six women in Middlesex, Kent, Cambridge and Salisbury preaching from "a stoole or a tub instead of a pulpit."[15] Such "stoole-" and tub-preachers are also the object of scathing ridicule in *Tub Preachers Overturned: Or, Independency to be Abandoned and Abhorred* (1647):

> And that her zeal, piety, and knowledge,
> Surpass'd the gravest student in the College
> Who strive their human learning to advance;
> She with her Bible and a Concordance
> Could preach nine times a week morning and night
> Such revelation had she from New Light.[16]

Edwards similarly protests against the audacity of "mechanicks taking upon them to preach and baptize, as Smiths, Taylors, Shoomakers, Pedlars, Weavers . . . also some women in our times, who keepe constant lectures, preaching weekly to many men and women."[17] "Whom do they [Anabaptists, Brownists, Barrowists and Familists] begin with," writes Robert Burton as early as 1621, "but collapsed Ladies, some few tradesmen, superstitious old folks, illiterate persons, weak women, discontent, rude, silly companions, or sooner circumvent?"[18]

To be sure, not even the sectaries themselves were entirely comfortable with the astonishing fact of women preaching and publishing. The Muggletonians held as truth what Milton's fallen Adam falsely conjectures: that the ranks of heaven contained only masculine spirits. They actively discouraged women from prophesying or ministering. Most of the gathered churches, however, took the more moderate position that female prophets could address the congregation directly, but that other women must rely on men to assert their religious convictions for them. Dr Peter Chamberlen's church in London decreed that "a woman (maid, wife or widow) being a prophetess (I Cor. 11) may speak, prophesy, pray, with a veil. Others may not."[19] Even the very liberal Baptist congregation of John Rogers in Dublin wavered on the question of the proper role and rights of women in the church. Rogers accorded

women all the privileges of men and was careful not to bar women
from church government – "Most men," he writes "do arrogate a sovereignty to this point which I see no warrant for"; yet his position on
women seems to have led half his congregation to reject his ministry.[20]
Even with such constraints, however, separatist churches nevertheless
fostered a visible number of women visionaries, over 300 by Phyllis
Mack's count.[21]

In addition to encouraging (however reluctantly) women to take on
the role of prophet or preacher, the sects also inadvertently helped
women to abandon their traditional duties as wives and mothers and
to define themselves instead as independent thinkers and preachers by
demanding obedience to their church over obedience to their husband.
In 1658, Jane Adams was rebuked by the Baptist church at Fenstanton
when she blamed her failure to attend a meeting on her wifely duty to
respect her husband's disapproval of her religious calling; she was told
that her desire to be a good wife must not interfere with her desire to be
a good Baptist and that she was required to attend church meetings under
any condition except forceful physical restraint.[22] In *A Dissuasive from
the Errours of the Time* (1645), Robert Baillie deplores the fact that the
followers of the radical spiritist Gorton in New England saw fit to assert
that "it is lawful for a woman who sees into the mystery of Christ, in case
her husband will not go with her, to leave her husband and follow the
Lords House; for the Church of God is a Christian home, where she must
dwell . . . and in so doing she leaves not her husband, but her husband
forsakes her."[23] Katherine Chidley also questioned the "authority this
unbeleeving husband hath over the conscience of his beleeving wife."[24]
While this demand that wives must subordinate the authority of their
husbands to that of their church merely forced women to exchange one
form of male rule for another, it also paradoxically enabled some women
to gain a measure of self-determination. Mrs Attaway, for instance,
the lace-woman whom David Masson describes as "perhaps the most
noted of all women-preachers in London," acted in conformity with
the churches' position on wifely obedience when she saw fit to leave
her husband and take off with the married preacher, William Jenney.[25]

Such rethinking of wives' duties and of husbands' authority led to
a general loosening of the marriage bond. "Unequal marriages," as
Christopher Hill notes, were perceived as "antichristian yokes" by both
sexes, who, on this principle, abandoned and changed spouses with
increasing ease and frequency. It is precisely this principle that, as we
have seen, Elizabeth Poole invokes in her address to the parliamentary
army. "It seems indeed," Hill writes, "to have been perfectly simple for
any couple to team up together and wander round the country, preaching

and presumably depending on the hospitality of their co-religionists or those whom they could convince."[26]

More perhaps than anything else, however, it was the doctrinal emphasis placed on the spiritual equality of the two sexes by both the reformed and the separatist churches that helped women to achieve authority in the "male" role of preacher or prophet. The Protestant sense that the Holy Spirit bloweth where it listeth regardless of gender made male and female souls equally important sites of divine inspiration. This was particularly true of the Quakers who believed that the Crucifixion had spiritually redeemed women from their subjection to men, to which they had been sentenced after the Fall;[27] Quaker congregations allowed all Friends to be moved to speak, regardless of gender. "In this great work of the Lord Jesus Christ," Margaret Fell-Fox writes in *The Daughter of Sion Avvakened* (1677), "in which he hath given himself for his Body, which is his Church, he hath made no difference in this Work between Male and Female, but they are all one in Christ Jesus."[28] In *A Call to the Universall Seed of God* (1665), Fell-Fox, echoing Galatians 3:28, proclaims that "Christ in the Male and in the Female is one . . . and God hath said, that his Daughters should Prophesie as well as his Sons."[29]

Protestant emphasis on St Paul's doctrine of the spiritual identity between maleness and femaleness also enabled the kind of blending of sexual categories already noted in connection with Elizabeth Poole's prophetic vision. Whatever their corporeal differences, men and women had the same kind of souls, and so each sex could take on attributes of the other and structure its spiritual beliefs and practices in androgynous terms. If women became "male" preachers and prophets, male prophets and preachers consciously emulated and appropriated qualities traditionally associated with women – passivity, self-sacrifice, receptivity and nurturing – in their posture towards the deity and their congregations. Indeed, many Protestants, as Mack points out, "depicted prophecy as a feminine activity, whether the actual prophet was a man or woman."[30] For Puritans, the conspicuous openness of the female body to outside influences made women a natural type of prophet. The celebrity that the prophet Anna Trapnel, the daughter of a Poplar shipwright, acquired during the 1650s derived in part from her efforts to enhance the openness of her body to divine inspiration through fast-induced trances, which she believed facilitated God's direct presence within her. In one of the anti-Cromwellian prophecies she recounts in *The Cry of a Stone* (1654), Trapnel demonstrates her receptiveness to the penetrating influence of deity by contrasting her spiritual intimacy with Christ with the threats of physical laceration and sexual assault that she receives when she is confronted by "a great company of Cattel," one whose "Countenance was perfectly like unto *Oliver Cromwells.*" "He ran at me," Trapnel reports, "and as he was near with his horn to my breast, an arm and a hand clasped me round, a Voice said, I will be thy safety."[31] To receive Christ's rescuing embrace – if not from Cromwell then from worldly corruption in general – Puritan men needed to become as open and receptive to divine influence as women; they were required, in short, to acquire a kind of allegorical female body. Puritan ministers in New England turned themselves into "breasts of God" and their congregations into "New born babes desiring the milk of the Word (Lev. 146)."[32] "Ministers are your Mothers too," writes Cotton Mather in a funeral sermon for his father, "Have they not Travailed in Birth for you that a CHRIST may be seen formed in you? Are not their Lips the Breasts thro' which the sincere Milk of the Word has pass'd unto you, for your Nourishment?"[33]

Female models and symbols have always been central to the depiction and articulation of Christian belief.[34] Veneration of the Virgin Mary and the female saints was an important component of late-medieval devotion; biblical iconography in the Tudor period stressed the female nature of truth, mercy, peace and righteousness.[35] The "feminine" had, however, special resonance for Puritans, who, while de-emphasizing the figure of Mary as the embodiment of sanctity, intensified the significance of "female" interiority and receptivity as religious metaphors for the central Protestant doctrine of "inner light," or private inspiration of believers. Sectarian antagonism to the university-trained Anglican clergy also conspired to make "femaleness" – as an essential condition of unlettered lowliness – a prerequisite to true belief. Gerrard Winstanley epitomizes the sectarian attitude towards the scholarly elite when he argued for the Utopian society, in *The Law of Freedom in a Platform*, in which children should "not be trained up only to book learning and no other employment, called scholars, as they are in the government of monarchy."[36] The miserable and despised position of women made them perfect vessels for the unscholarly and purely inspired wisdom that sectarians like Winstanley championed as a corrective to what they saw as the "papist" corruption and worldly ambitions of the reformed English clergy.[37] It is for her unworldly and unselfmotivated preaching that George Keith thus celebrates the Woman of Samaria:

> Her preaching was not of any Human design . . . it was of the Lord alone . . . whereas their preaching [that of the Anglican clergy] commonly and generally is a human design and contrivance from first to last, to get money, and Worldly Honour and preferment with much ease.[38]

To become true servants of God, Puritan men needed to abandon scholarly and self-promoting "male" forms of sermon-writing and to turn themselves instead into untutored and unselfinterested "female" vessels "of the Lord alone."

Puritan efforts to de-institutionalize the church further deepened the significance of female qualities and roles for male believers. In their desire to rid the church of its institutional "scaffolding," as Milton terms it in *The Reason of Church Government*, radical Protestants succeeded also in allegorizing the church, abstracting it from actual physical sites and structures and locating it instead in spiritual constructs and foundations. With the diminished stature of the visually impressive church, the metaphorical description of the church as a wife in Ephesians 5:23 – "For the husband is the head of the wife, even as Christ is the head of the church" – took on new importance as a central principle of Puritan devotion. As Maureen Quilligan points out,

> If each believer had become his own priest, and was no longer a member of an institutionally visible church, the priest found his congregation had shrunk to the literal foundation upon which Paul had based his metaphoric description of Christ's relationship to his church: the love of a husband for his wife.[39]

In spiritual terms, both men and women were "wives" of Christ, the Bridegroom. "Christ," writes Fell-Fox, "is the Husband, to the Woman as well as the Man, all being comprehended to be the Church."[40] By adopting the wifely posture of submissiveness in relation to God, Puritan men could internally literalize the Pauline metaphor of the church as beloved helpmeet. It is precisely this male wifely role that Milton celebrates at the end of *Paradise Lost* when he has the "domestic" Adam proclaim his devotion to God:[41]

> Henceforth I learn, that to obey is best,
> And love with fear the only God,
> . . . . and by small
> Accomplishing great things deem'd weak
> Subverting worldly strong, and worldly wise
> By simply meek; that suffering for Truth's sake
> Is fortitude to highest victory.[42] (12: 561–70)

Conversely, Satan impugns such goodwifely devotion to God as "ignominy and shame":

> That Glory never shall his wrath or might
> Exhort from me. To bow and sue for Grace
> That were ignominy and shame beneath
> This downfall. (1: 106–16)

Satan's disdain for male-wifely submissiveness condemns him to the eternally unregenerate manliness of the classical epic hero.

Images of feminized manhood occupy a central position in political as well as religious discourse, as demonstrated by the attempts of Cromwell's apologists to depict the Lord General in female, and more specifically, maternal terms. In the words of the annalist of a Cockermouth congregation, Cromwell is "that most eminent Servant of the Lord, and nursing father of the churches."[43]

This image of Cromwell as a male mother draws on Isaiah 49.23: "And kings shall be thy nursing fathers"; however, it also represents a republican adaptation of the maternal qualities that the Stuart monarchy attached to its royal sovereignty. Cromwell's male motherhood is, for the Cockermouth annalist, a measure of his (partially politically motivated) tolerance for religious diversity, or what Claire Cross describes as his "vision of the English Church as a multitude of congregations."[44] By contrast, James I's depiction of himself as a "louing nourish father" who feeds and nurtures his subjects with "nourish milk" allegorizes his sense of the all-inclusive and undifferentiated unity of his royal power.[45] James's role as both father and mother also reinforces his desire for empire and his absolutist sense of his imperial sovereignty. His sexual completeness as androgyne emblematically asserts that "the king is beyond comparison because that which is other – other people – or sexually other . . . are nonetheless his."[46] In Cromwell, the Stuart image of male motherhood is reconfigured to idealize a republican vision of balance between central and local authority, between state power and individual conscience.

Also underpinning Cromwell's maternal relation to the various sects is the paradigm of the tender, nursing mother frequently invoked in Puritan family guidebooks. Breast-feeding was vigorously urged upon Puritan mothers as an ideal way to nurture babies. "How can a mother better expresse her love to her young babe," asks William Gouge in *Of Domesticall Duties* (1622), "then by letting it suck of her owne breasts?"[47] An ordinary woman, as Laurel Thatcher Ulrich points out, "had no choice, or course, since the only alternative was to hire another mother to do it for her."[48] In the pro-nursing manuals, however, breast-feeding ceases to function as a sign of a woman's lower-class standing; nursing one's own baby becomes instead a symbol of high moral stature and ethical advantage. Unlike the aristocratic practice of wet-nursing, breast-feeding would establish proper ethical patterns of behaviour upon which children could build in later life. In the *Doctrine of Superiority* (1609), a title that encapsulates the class argument that underpins Puritan emphasis on breast-feeding, Robert Pricke insists that the "tender care of noursing & bringing [children] up in their younger & more tender yeares" is the best way to foster good citizens.[49] As David Leverenz points out, Puritans maintained that "Tender mothers and tender children go together. Mothers should not be surprised if children deny them later in life, ran the warnings [in the guidebooks], when they deny children the breast early in life. Strange milk would lead to strange manners."[50]

The same anti-aristocratic equation between nursing mothers and right-mannered children informs Cromwell's perception of his "maternal" relationship to the various separatist churches in the early years of the Civil Wars, for he seems to have held the protection, nurturing and cultivation of what he termed the "tender consciences" of the radical sects as an essential part of his mandate as Lord General. In September 1644, he successfully lobbied the Commons on behalf of his largely Independent army to accept a motion that would force the parliamentary committee appointed to convene with the Westminister Assembly, which generally favoured a Presbyterian form of church government, to tolerate Independent and other separatist congregations who refused to conform to the Scottish model. He urged parliament to "endeavour the finding out some ways how for tender consciences, who cannot in all things submit to common rule which shall be established, may be borne with, according to the Word, and as may stand with the public peace." Such nurturing or "nursing" of the various sects would not only cultivate their goodwill but encourage them to stay within the parliamentary fold, where Cromwell could (ultimately unsuccessfully) contain and control the threat of revolt within the Revolution he had helped to engineer. For Cromwell, Parliament's role was to extend his motherly love and protection to the sects as a way to preserve the coalition between the disparate religious and political factions that had forged an uneasy alliance with him against the king. "Therefore I beseech you," he tells the Barebones Parliament, ". . . have a care of the whole flock! Love the sheep, love the lambs; love all, tender all."[51]

III

The Civil War period thus witnesses a loosening of gender categories as women preachers and spiritually feminized men appear as comprehensible figures on the social scene – symbols of the new anti-traditional society and anti-institutional paradigms of belief that sectarians hoped the Revolution would initiate and support. The same desire for a radically new, anti-traditional cultural order also drives the tremendous proliferation of utopian proposals, platforms and manifestos during the two revolutionary decades, "a rich harvest of [utopian tracts] that is not matched anywhere in Europe until the first half of the nineteenth century in France."[52] Against the unthinking acceptance of ancient custom and tradition and the pretences of mystical sovereignty assumed by the Stuart monarchy, Puritan utopists tried to reshape the English body politic according to rational, and hence "objective," principles of organization.[53] While seemingly contradictory, the utopian effort to rationalize statecraft and to draft perfect laws and optimum constitutions in fact complements the challenge to the old order offered by the visionary activities of women and the spiritual feminization of men; but it also reasserts the very same strict demarcations between the two sexes that are simultaneously relaxed by the new "male" authority exerted by women as prophets and preachers and the "female" qualities and roles adopted by men as signs of their spiritual regeneration.

If the anti-customary impulse of seventeenth-century utopianism led to a demystification of social and political relations, it also preserved the mystique of paternalism through a new mechanics of male domination more efficient than the traditional and customary supports for patriarchalism that sectarian utopianism endeavoured to undermine. Bacon's *New Atlantis*, upon which many of the sectaries derived the principles of their utopian ideals and practices, is a case in point. In his utopia Bacon imagines the College of Six Days' Work, or Salomon's House, an academy of male Elders dedicated to demystifying the mysterious reproductive and generative powers of Mother Earth by forcing nature to yield up its secrets under the discipline of the new science. Unlike the "Ceremonies, Characters, and Charms" of the old occult and mystical philosophies, the "pretended Natural Magic," which for Bacon fostered illicit and unreliable means for gaining power over nature, the new "masculine" science was to offer lawful, systematic and foolproof measures for treating "nature under constraint and vexed; that is to say, when by art and the hand of man she is forced out of her natural state, and squeezed and moulded."[54]

Bacon's natural science appealed to English Puritans "by virtue of its freedom from authoritarian influence, sound inductive foundation, and great utilitarian potential," but his Puritan disciples also enlarged upon the anti-female implications of his efforts "not only to bend nature gently, but to conquer and subdue, even to shake to her foundations";[55] they dedicated themselves to "the eviscerating of nature, and disclosure of the springs of its motion."[56] In *Oceana*, the republican James Harrington changes Bacon's metaphors of rape and conquest to ones of courtesy and benevolence, but he remains a Baconian in his gendered delineation of the relations between agrarian legislation and nature:

if a river have had many natural bed or channels, to which she hath forgotten to reach her breast and whose mouths are dried up or obstructed, these are the dams which the agrarian doth not make but remove; and what parched fortunes can hereby hope to be watered by their only, whose veins having drunk the same blood, have a right in nature to drink of the same milk?[57]

While tactful and gentle rather than violent and rapacious, Harrington's "masculine" legislation, like Bacon's masculine science, appropriates and co-opts the nurturing powers of "feminine" nature. By devising innovative measures for distributing the "milk" of the maternal earth to her "forgotten" progeny, Harrington's Oceanic agrarian not only assumes nature's nursing faculties, but he also proves to be a more effective "mother" than Mother Nature. The "masculine" desire to control nature enters into Royalist as well as republican constructions of state power. After the Restoration, Bacon's disciples in the Royal Society turned the scientific argument for male domination to imperial ends. In *Plus Ultra* (1668), Joseph Glanvill celebrates natural science for increasing "the empire of man over inferior creatures."[58] Brian Easlea's comments on the sexual undercurrents of seventeenth-century science are apt: "It would appear that after a long historical development a class of men had emerged in western Europe who would sever ties with 'mother earth' in pursuit of a compulsive drive to prove their masculinity and virility."[59]

In *New Atlantis*, Bacon turns the celebration of virility into a ritual event through the "Feast of the Family." "A most natural, pious, and reverend custom," the Feast is granted, at the behest of the state, to any temperate and monogamous man who lives to see 30 descendants above three years; the mother of the patriarch's (the "Tirsan") sons and daughters, if present at the ceremony, is "placed in a loft above the right hand of the chair, with a privy door and a carved window of glass, leaded with gold and blue, where she sitteth but is not seen."[60] This ceremonial highlighting of male potency and masking of female creativity allegorizes Bacon's celebration of the intellectual fecundity he believed would result from his methodological cure for distempered learning, learning that is not "steadily fixed upon the facts of nature." In Bacon's new science, and in the utopian world he designs to demonstrate the social impact of the advancement of learning, there is no room for the speculative, the visionary, the divinely inspired, or any other form of non-rigorous and soft "female" truth – the very forms of truth by which the female prophets of the 1640s and 1650s were to gain at least some measure of cultural authority and acceptance.[61]

Bacon's emphasis on the primacy of "male" over "female" knowledge and authority is reasserted in explicitly political terms by Puritan utopists, even those like Gerrard Winstanley who insisted that women have an "equall privilege to share with [men] in the blessing of liberty."[62] Winstanley's anti-customary argument for the creative and redemptive force of "Reason," which "made the earth a common treasury" of masters and servants, men and women, is combined with "a strong element of patriachalism" in his utopian reconstruction of society.[63] For Winstanley, the proper magistrate is the father; just as children consent and submit to paternal power and protection as a way to stave off the threat of personal destruction, so men and women will contract to give the magistrate, as a good father, their obedience so long as he preserves their safety and well-being. Within the sphere of the family itself, the role of the father is to discipline his children, "to reprove by words, or whip those who offend," as a way to mould them into "rational men, experienced in yielding obedience to the Laws and Officers of the Commonwealth."[64] Phyllis Mack may be overstating the case when she argues that Winstanley's utopia, "while radical in terms of class relationships, is conservative to the core in terms of gender."[65] The optimum constitution set out in *The Law of Freedom in a Platform* is remarkably innovative in its inclusion of laws that proscribe capital punishment for rape and compel men to marry women who bear them children out of wedlock. Yet, while Winstanley's conservatism on gender issues is not as thorough-going as Mack contends, his utopia remains, despite its proto-feminist legal safeguards for "a womans bodily Freedom" and her illegitimate children, a society that reinforces sexual inequity by reinstating patriarchy in a new anti-customary mode.[66]

The increasing polarization of the two sexes during the Civil War period is performed not only by the new mechanics of male dominance contained in Baconian science and Puritan utopianism, but also by the sexual inequities built into emergent capitalism's rational system of calculable work. The new economy was to force radical distinctions between the commercial labours of husbands and the domestic duties of wives. These distinctions are assisted in part by Puritan emphasis on the spiritual and psychological partnership that wives were to offer their husbands. The image of the wife as a companion of her husband's soul recurs frequently in Puritan family guidebooks. Dorothy Leigh insists that "If she be thy wife, she is always too good to be thy servant, and worthy to be thy fellow."[67] "She shall be a fellow helper to [her husband]," writes John Dod in *A Plaine and Familiar Exposition of the Ten Commandments*, "& bring a blessing upon the family, by her labour," which is to awaken the divine spark in her spouse.[68] Yet, while the companionate nature of the helpmeet's role would appear to promote greater equality, or at least greater mutuality, between husbands and wives than in earlier models of marriage in which wives were simply the property of husbands, it in fact had the opposite effect of reinforcing the divisions between the two spouses. As Roberta Hamilton has argued, the spiritual services of wives did not register as real labour in the emergent capitalist economy of seventeenth-century England, for such services could not be accounted for by the new calculus of labour; as a result, only men were visible in the market-place and the public orbit, while the domestic sphere became an exclusively female world.[69]

The interpretive activities of leading Protestant exegetes were to conspire with the economic and intellectual imperatives of the new bourgeois culture to produce scriptural readings that helped to reinforce the inequities between men and women. The ideological conflicts underpinning Reformed readings of Scripture are especially discernible in Protestant efforts to reconcile the two accounts of creation in Genesis. Margaret Fell-Fox turns to the "P" or Priestly text, in which male and female are created simultaneously in the image of God, for justification of an egalitarian interpretation of the relationship between the two sexes:

> And first, when God created Man in his owne Image: in the Image of God created he them, Male and Female: and God blessed them, and God said unto them, Be fruitful and multiply: And God said, Behold, I have given you of every Herb, &c. Gen. 1. Here *God* joyns them together in his own Image, and make no such distinctions and differences as men do.[70]

Daniel Rogers finds proof of sexual equality in the "J" account of Eve's secondary creation from Adam's rib: Eve, he argues, was made from Adam as "woman of man, equall to him in dignity."[71] Leading Puritan exegetes like Calvin and Pareus, however, subordinate the "P" account to "J" account by treating "J" as an expanded version of "P". By this reconciliation of the two texts, the verse "male and female created he them" in the first chapter of Genesis is, as Mary Nyquist points out, "taken to refer to the creation from Adam of his meet help, Eve," and the relationship between the two sexes is understood to be not physical or metaphysical likeness but spiritual companionship in marriage – "It is not good that the man should be alone" (Genesis 2:18) – as in the prevailing Puritan paradigm. It is also this reading of the "P" and "J" accounts of creation, Nyquist argues, upon which Milton relies in the divorce tracts, where his defence of psychological and spiritual incompatibility as the leading grounds for divorce is the "outcome of the deeply masculinist assumptions at work in Milton's articulation of a radically bourgeois view of marriage."[72]

Yet, while Milton's divorce tracts celebrate a model of marital companionship that teaches the essentially domestic and private nature of female experience, they also, especially in the celebrated instance of Mrs Attaway, enable sectarian women to justify the independent assertion of private conscience by which they not only discarded ungodly husbands but also proclaimed their spiritual equality with men. Mrs Attaway, Edwards tells us, discussed "Master Milton's doctrine of divorce" with two gentlemen after one of her sermons, for she felt "it was a point to be considered of; and that she for her part would look more into it, for she had an unsanctified husband, that did not walk in the way of Sion, nor speak the language of Canaan."[73] Mrs Attaway apparently found in the divorce tracts arguments of which she could make use, for she shortly left her husband and took up with William Jenney.

It is precisely this kind of paradox that we seem to meet at every turn when we inquire into gender relations in the Civil War period: irrational and ecstatic modes of female inspiration are sanctioned alongside rationalist and new scientific efforts to control and domesticate "female" nature; the emphasis upon the spiritual identity between male and female souls leads both to a loosening of the bonds of marriage and to a new sense of the companionate role of the helpmeet, which in turn deepens the polarization of men and women by confining wives to the domestic arena. Similarly paradoxical are the seemingly discontinuous cultural imperatives that led Milton to structure the presentation of gender in *Paradise Lost* according to the paradigm of "he for God only, she for God in him," and that also drove him to conclude his epic by evoking the culturally subversive Civil War figure of the woman prophet in the form of the enlightened post-lapsarian Eve. Eve's sense of her prophetic powers and central role in humankind's redemption lends renewed credibility to the Elizabeth Pooles and other women visionaries, who had faded into oblivion along with the revolutionary vision of a new anti-monarchical order of which they were an emblem:

> For God is also in sleep, and Dreams advise,
> Which he haith sent propitious, some great good
> Presaging. . . . .
> . . . . though all by mee is lost,
> Such favour I unworthy am vouchsaf't,
> By mee the Promise Seed shall all restore. (12: 611–22)

Like the story of Elizabeth Poole, Milton's epic registers the ideological "double bind" that structures gender relations in the Civil War years.

While the sectarian impulse to dismantle the old order thus facilitates public acceptance of the ministerial authority of women and the spiritual maternity and wifeliness of men, the deep residual attachment, even among radicals, to a patriarchal power structure helps to foster the covert strategies for sustaining male dominance contained within Puritan utopianism, science and theology – strategies that produce even firmer supports for male supremacy than the ancient customs and traditions that they challenge and supersede. In the Civil War period, the desire for change and the nostalgia for tradition achieve a fragile equilibrium, one that enables women to occupy centre stage, but that compels new behind-the-scenes tactics for subordinating and, as in the case of Elizabeth Poole, exploiting and obscuring female power and authority. Such tactics successfully drive women like Poole out of the public arena and reinstate conventional sexual roles; but even as it is repressed by the new mechanics of male power, the undeniable elevation of the "feminine" during the 1640s and 1650s points to a genuine reconstruction of gender identity, one that defines the Interregnum as a transforming, if embattled, moment in the history of gender relations.

NOTES

1. For an account of David as a political archetype of Cromwell, see Joseph Anthony Mazzeo, "Cromwell as Davidic King," in *Renaissance and Seventeenth-Century Studies* (New York: Columbia University Press, 1964), 183–208.
2. Elizabeth Poole, *A vision Wherein is Manifested the disease and cure of the Kingdome* . . . (London, 1648), 2, 6, 5; *The Clarke Papers*, C.H. Firth, ed. (1884; reprinted. London: Johnson Reprint Company, 1965), v. 54, 154.
3. Poole attempts to justify herself against her attackers in *An Alarum of War, Given to the Army, and to their High Court of Justice (so called) by the will of God* (London, 1649). Accounts of Poole's vision and the circumstances surrounding her delivery of it can be found in David Underdown, *Pride's Purge: Politics in the Puritan Revolution* (Oxford: Clarendon, 1971), 183, Margaret George, *Women in the First Capitalist Society: Experiences in Seventeenth-Century England* (Urbana: University of Illinois Press, 1988), 98–101.
4. The most important studies of women prophets during the revolutionary decades are Ethyn Morgan Williams, "Women Preachers in the Civil War," *Journal of Modern History*, 1 (1929), 561–9; Keith Thomas, "Women and the Civil War Sects," *Past and Present*, 13 (1958), 42–62; Phyllis Mack, "Women as Prophets During the English Civil War," *Feminist Studies*, 8.1 (1982), 19–45 and "The Prophet and Her Audience: Gender and Knowledge in the World Turned Upside Down," in *Reviving the English Revolution: Reflections and Elaborations on the Work of Christopher Hill*, Geoff Eley and William Hunt, eds. (London: Verso, 1988), 139–52; Nigel Smith, *Perfection Proclaimed: Language and Literature in English Radical Religion 1640–1660* (Oxford: Clarendon Press, 1989), especially 45–53; and George, chap. 5. On the general prophetic climate of seventeenth-century England, see Smith and Keith Thomas, *Religion and the Decline of Magic* (New York: Scribner, 1971), 128–46.

5. Poole's transformation from prophet to heretic recalls Anne Hutchinson's career. For a contemporary account, see John Winthrop, *A short story of the rise, reign, and ruine of the Antinomians, Familists & Libertines, that infected the churches of Nevv-England . . . and the lamentable death of Ms. Hutchison* (London, 1644). Anna Trapnel's prophetic career followed a similar course: she was accused of witchcraft after prophesying against Cromwell. See Smith, 49–53.
6. Williams, 561; Margaret Masson, "The Typology of the Female as a Model for the Regenerate: Puritan Preaching 1690–1730," *Signs*, 2 (1976), 304–15.
7. Carolyn Merchant notes that "The English Parliament continued passing [sumptuary] laws until the early seventeenth century" in *The Death of Nature: Women, Ecology, and the Scientific Revolution* (San Francisco: Harper and Row, 1980), 175.
8. Angeline Goreau, *The Whole Duty of a Woman: Female Writers in Seventeenth-Century England* (Garden City: Doubleday, 1985), 91. On 9 February 1620, shortly after the king delivered his order against cross-dressing women to the London clergy, the anonymous author of *"Hic Mulier"; or, The Man-Woman: Being a Medicine to cure the Coltish Disease of Staggers in the Masculine–Feminines of our Times* decried the "monstrous deformity" of women in male clothing and accessories. One week later, another anonymous pamphlet, *"Haec Vir"; or, The Womanish Man: Being an Answer to a late Booke entitled "Hic Mulier,"* Expressed in a brief Dialogue between "Haec-Vir," the Womanish man, and "Hic Mulier," the Man-Woman, defended female cross-dressing by attacking men who favoured feminine attire. The two pamphlets are anthologized in *Half Humankind: Contexts and Texts of the Controversy about Women in England, 1540–1640*, Katherine Usher Henderson and Barbara F. McManus, eds. (Urbana: University of Illinois Press, 1985), 264–89. See Linda Woodbridge, *Women and the English Renaissance: Literature and the Nature of Womankind, 1540–1620)* (Urbana: University of Illinois Press, 1984), 143–51, for useful commentary on these pamphlets.
9. George, 43.
10. See Ian Gentles, "London Levellers in the English Revolution," *Journal of Ecclesiastical History*, 29 (1978), 281–94; George, 94–6; and Williams, 566–9, for accounts of Chidley's career.
11. Thomas Edwards, *Gangraena* (London, 1646) Book 1, 170, 79–80.
12. Commentary on Davies' appropriation of the printing press can be found in Beth Nelson, "Lady Elinor Davies: The Prophet as Publisher," *Women's Studies International Forum*, 8 (1985), 403–9; for a study of Davies' life and career, see Esther S. Cope, "'Dame Eleanor Davies Never Soe Mad a Ladie'?" *Huntington Library Quarterly*, 50 (1987), 133–44.
13. Katherine Chidley, *The Iustification of the Independent Churches of Christ* (London, 1641); Williams traces a progressive narrowing of Chidley's views on toleration between 1641 and 1645. See Williams, 568–9.
14. Thomas, "Women and the Civil War Sects," 45.
15. *Thomason Tracts*, E. 166 (London, 1641).
16. *Thomason Tracts*, E. 384 (10) (London, 1647).
17. Edwards, *Gangraena*, Book 1, 84.
18. Robert Burton, *The Anatomy of Melancholy* (London: Dent-Everyman, 1968), 3: 339.
19. Quoted in Claire Cross, "The Church in England 1646–1660," in *The Interregnum: The Quest for Settlement*, G.E. Aylmer, ed. (Hamden, Conn.: Archon-Shoe String, 1972), 117.
20. Thomas, "Women and the Civil War Sects," 47.
21. In "Women as Prophets," 24, Mack writes that during the Interregnum there were "over 300 women visionaries of whom about 220 were Quakers"; in "The Prophet and Her Audience," 150, she notes that "Over four hundred women prophesied at least once during the second half of the seventeenth century, about 375 of whom were Quakers."

22. Thomas, "Women and the Civil War Sects," 52.

23. Robert Baillie, *A Dissuasive for the Errors of the Time* (London, 1645), 145.

24. Katherine Chidley, *The Iustification of the Independent Churches of Christ,* 26.

25. David Masson, *The Life of Milton: Narrated in Connexion with the Political, Ecclesiastical, and Literary History of his Time* (London: Macmillan, 1873), 3, 189.

26. Christopher Hill, *The World Turned Upside Down: Radical Ideas During the English Revolution* (New York: Viking Press, 1972), 251, 255.

27. See George Fox, *A Collection of Many and Select Epistles*, Vol. II (London, 1698), 33: "Man and Woman were helps meet . . . before they fell; but after the Fall, in the Transgression, the Man was to rule over his Wife; but in the restoration by Christ . . . they are helps meet, Man and Woman, as they were before the Fall."

28. Margaret Fell-Fox, *The Daughter of Sion Avvakened, And Putting on her Strength . . .* (London, 1677), 18.

29. Fell-Fox, *A Call to the Universall Seed of God* (London, 1665), 13.

30. Mack, "Women as Prophets," 24.

31. Anna Trapnel, *The Cry of a Stone, or a relation of something spoken in Whitehall by Anna Trapnel, being in the visions of God . . . uttered in prayers and spiritual songs, by an inspiration extraordinary and full of wonder* (London, 1654), 13. Commentary on this vision can be found in Smith, 90.

32. John Cotton, *A Practical Commentary . . . [on] John* (London, 1656), 338.

33. Cotton Mather, "A Father Departing . . ." (Boston, 1723), 22–3; see David Leverenz, *The Language of Puritan Feeling: An Exploration in Literature, Psychology, and Social History* (New Brunswick: Rutgers University Press, 1980), 1; and Mack, "Women as Prophets," 24, for useful commentary on this passage.

34. See Donald N. Maltz, "The Bride of Christ is Filled With His Spirit," in *Women in Ritual and Symbolic Roles*, J. Hoch-Smith and A. Spring, eds. (New York: Plenum, 1978), 27–44, for a helpful discussion of female religious tropes and symbols.

35. For analysis of the ways in which this iconography is transformed into political emblems of the monarchy of Elizabeth I, see John N. King, *Tudor Royal Iconography: Literature and Art in an Age of Religious Crisis* (Princeton: Princeton University Press, 1989), 233–8.

36. Gerrard Winstanley, *The Works of Gerrard Winstanley*, George Sabine, ed. (Ithaca: Cornell University Press, 1941), 577.

37. Protestant writers are inconsistent on this point since they also personified papal corruption in female terms. The scarlet attire of Spenser's Duessa makes her an embodiment of the "harloty" of Rome; Milton's indictment of Delilah as "so bedeckt, ornate, and gay" similarly identifies her as a personification of papal excess and extravagance.

38. George Keith, *The Woman Preacher of Samaria* (London, 1674), 9.

39. Maureen Quilligan, *Milton's Spenser: The Politics of Reading* (Ithaca: Cornell University Press, 1983), 224.

40. Margaret Fell-Fox, *A Call to the Universall Seed of God*, 16–17.

41. On "male" androgyny in *Paradise Lost*, see my "'The Single State of Man': Androgyny in *Macbeth* and *Paradise Lost*," *Papers on Language and Literature*, 26 (1990), 319–30.

42. All quotations from *Paradise Lost* are taken from *John Milton: The Complete Poems and Major Prose*, Merritt Y. Hughes, ed. (New York: Odyssey, 1957) and are noted in the text.

43. Quoted in Cross, 120.

44. Cross, 103.

45. C.H. McIlwain, *The Political Works of James I* (Cambridge: Harvard University Press, 1918), 24.

46. Jonathan Goldberg, *James I and the Politics of Literature: Jonson, Shakespeare, Donne, and their Contemporaries* (Baltimore: Johns Hopkins University Press, 1983), 143.

47. William Gouge, *The Works of William Gouge* . . . (London 1626), 287–8.

48. Laurel Thather Ulrich, *Good Wives: Image and Reality in the Lives of Women in Northern New England* (New York: Knopf, 1982), 138.

49. Robert Pricke, *The Doctrine of Superiority, and of Subjection, Contained in the Fifth Commandment* . . . (London, 1609), section H 3.

50. Leverenz, 73. My discussion here owes much to Leverenz's wonderfully rich treatment of Puritan nursing fantasies and principles of child-rearing.

51. Quoted in Cross, 102, 103.

52. Frank E. and Fritzie P. Manuel, *Utopian Thought in the Western World* (Cambridge: Belknap-Harvard University Press, 1979), 335.

53. For an evocative study of Puritan utopias as "rational" paradigms for containing displaced populations and colonizing new worlds, see James Holstun, *A Rational Millennium: Puritan Utopias of Seventeenth-Century England and America* (New York: Oxford University Press, 1987).

54. Francis Bacon, *The Works of Francis Bacon*, James Spedding, Robert Leslie Ellis and Douglas Denon Heath, eds., 14 vols. (London: Longman, 1860), 3: 381; 4: 29.

55. Charles Webster, *The Great Instauration: Science, Medicine and Reform 1626–1660* (London: Duckworth, 1975), 515; Bacon, "Thoughts and Conclusions on the Interpretation of Nature or A Science of Productive Works," trans. Benjamin Farrington, *The Philosophy of Francis Bacon* (Liverpool: University of Liverpool Press, 1970), 93.

56. Joseph Glanvill, *Plus Ultra* (Gainesville: Scholar's Facsimile Reprints, 1958), 13.

57. James Harrington, *The Political Works of James Harrington*, J.G.A Pocock, ed. (Cambridge: Cambridge University Press, 1977), 468; for Holstun, this passage modifies the strong element of male domination in Machiavelli's delineation of the relationship between *virtu* and *fortuna*, 194.

58. Joseph Glanvill, *Plus Ultra*, 104.

59. Brian Easlea, *Witch-hunting, Magic and The New Philosophy: An Introduction to the Debates of the Scientific Revolution 1450–1750* (Brighton: Harvester Press, 1980), 248

60. Bacon, *Works*, 3: 147, 148–9; see also Merchant, 172–5.

61. Bacon, *Works*, 4: 32.

62. Gerrard Winstanley, "Truth Lifting Up Its Head Above Scandals" (London, 1649), quoted in Mack, "The Prophet and Her Audience," 143.

63. Winstanley, *Works*, 251–2; J.C. Davis, *Utopia and the Ideal Society: A Study of English Utopian Writing 1516–1700* (Cambridge: Cambridge University Press, 1981), 197.

64. Winstanley, *Works*, 532.

65. Mack, "The Prophet and Her Audience," 144.

66. Winstanley, *Works*, 599.

67. Dorothy Leigh, *The Mother's Blessing. Or the godly counsaile of a Gentlewoman not long deceased, left behind for her Children* (London, 1616), 55.

68. John Dod, *A Plaine and Familiar Exposition of the Ten Commandments* (London, 1603), 128. Discussion of Puritan marriage doctrine can be found in W. Haller and M. Haller, "The Puritan Art of Love," *English Literary History*, 5 (1941–42), 235–72; W. Haller, "Hail Wedded Love," *English Literary History*, 13 (1946), 79–97; James T. Johnson, *A Society Ordained By God: English Puritan Marriage Doctrine in the First Half of the Seventeenth Century* (Nashville: Abington, 1970); Alan Macfarlane, *Marriage and Love in England: Modes of Reproduction 1300–1840* (New York: Blackwell, 1986); James Grantham Turner, *One Flesh: Paradisal Marriage and Sexual Relations in the Age of Milton* (Oxford: Clarendon, 1987).

69. Roberta Hamilton, *The Liberation of Women: A Study of Patriarchy and Capitalism* (London: Allen and Unwin, 1978).

70. Margaret Fell-Fox, *Womens Speaking Justified* . . . (1667), in *First Feminists: British Women Writers 1578–1799*, Moira Ferguson, ed. (Bloomington: Indiana University Press, 1985), 114.
71. Quoted in Turner, 108.
72. Mary Nyquist, "The Genesis of Gendered Subjectivity in the Divorce Tracts and in *Paradise Lost*", in *Re-membering Milton: Essays on the Texts and Traditions*, Mary Nyquist and Margaret W. Ferguson, eds. (New York: Methuen, 1988), 106, 102–14; see also Turner, 106–23.
73. Edwards, *Gangraena*, Book 2, 10–11. See also Joseph Wittreich, *Feminist Milton* (Ithaca: Cornell University Press, 1987), 138–43.

"Adam, the Father of all Flesh," Porno-Political Rhetoric and Political Theory in and After the English Civil War

SUSAN WISEMAN

What follows is an investigation of the role of the theory of patriarchy and republicanism in the political theory and prose fiction of the Civil War and early Restoration. The question that I seek to answer is, what is the relationship between satirical sexual slander and political theory and polemic in the prose pamphlets, dialogues and short fictions of the English Civil War and its aftermath? Underlying this question is an assumption that in the period of the Civil War what might be seen by twentieth-century critics as disparate and unrelated discourses were interwoven and even interdependent, since abstract political theory shared interests, modes of address and even genres with "popular" political satires. Historians and bibliographers are still disputing whether the end of censorship in 1641 actually precipitated, or even registered, a politicized publishing revolution.[1] This essay assumes that, in the early 1640s, the appearance and persistence of not one but many newsbooks and short fictional and political pamphlets are testimony to an awakened qualitative sense of participation in political destiny. The large number of short and long printed publications suggests that the sphere of political debate was reaching a range of readers in a culture of active political debate. Moreover, the connections between political theory and prose narrative endorse the notion that during this period politics was "popular" reading and vice versa – whatever problems there might be with the term "popular."[2]

During the Civil War fictional narratives, dialogues and anti-Puritan polemic cannot be perceived as wholly distinct from a notionally "elite" corpus of political writing found in political pamphlets, such as those of Henry Parker or Robert Filmer.[3] The range of printed replies to the political pamphlets indicates that a reading public for political theory existed, and suggests substantial public interest and even participation. In the army debates, which brought together men of very different social backgrounds, Ireton (himself no radical) articulated the possibility of a transformation of the political sphere: "If God saw it good to destroy, not only Kings and Lords, but all distinctions of degrees – nay if it go further, to destroy all property . . . that there be nothing at all of civil constitution left in the kingdom – if I see the hand of God in it I hope I shall with quietness acquiesce."[4]

Even more important, as part of the war of words each pamphlet was involved in persuasion, attempting to convince the same audience of political truths. Texts dealt with political events and issues in rhetorics which we would not necessarily recognize as political (dialogue, playlet, narrative), but these texts participated in constituting the nature of the political-literate (and literary) sphere. In the 1640s and 1650s, political theory and scurrilous polemic must be seen as part of a continuum of political discourses using a range of rhetorical persuasive techniques.

Methodologically, therefore, this essay responds to revisionist history which, by situating the political theory and agency of the Civil War firmly in a Royalist camp, has tended to marginalize any theorization of the situation of republicans or the literate non-elite, and therefore to marginalize the social currency and extent of political thought and writing.[5] In literary methodology, the new historicism has brought non-literary writing into focus, but such writing has characteristically been used as corroboration of iconic (and canonical) literary texts and as "shocking examples" of surprising and often violent incidents taken, for instance, from travel narratives. It serves to hold and fascinate the reader but, in doing so, is used as a prelude to extended analysis of a canonical text.[6] Thus, while it might appear to be gaining in status, the non-canonical text is sometimes (habitually?) reproduced in critical discussions of the early modern period to corroborate an argument about canonical writing; and such texts are often reinscribed in a factitious differentiation between text and contextual text. Therefore this essay is an attempt to consider non-canonical texts in which, I think, can be traced a sequence of sophisticated political and literary disputes in the Civil War period. I attempt to trace a link between what might be called imaginative writing – narrative satire – and political theory, and suggest that such a connection might have been made by a contemporary reading public.

Specifically, I hope to illuminate some of the interconnections between sexual satire and political theory during the crises of government by looking at writing by and about Henry Marten and Henry Neville, both republicans and both involved (in different ways) in political theory and sexual satire. They were both active republicans – "Commonwealths-men" as Ludlow called them – in the 1640s and throughout the Protectorate, and both were part of the group thinking through the possibilities of an English republic which found its focus in Harrington's circle and proposals to Parliament in 1659.[7] I begin with a discussion

of the porno-political satires against Henry Marten and end with a
reappraisal of Henry Neville's fantasy, *The Isle of Pines* (which he
published under the pseudonym Cornelius van Sloetten in 1668, long
after the wars of words were over[8]), using the sexual satire on and of
republicans from the Civil War years to re-read this text in relation to
contemporary theories of patriarchy.

The crisis of the English Civil Wars necessitated an elaboration of
political theory in relation to position and material advantage which, to
an extent, had hitherto been assumed. Patriarchal theory and republican
theory at this point developed in intense dialogue with each other.
Republican thought denied the rights of monarchy, using a range of
arguments to do so, and some monarchist theorists chose the Bible as
their stronghold. One of the most important developments of Royalist
political theory during the war was made by the Kentish peer, Sir Robert
Filmer, whose analysis of the basis of government, the "Patriarcha,"
remained in manuscript throughout the Civil War and the Interregnum.[9]
However, Filmer did publish three texts in which he worked out his
theory of the rights of kings as fathers in relation to the contemporary
English situation. His first political publication was *The Freeholders
Grand Inquest*, published after his imprisonment in Leeds Castle. In
April 1648, he published a critique of Philip Hunton's *Treatise of
Monarchy* in a pamphlet called *The Anarchy of a Limited or Mixed
Monarchy* and after the Kentish rebellion he published *The Necessity of
the Absolute Power of all Kings and Especially the King of England*.[10]

In accounting for his theory of political obligation in which all men
were subject to one king who was the rightful heir to the throne,
found by succession (or, *in extremis*, elected by the nobility), Filmer
constructed the form of his political debate as a history, or narrative, of
right. His insistence on the centrality of right and, therefore, of history
(especially the Old Testament read as history) in understanding the
rightful distribution of political power meant that, in Filmer's hands,
politics became a narrative of origins, beginning with God the Father
who gave the power of inheritance to Adam. This narrative is, at
times, close to something a late-twentieth-century reader might read
as a psychic fantasy of origins, preserving the power of masculinity
from dangerous incursions by any other agency. The importance of
a narrative of generations in Filmer's theory of monarchy provides
a theoretical religious system which underpins monarchy and serves
as a counter-formulation of the place of political power in response
to populist theories of government. Crucially, where populist theories
refuse to accept the contiguity of the structure of the family with that
of the state – claiming, for example, that "allegories are good only

as far as the likeness hold" – Filmer's theory of kingship insists upon it.[11]

The narrative of power in the family and the narrative of political right are contiguous and virtually coterminous in Filmer's writings. I have taken examples from *The Anarchy of a Limited or Mixed Monarchy*, where he is writing in response to theories which refute the absolute patriarchal power of the king as equated with father. Filmer uses the etymology of "monarch" to prove that every monarch must have "supreme power" if monarchy is not to be a mere contradiction in terms (*Anarchy*, 281). He continues:

> So that if our Author will grant supreme power to be the ordinance of God, the supreme power will prove itself to be unlimited by the same ordinance, because a supreme limited power is a contradiction.
>
> The monarchical power of *Adam* the Father of all flesh, being by a general binding ordinance setled by God on him & his posterity by right of fatherhood, the form of Monarchy must be preferred above all other forms, except the like ordinance for other forms can be shewed. (*Anarchy*, 284–5)

In this way Filmer makes biblical narrative a narrative of family which invests all power in the father, and in a second movement he insists on the Bible as the only true narrative and justification of government. As for other forms, he regards them as "brought in or erected by rebellion" (285). Filmer's argument against populist theories of government which assert that rulers must be elected because of the "natural freedom of mankind" once again resorts to the model of the family: "For if it be allowed, that the acts of the Parents bind the Children, then farewell the doctrine of *the natural freedom of mankind*, where Subjection of Children to Parents is natural, there can be no natural freedom" (*Anarchy*, 287).

This epitomizes Filmer's argumentation: in order to refute his opponents he makes the family stand synecdochially for the state and then points out that the populist arguments do not work for the family. As I indicated above, and as Henry Parker's theories illustrate, the most thoroughly worked out of the populist arguments were busy rejecting that very step whereby the family *could* stand for the state. The second essential ingredient of Filmer's theory (for the purposes of demonstrating the interconnections of popular polemic and political theory in dealing with political topics) is the fact that his political theory operates not by the description of an ideal state but by tracing back a line of right to the past. The contravention of this line is an usurpation of God's ordinance. Filmer makes this absolutely clear in an answer to an imagined objection to his theory:

> To all this it may be opposed, what need dispute how a People can choose a King, since there be multitude of examples that Kings have been, and are now adays chosen by their People? The answer is 1. The question is not of the *fact*, but of the *right*, whether it have been done by a *natural* or by an *usurped* right. (*Anarchy*, 387–8)

Although Filmer goes on to modify this to allow the nobility to elect kings, he repeats his claim with direct reference to descent from Adam:

> If it be objected, That Kings are not now (as they were at the first planting or peopling of the world) the Fathers of their People, or Kingdoms, and that the Fatherhood hath lost the right of governing. An answer is, That all Kings that now are, or ever were; are, or were either Fathers of their People, or the Heirs of such Fathers, or Usurpers of the right of such Fathers: It is a truth undeniable that there cannot be any multitude of men whatsoever, either great, or small, though gathered together from the several corners and remotest regions of the world, but that in the same multitude considered by itself, there is one man amongst them that in nature hath the right to be King of all the rest, as being the next heir to *Adam*: and all the others subject unto him, every man by nature is a King or a Subject: the obedience which all subjects yield to Kings is but the paying of that duty which is done to the supreme fatherhood. (*Anarchy*, 288–9)

This is a clear statement of the logic of patriarchal thought. But what is important here is the way patriarchal theory produced in the war years focuses on the intimate link between father and son in determining who is king. And it is a narrative of right rather than a theory of might, arguing from first moments rather than first principles. Filmer's theories supported monarchy by making the state into the family.

Contemporaries reacted strongly to Filmer's arguments, which became especially influential after the Restoration when they became the support of the new Stuart order, but the publication of Filmer's patriarchal theory in the late 1640s endorsed and elucidated a monarchist position which was implicit in many defences of Charles I. Along with Milton's publications on liberty and government but on the other side, Filmer was at the centre of the raging controversy over patriarchalism. In its insistence on the importance of the biblical original of the link between fathers of families and the power of heads of state, his theory (or story) provides a picture of government rather like a double-exposure photograph, the most obvious picture being that of the patriarchal control of the state, but this picture overlapping in its outlines with the issue of sexual control in the family. The area of leakage from one issue into the other became one of the defining spaces of Civil War politico-sexual satire.

Sexual satire was applied to political objectives throughout the Civil War, as in satires on puritan mores such as *A Brief Dialogue Between a Zelotopist, one of the Daughters of a Zealous Round-head, and Superstition, a Holy Fryer, newly come out of France* (in which a young Puritan woman exposes her sexual laxity to a lascivious friar) or in the three Antibrownistus satires, in which a Puritan city warden, his wife and her maid expose their sexual and political schemes.[13] Attacks were also made on republicans, especially Henry Marten who was one of the first members of the Parliament of 1640 to declare himself as a republican. That Marten saw republicanism as the primary, natural order of government is proved by his example of the man blind from birth whose sight was "restored": for Marten, republicanism was every man's liberty and a republic was, indeed, the natural state. He played an important part in the Commons, being a member of the Committee of Safety set up in 1642.[14] Clarendon had recorded his opinion that one man was not wise enough to govern all, and Bishop Burnet wrote that "Henry Marten was all his life a most violent enemy to monarchy, but all that he moved for was upon Roman and Greek principles."[15] Marten's outspoken opinions against monarchy led to his expulsion from the House and imprisonment in the Tower in August 1643, after he had spoken in defence of the divine, John Saltmarsh. Although he was released from the Tower two weeks later, he was not readmitted to the Commons until January 1645/1646.[16] Throughout his period in the public eye, he was abused as a libertine, partly because he lived with a woman who was not his wife. However, attacks on Marten for whoring were standard issue in journalistic and polemical writing. For instance, two whores conversing before the displaying of the "monster" of the new post-regicidal commonwealth in the playlet *The terrible, horrible monster of the west* accuse one another of having slept with Marten.[17]

Several satires were entirely devoted to Marten and these provide examples of the way in which Marten's reputation for sexual incontinence was set alongside his republican politics. For instance, *Mr Henry Marten His Speech In the House of Commons Before his Departure Thence* (1648) pretends to be Marten's speech to the House against sending reinforcements to the parliamentary army in Wales. It begins:

Mr Speaker, you know how forward I have beene always from the beginning, to act and speake Treason. I was not like Adam, that old fool, to hide my transgressions in my bosom. I am an Achan in part but not in whole: for he confessed his sinnes troubled Israel, in a penitent way, but I scorn his baseness: I have troubled Israel, and I glory in it. I hate the traytor Judas, who will repent of his Treason and restore that money which was the price of Christs bloud: what base principles had these blades? Had I received the 30 pieces of silver I would have gone with it straight to a Bawdy-house, and have had a gallant young Wench for it. I was once in the way to have spent the King's Revenue in this way.[18]

Putting biblical examples into his mouth situates Marten, the wit and classical republican, in relation to the religious discourses which here imply an analogy between Charles I and Christ. It also makes an association between Marten and the first human, particularly in this case the first human rebel and the "father of mankind", Adam, who was (paradoxically) a crucial figure of authority for patriarchal theory. Marten's outspoken republicanism is presented as revealing the true plans of the whole House: "I know, Mr Speaker, the King likes me better than he doth *Vane*, or *Perpoint*, or *Mildmay* or *Haslerigge* . . . because I am plain with him, and tell him and the world the truth of our intentions" (*Speech*, 4). But this republicanism sits alongside a demand for money to cure him of syphilis. He needs money "to keep and preserve my life; which if it bee denied me, the French scab will eat out my bowels: and if you vote for me today for that money, I will vote for you tomorrow, for as much as will buy you a whole County in New England" (*Speech*, 5).

The words that this pamphlet puts into Marten's mouth do include his republicanism, and link sexual desire to the peopling of colonies, but, more emphatically, they satirize his allegedly promiscuous (hetero)sexual appetite. How does such satire relate to Marten's opinions? In one sense, it seems to be very close to articulating his actual republican position, but this is continually mixed with sexual slurs and the two are presented as intimately interwoven, as when Marten says "Had I received the 30 pieces of silver I would have gone with it straight to a Bawdy-house." The unrepentant irreligion which the text attributes to Marten is elided with his sexual looseness, which in turn runs into his republicanism, and the three terms of attack – atheism (or at least lack of religious feeling), sexual misbehaviour and republicanism – are fused to undermine Marten. Thus, his political position is discredited by association with sexual licence, and his political programme is translated into sexual scheming; for example, to punish the Kentish rebellion by cuckolding the Kentish country gentlemen (*Speech*, 3). The anti-republican rhetoric does not employ arguments about government but rather satirizes crimes against the accepted mores of the family: Marten figures as a disruptor of marriage, the psycho-sexual-economic unit of social stability.

But why is the attack mounted in the region of the family when Marten's republican politics were so well known and provide such an obvious place of attack? One answer is that Marten's licentious behaviour was well known (precisely because of his prominence as a republican) and provides an equally obvious place of attack. Certainly, we hear of the republican Marten as a usurper of the rights of the husband, a cuckolder, invader and occupier of wives – "under Venus banner" (*Speech*, 2). But I think the significance of the displacement can be taken further, in that it points towards the multivalent importance of the idea of family in both the theory underpinning royalism and in the perceptions of the Civil War years. As David Underdown has noted, mid-seventeenth-century English society perceived itself to be involved in a gender crisis.[19] However, what was at issue was the practice of gender roles rather than their ideological status; the theory of the family (as opposed, perhaps, to the practice) seems to have remained relatively stable. In politics, the very link between the metaphor of the family and the state was being questioned by parliamentary theorists such as Henry Parker who wrote:

> But to look into terms a little more narrower, and dispel umbrages; *Princes are called Gods, Fathers, Husbands, Lords, Heads etc., and this implies them to be of more worth and more unsubordinate in end, than their Subjects are, who by the same relation must stand as Creatures, Children, Wives, Servants, Members etc.*, I answer, these terms do illustrate some excellency in Princes by way of similitude, but must not in all things be applied, and they are most truly applied to Subjects taken *divisum* but not *conjunctum*: Kings are Gods to particular men, . . . and are sanctified with some of God's royalty; but it is not for themselves, it is for an extrinsical end, and that is the prosperity of God's people, and that end is more sacred than the means; as to themselves they are most unlike God, for God cannot be obliged by any thing extrinsical, no created thing whatsoever can be of sufficient value or excellency to impose any duty or tie upon God, as Subjects upon Princes: therefore granting Prerogative to be but mediate, and the Weal Public to be final, we must rank the Laws of liberty in the first Table, and Prerogative in the second, as Nature doth require; and not after a kind of blasphemy ascribe

that unsubordination to Princes, which is only due to God; so the King is a Father to his People, taken singly but not universally; for the father is more worthy than the son in nature, and the son is wholly a debtor to the father, and can by no merit transcend his duty, nor challenge any thing as due from his father. . . . Yet this holds not in relation between King and Subject, for it's more due in policy, and more strictly to be challenged, that the King should make happy the People, than the People make glorious the King. The same reason is also in relation of Husband, Lord etc., for the wife is inferior in nature, and was created for the assistance of man, and servants are hired for the Lord's attendance; but it is otherwise in the State betwixt man and man, for that civil difference which is for civil ends, and those ends are, that wrong and violence may be repressed by one for the good of all, not that servility and drudgery may be imposed upon all for the good of one.[20]

Parker challenges the very resemblance between family and state as a system for structuring authority and distributing meaning. The family is the stable term for Parker, and the metaphors of the state are those contested. For Parker, the relationship between citizens and the state could not correspond to the relationship between an individual and a family. Conversely, the satires on Henry Marten operate as a defence of the integrity of the family, moving his transgression away from contested political ideas involving the state (and contesting its analogy with the family) to the family alone, an area where all readers could agree on proper conduct. Such scandal operates in a political sphere precisely by suppressing the exact nature of the (assumed) connections between the family and the state, and by refusing to map the precise connections between Marten's republicanism and his libertinism, which remains a sketchy translation of the "political" into the "private." The first connections were exactly the links which the populist theorists such as Parker (in his insistence on the separation of family and state) were challenging and which had become visibly "artificial." Indeed, the severing of these naturalizing links implies the recognition of the state itself as "artificial" rather than organic, as expressed by Hobbes.[21]

In another parodic pamphlet from 1648, *The Remonstrance or Declaration of Henry Marten and all the Society of Levellers*, it is suggested that the Levellers will make an alliance with criminals and be supported by unruly women, thus associating their demands with general marginal elements.[22] Besides being corruptors of women, Levellers are made equivalent *to* women as figures of insurgency, and hence in alliance with law-breakers and, especially, rebellious wives:

[we] doubt not but we shall have the assistance of all Rebels, Arch-rebels, Thieves, petty-Thieves, Whore-masters, Whore-mongers, drunkards, tiplers, covetous persons, greedy Epicures, as also the prayers of all women who have poisoned their husbands, murdered their children, bawdy house keepers, Whores, secret and public, and all others who desire to live as they list. (*Remonstrance*, 3)

The association between subversive feminine agency (here characterized as criminal) and radical political programmes is made explicit. The family, which "ought" to be stable, is threatened by rebellious women as the allies of the Levellers. The political aims of the Levellers and Marten's republicanism are transformed into commonplace social ills and excesses. But the spoof attributes to them a more important refusal:

We first declare against God the Father, as being nothing to us, who never had, nor never shall have any thing to doe with us; if there be any such power as the ignorant speak of and prate so much of: and we do steadfastly believe we had our original and first being in this world, as flies come in Butchers meat, only blown there by bad and unseasonable weather. (*Remonstrance*, 3)

As a myth of origins, flies appearing in butchers' meat is, of course, in direct conflict with all dicta of church and family, and it is striking that, in parodies and critiques of Ranter and Leveller politics, attempts to undermine the family (as in the first quotation) are consistently combined with attempts to undermine the state (as in the second quotation). By putting a refusal of God the Father into the mouths of Marten and the Levellers, the text positions them as rejecting both state and religion in one sentence. God the Father is replaced by flies and accident in an extreme caricature of the republican and Leveller refusal of the predominantly patriarchal and hierarchical assumptions which supported kingship. These assumptions had also been rejected by theorists of parliamentary sovereignty, particularly by Henry Parker. Indeed, by 1648, debate had moved on to the question of engagement. As Wildman asked in the *Army Debates*, if a Parliament "doth anything unjustly" were men forced to obey?[23] As a gross parody of developing political positions, the blasphemous and abhorrent idea that men grew like flies calls attention to the way the Levellers are being constructed as in a polar opposition to patriarchal theory which accounted for every man by his father.

These were satires against Marten as a republican during the Civil War. In the post-war publication, *Coll. Henry Marten's Letters to his Lady of Delight*, the editor, Gayton, claimed to be punishing Marten for his part in sponsoring the publication of the seized letters between Charles and Henrietta Maria in *The King's Cabinet Opened*.[24] Gayton, who published the letters, wrote:

> These letters of Yours to Yours, had not seen the world, if you yourself had not given just occassion for the incivility. There was a time (I would it had never been) when you voted and principaly caused the Sacred Letters of your Soveraign, and his Queen (the Cabinet as it was stated) to be made public. . . . Pretty devices these (Colonel;) but now you see the times of retaliation are come: I am very glad they are come, that such rebellious and inhumane persons may be in their kind requited. (*Letters*, A3r)

Once again the scene of the crime is the closet rather than the Commons chamber. The connection between Marten's publication of the king's letters and his "punishment" is put in terms of privacy rather than politics – although, once more, the crime was the publication of political letters, not solely "intimate" ones as is suggested. It is also, in each of the cases I have examined, mediated through the body of a woman, usually figured as Marten's sexual partner.

The construction of Marten – a republican – as threatening the family directs attention to his political ideas at the point of the origin of the satire – he is being libelled sexually not because he is a libertine, but because he is a republican. Therefore the displacement of the attack cannot fully obscure its connection with politics but reads as a figure for it: Marten's sexual deviance stands for his political deviance. The significance of the sexual satires rests on the semi-suppressed information of Marten's republicanism and his political activities, even as they insist on attacking his sexuality. Reprehensible sexual activity becomes a register of political activity which, inevitably, confirms the political nature of Marten's activities, and his own political status, in the very displacement used to deny them. Thus the attacks on Marten displace his political transgression but cannot conceal it. What Marten refused, as a classical republican, was the analogy between the state and the family fundamental to patriarchal monarchist theory during the English Civil War. Even as republican theory developed, patriarchal theory was being refined to support monarchy. The order of the family in 1648 *was* connected to the state by patriarchal defenders of monarchy, especially Sir Robert Filmer.

Patriarchal theory enmeshed family and state, and crucial to this enmeshing was that men should agree about the social disposition of women.[25] To move to a more abstract statement of patriarchal theory, Luce Irigaray characterizes a patriarchal society as one in which "exchanges . . . take place exclusively among men. Women, signs, commodities and currency, always pass from one man to another; if it were otherwise, we are told, the social order would fall back upon the incestuous and exclusively endogamous ties that would paralyse all commerce." Irigaray is careful to emphasize the *theoretical* rather than the "natural" status of such systems of exchange, and I wish to use her insight with regard to the theory of a "homosocial" system of exchange, especially a patriarchal one in which the exchange of women organizes or disrupts the cultural (and therefore political) order.[26] Under such patriarchal theory, homosociality designates "the assignment of economic roles: there are producer subjects and agents of exchange (male) on the one hand, productive earth and commodities (female) on the other" (*This Sex*, 192). This describes a theoretical political system and places women in patriarchal political theory as the goods exchanged between men – of course, as the contemporary polemical texts suggest, actual social relations were infinitely more complicated. But in such an imagined, purely patriarchal society, men order the exchange of goods, including women, through space and time and decide on the relative values ascribed to particular goods: women do not need to appear in descriptions of patriarchal society; the method for describing their value decides their significance and this has been agreed between men who exchange them.

However, as Irigaray also notes, the utterly rigid (patriarchal) differentiation between masculine subject and relegation of women to the twin categories of nature and commodity in itself implies that, in being designated the defining other of the masculine, women "come to represent the danger of a disappropriation of masculine power" (*This Sex*, 185), a comment which illuminates the theoretical and polemical texts of the English Civil War. Events and theories from 1640 onwards had led to the impasse of 1648 in which the king, theoretically head of a patriarchal order, had no power and had his value decided by competing groups. Presbyterians, Independents, Levellers and the Army did not find themselves in agreement on the system whereby social place and value might be determined and how Charles I might play a role: after the second Civil War, a crisis developed in the understanding of government, leading to the king's death and the establishment of the new order of government of the 1650s. If, as Irigaray suggests, women are patriarchally designated as commodities, then what happens when the system by which value can be assigned is disputed, as republicanism disputes monarchy? It would seem that once homosocial groups disagree among themselves (as in civil struggle or civil war), this might unleash the latent dangers of women as imagined or figured dangerous disappropriators, precisely as it does in the political satire of the late 1640s.

In part, what seems to have happened in the 1640s and 1650s is that, from being an invisible element in the operation of patriarchy, women became visible in discourse as obstructions, channels which took virtue, semen, money out of the proper routes, no longer recombining these elements so as to fuel the patriarchal economy of status. If, as in the 1640s, the way in which power should be arranged and determined is disputed, then the status and significance of women becomes radically unstable. Marten's challenge to patriarchal values is figured in terms of his relationships to women – as a "libertine" he is placed outside patriarchal exchange with regard to the family. But as a republican he also threatens the very link between family and state – a vital link in the patriarchal designation of political meaning. This particular rebelliousness also placed him in a position which threatened the system of values whereby women are assigned meaning and value, because republicanism disputed this ordering of perceived social value. The conflict of these two possibilities was acute in England after the end of the second Civil War and during the trial and execution of the king and the establishment of the republic, changing as an issue when Cromwell established the Protectorate in the early 1650s. In 1648, however, the presence of contradictory possibilities of political order meant that women, no longer easily assigned value, were figures for the crisis in scurrilous, rather than theoretical, political pamphlets.

However, satire against Marten is only one example of the inter-relationship of the sexual/political during the 1640s and 1650s. Civil War disputation over the assignation of social meaning also brought women into focus in political satire. This can be shown in the scurrilous political pamphlets which have been attributed to the second republican figure discussed here, the politican, theorist and prose writer, Henry Neville. The value of the female in relation to differing systems of status is self-consciously explored in several prose pamphlets on the topic of the "Parliament of Ladies," attributed to Neville. These appeared at a time when the idea of parliamentary sovereignty and freedom counterposed to patriarchal theory illuminated women who, as objects exchanged, were necessary, silent and a part of the analogy of the family and the state, and when the control over women in the analogy between family and state government was seen to break down. Irigaray describes the place of women in patriarchal thought as existing as bodies which "– through their use, consumption and circulation – provide for the condition making social life and culture possible, though they remain an unknown 'infrastructure' of the elaboration of that social life and culture" (*This Sex*, 171). But in these texts the gendered order of society is shown as inverted, or in danger of inversion, as the competition between different modes by which value could be assigned (monarchist versus republican, for example) made women visible counters in the Civil War. At the most basic but socially central level, they acted as the link joining opposed branches of families, but in these pamphlets they are at times seen as autonomous agents who might choose a lover from either side. The pamphlets describe parliaments of "malignant" and "well-affected" ladies.[27] They show women assigning value to the men who have taken part in the war, representing women-as-agents as signs of the disruption of the socio-political and economic assignation of value.

In *The Parliament of Ladies*, rebellious women have benefitted from social disruption and have gained socio-sexual power; in fact, they are presented as busy converting the political sphere (masculine space) into sexual irregularity (the crime of women against the family). This is seen as a product of the politically volatile situation, though the exact political or factional position of the pamphlets themselves is difficult to pin down. The satires address the problems of socio-sexual policing of women and/in the state. For instance, in *The Ladies a Second Time Assembled* the women become agents in political issues which they see entirely in sexual terms. The satire is directed against the inability of women to think politically or discern the differences between one political system and another, because their judgement is made only by the standards of the sexual conduct of the men in question. They tackle the issue of the redistribution of bishops' lands as follows:

> That the Bishoprick of Lincolne, of Worcester, of Ely, and Durham, should remain intire; for that though the Bishops of those Sees, had in other matters of concernment, shewed themselves very averse, yet to those Ladies assembled, they had beene very free and cordiall, even to their utmost abilities, and had in some private performances, ayded them more strongly than any secular man whatsoever.[28]

Women's decisions favour the sexual over the political, and the crisis of the Civil War can be seen here making women appear dangerous when men are not fully in control nor in agreement about their theoretical place. There is an evident articulation between sexual satire and political discourse and the whole pamphlet offers a parodic perspective on the war which takes account of no political or religious issues, but only of adulterous possibilities. It critiques the situation consequent upon the disputes about government, once again (as in the satires on Marten) using sexual satire – here of women MPs – to signal the situation of political crisis.

In *News From the New Exchange* (1650), the pamphlet sets the scene and describes the cause for concern explicitly – "there was a time in *England*, when men *wore the Breeches*, and debar'd women of their *Liberty*" (1) – and goes on to contrast this with the present, when the power of women to drink and smoke signals a new commonwealth indeed. However, by the end of the pamphlet, the anxieties expressed about "the *Ladies Rampant*" have been dissipated into recommodification of women as whores, available to be bought, used and circulated just like the pamphlet itself. Both women and this narrative about them are replaced by the story in a social order dominated by men, enabling it to end: "These, and many more you may buy; but beware you repent not your Bargain. In our next *Annals* (if your humour hold) we will give you more particular relation" (21). Thus, the narrative strategy first raises the problem of female autonomy and then reduces women to subordinates, even within an acknowledgedly disrupted political sphere, by displaying their subjection to traffic between men.

How seriously can we take such satirical attacks on women as signs of political disruption? It seems to me that we need to read them in two ways, first, as pointing towards a crisis among men in which women were also participating and, second, as an index of the kind of discourse felt to be applicable to political situations in the 1640s and 1650s, indicating that the ambivalent relationship between political and familial rhetoric was apprehended and articulated in such populist socio-sexual satire. These pamphlets, whether they are by Neville or not, fuse popular and political polemic to critique the situation *consequent* on the breakdown of agreement in the masculinist ordering of society and respond to the competing rhetorics of patriarchal and populist political theory. Neville had been concerned with the relationship between gender and politics in the 1640s (when he may have been engaged in writing political theory) and this concern continued into the 1660s, as I shall argue, through an engagement with Filmer's patriarchal theory. Soon after the Restoration, Henry Neville returned to England and in 1668 he published a prose fantasy called *The Isle of Pines* which, like the Civil War porno-political polemic about Marten and, by Neville, about the crisis in government, needs to be considered as *both* a scurrilous narrative and political polemic.

The assertion that such fictional writing could be and was seen as, at least in part, political is reinforced by the outline of Neville's career. He continued to be a political writer, publishing the anti-Cromwellian satire *Shuffling, Cutting and Dealing* in 1659 and resuming his role as a republican theorist in 1680–81, when the climate once more seemed to offer hope for republicans.[29] His republican tract *Plato Redivivus* was greeted with alarm and provoked two book-length replies, attacking him for his republican principles and for the stylistic sophistry whereby he pretended to support monarchy. "W.W." took a Filmerian line in his assertion that Neville's design was "to turn Monarchy into Anarchy"[30] and Thomas Goddard, in his *Plato's Demon*, was equally scandalized.[31] Clearly, Neville had not abandoned any of his republican aspirations in the 1660s. As he said in *Shuffling, Cutting and Dealing*, he was still dreaming of a different game altogether – the possibility of a real republic. Therefore, it seems probable that, like the rest of his writing, *The Isle of Pines* – which when it has been considered at all has been considered *only* as a pornographic fantasy of polygamy – addresses political questions.

The Isle of Pines, like Neville's other political writings, takes the form of a framed narrative in which events from the past are related in (and, implicitly, to) the present. In this case, the present is 1668. A Dutch captain is said to have come upon some 2,000 English people living on an island where one man and four women had been shipwrecked in the reign of Elizabeth I. The first part is a narrative by the founding father, George Pine, who tells of his sexual relations with the women and of the gradual establishment of legal strictures to protect persons and property as the neo-Adamic settlement grew. The second part tells the story of the Dutch intervention in the present, and of their helping the king (like Machiavelli's foreign army) to put down an insurrection. Thus, the piece combines political discourse, traveller's tale and scurrilous sexual narrative. One interconnection between the three is the possible pun on "pine"/"penis," in which the phallic order of patriarchy (resting, literally, on the male organ) is linked with rebellion and disorder in the multiplication of "pines"/"penises" on the Isle of Pines.

As I have suggested in my brief analysis of some of the parliament of women tracts, there are good reasons to see Neville's satires as part of a political commentary and *The Isle of Pines* offers a place in which we can trace the interconnections between sexual slander and political polemic a little more clearly. It delineates what Christopher Hill calls "the Robinson Crusoe situation," but, as James Holstun notes, the text works in part as a "masculine fantasy . . . [of] utopian isolation and reproduction."[32] However, the text's relationship to the situation it describes and its commentary upon it are ambiguous. Just as satires on Marten strove to efface political questions by substituting sexual questions on which agreement would be general, Neville's fictional patriarchal colony serves to move in the other direction, taking the reader from the family to the state in a demonstration that the authority of the father is not enough to rule alone, without law.

The narrative interests itself in other issues too, but what I shall concentrate on is the story of the shipwreck and the extensive procreation that ensues. The ship set off during the reign of Elizabeth but the narrative is told three generations later, during 1667. The book was published in 1668, the year after the end of a war with the Dutch which had been disastrous for Britain, and had culminated in the bombardment of the fort at the mouth of the Medway and the firing of the English navy at Chatham. But even before the blockade in June 1667, Charles II had beeen desperate to end the war.[33] Intriguingly, the narrative of *The Isle of Pines* is said to have been given to a Dutch seaman – "the whole Relation [was] written, and delivered by the Man himself a little before his death and delivered to the Dutch by his Grandchild" – after "a Dutch ship making a voyage to the East Indies" came upon the progeny of the original George Pine.

The significance of the narrative being given to a Dutch seaman (presumably Neville's pseudonymous Henry Cornelius van Sloettan) is difficult to determine. What can be said is that the presence of a Dutch sailor as the receiver and publisher of the narrative does alert us to an engagement with contemporary political questions. This is reinforced in a later reprint in which a footnote indicates that when Neville's tract was reprinted in the eighteenth century it was felt to figure in a political (as well as a literary) tradition of anti-absolutist writing. The footnote implicitly places the story in the republican tradition by also mentioning Locke's *Two Treatises of Government*, the first of which was a lengthy, point-by-point refutation of Filmer, in which the very detail of the refutation testifies to the importance of Filmer's theory as a support to monarchy.[34] The fact that it was reprinted in such a context strongly suggests that *The Isle of Pines* was read, at least by a subsequent reading public, as a politicized text taking a place in post-war debates.

This brings me back to the original question about the relationship between political theory and scurrilous narrative. Roger Thompson, in his outline of seventeenth-century pornographic writing, asserts that there was much contemporary interest in polygamy and bigamous marriage, and that this was reinforced by the behaviour of Charles II and worries about the lack of an heir.[35] However, I would argue that a close analogue is offered by patriarchal political theory. *The Isle of Pines*, although it presents itself as a fictional/verisimilar narrative, or fantasy of origins, also continues Neville's preoccupation with the proper ordering of government as worked out through fictions using politically charged constructions of heterosexual exchanges. In constantly tracing political authority back to Adam, Filmer produced a vision of the first fathers establishing something very like colonial plantations. The link between this version of the story of the way the earth was populated and colonial theory is helpfully explicated by Francis Bacon: "Plantations are amongst ancient, primitive and heroical works. When the world was young it begat more children; but now it is old it begets fewer: for I may justly account new plantations to be the children of former kingdoms."[36]

Bacon is using the analogy of the family and its generations to justify colonialism as an ancient practice. We can see biblical narrative, seen as the story of the first family, reproduced in the "planting" of new colonies. *The Isle of Pines* takes a similar metaphor and disfigures it, reproducing a bastard version of the biblical narrative and the notion of colony as family. First, a "family" sets out to run a colonial "factory." At this point "family" is used in its extended sense of multiple relationships between a master and his wives, daughters and servants. The shipwreck produces what comes to be a rather different version of the family. The master is killed, leaving a male servant, George Pine, to found the colony (in this we can see the lineaments of Filmer's rights of kingship), using the bodies of his master's wife and daughter, a maid and a black "slave." This is a parodic version of Eden – as the narrator tells us, the island is like Eden before the fall: "the country so very pleasant, being always clothed in green, and full of pleasant fruits, and variety of birds, ever warm, and never colder than England in September; so that this place, had it the culture that skilful people might bestow on it, would prove a paradise" (65–6).

The colony takes shape as George Pine begins to have sex with all the women. A sub-text rapidly develops about the black slave and the founding father's lack of desire for her (he will only sleep with her in the dark). She is the mother of a child who rebels in the second part of the narrative. Although the story is "about" reproduction, the narrative does not interest itself in the nature of women. On the other hand, it does give us numbers of the children produced – 1,789 by the fifty-ninth year that Pine had been on the island. And it explains how Pine rules his offspring and sends them to other parts of the island in small colonies. Moreover, the story parallels Filmer's biblicized narration of the establishment of the first monarchy, on which patriarchal theory was based. As a fantasy of literal patriarchy in the present (1668), it can be read as delineating the polygamous (and implicitly incestuous) implications of bringing the Bible story to bear on the contemporary situation.

Because of the desert island situation, the narrative works in two ways. First, it presents polygamy as an acceptable (or, rather, pragmatic, "necessary") possibility, posing the problem in a way which offers the reader a safe position from which to regard multiple marriage. Second, the very secularity of the working out of polygamous (and incestuous) relations points back to the sacred construction of sexual relations in which such affairs are prohibited: by implict comparison between biblical narrative of origin and the present, it illuminates the discontinuity between the two and the inapplicability of literal biblical narrative to the present. The story is, at least, a version of the patriarchal theory in which kings are founding fathers to their people. Polygamy is not condemned in biblical terms (rather it is secularized): instead, patriarchy, on the quasi-biblical model of the Adamic founding father, is shown to be inadequate to the political needs of the community. Ultimately, the narrative demonstrates that without law and reinforcements – without "property" and arms – a ruler is unable to quash rebellions. Fatherhood is demonstrated as inadequate as a guarantee of government in rebellion against the authority of patriarchy which, as it is repeated and followed by the invention of the rule of law, implies the inadequacy of a mere patriarch to govern in ethical, legal and, above all, political terms.

The foundation of the colony was laid by Pine but when he dies and passes on control of the family/colony to his son, trouble begins. The families have now extended to become semi-separate dynasties and "in multitudes disorders will grow, the stronger seeking to oppress the weaker; no type of Religion being strong enough to chain up the depraved nature of mankinde" (71). Rebellions ensue, commencing with that of the son of the black slave. Later, rebellion takes a form which treads the line between family transgression and political rebellion: we hear of sex-crimes against the family – which, in this context, are also crimes against the state: "The sense of sin being quite lost in them, they fell to whoredoms, incests and adulteries; . . . nay, not confining themselves within the bound of any modesty, but brother and sister lay openly together" (72). The power of the patriarch alone is not enough to prevent such crimes against family-and-state, so he delegates some executive responsibility and, crucially, sets up autonomous *laws* for the regulation of sexual and social behaviour. Thus, rebellion against the family as state in the patriarchal Isle of Pines brings about partial abandonment of patriarchy and recourse to the separation of state and family, shown to be necessary and exemplified in the appearance of law. The laws primarily regulate the family, condemning rape as well as theft and blasphemy. Problems because of the inability of one ruler to control rebellions continue and, in the end, the patriarch only remains in control because of the guns and powder of the Dutch. But on rebellion and the transition from pure patriarchy to a legal state, the narrator comments: "Now as Seed being cast into stinking Dung produceth good and wholesome Corn for the sustenation of mans life, so bad manners produceth good and wholesome Laws for the preservation of Humane Society" (73).

The Isle of Pines is a fiction of the origins of a nation in patriarchal dominance and draws on patriarchal theory, but the second generation is seen to be forced to make the transition from patriarchy to a state based on law. Certainly, *The Isle of Pines* reproduces the power of the phallus to order a kingdom in its concentration on the story of these father-governors. But it simultaneously parodies and ironizes that power, undercutting it by presenting its ultimate inability to control the state. More abstractly, we can say it brings to bear satirical techniques of the Civil War on the patriarchal theory which came to prominence after it, and which was available for such fictional caricature because of its literal use of biblical narrative to the point of the collapse of all political theory into the story of the (first) family. This illuminates only one aspect of *The Isle of Pines*. It can be read as a story of shipwreck and sex, a verisimilar fiction often genericized (problematically, as I hope I have suggested) as a pornographic narrative. It can also be read as a part of the colonial writing and as an important point of convergence between colonial description, utopia and verisimilar fictional narratives of colonial dominance. One way of "placing" the text is to see it as part of a tradition which joins Elizabethan colonial narratives to *Robinson Crusoe*, set in the Interregnum. Republican possibilities lurk in *Crusoe* simply because of the time when it is set, redoubling the text's engagement with the re-ordering of a new patriarchal society. But though *The Isle of Pines* is part of such traditions, it is also interwoven with a political context and with the context of the politico-literary writing of the Civil War and its aftermath. It also exists in the space inaugurated by the conflicting politics of the Civil War, at the uncomfortable and disputed border between the family and the state, between the sexual and the political. In this context, I would suggest, not only political theory but also narratives, plays, poems and dialogues were "read politically," and polemic addressed a reader in several simultaneous registers, or even discourses, without these being fully separate but joined in persuasive polemic.

The interconnections I have traced between conflicting political theories and sexual satire do, I hope, suggest another way to read popular rhetoric of the Civil War and seventeenth-century fictions, that is, politically. In tracking the movement of political ideas through different discourses and registers, I have traced a sequence of displacements, or translations, at the level of discourse to put in place some connections between the different kinds of political or politicized language in the Civil War and its aftermath. In taking a small group of writings to illuminate ways in which texts construct meanings, I have tried to illuminate the way such meanings – political meanings – are not generated solely by political discourse but are registered, transformed, modified and contested in a range of different discourses – which construct them differently and operate in relation to a continuum of different texts and different ways of reading.

NOTES

For Jack. My thanks to Jim Holstun, Tim Armstrong and participants in Peter Brown and Andrew Butcher's "Literature and Society" seminar, January 1991.

1. The debates between "revisionist" historians of the Civil War and others, perhaps post-Marxist historians of the period, are summarized from the latter perspective in the introduction to Richard Cust and Ann Hughes, eds., *Conflict in Early Stuart England* (London: Longman, 1989), 1–47. Cust and Hughes note that revisionist histories offer multiple and inconsistent versions of the period and they argue for a combination of detailed research with an acknowledgement that the society of Stuart England did hold the potential for conflict (16–17). For a summary of debates up to 1977 see R.C. Richardson, *The Debate on the English Civil War* (London: Methuen, 1977).

2. See David Norbrook (forthcoming) on the creation of a political and literary public sphere in the 1640s. On the issue of the "popular" sphere, see Tim Harris, *London Crowds in the Reign of Charles II* (Cambridge: Cambridge University Press, 1987), 14–35. Harris finds the isolation of a "popular" sphere from an "elite" sphere problematic; he does not argue that the masses had no political consciousness but that "ordinary people had a more important role than is usually conceded" (15). His considered analysis of "popular" political action provides a salutary contrast to Anthony Fletcher's treatment of crowds (e.g., pages 170–3) in his otherwise immensely detailed *The Outbreak of the English Civil War* (London: Arnold, 1981).

3. Gordon J. Schochet, *Patriarchalism in Political Thought* (Oxford: Blackwell, 1975). Schochet refers to the "pamphlet war on the nature of the English commonwealth" (158). In defining the "war" as of "pamphlets," Schochet implicitly acknowledges the range of discourses implicated in the debate and gestures towards its potentially wide circulation.

4. Excerpt from the Army Debates in *Revolutionary Prose of the English Civil War*, Howard Erskine-Hill and Graham Storey, eds. (Cambridge: Cambridge University Press, 1983), 69.

5. Jonathan Clark, *Revolution and Rebellion* (Cambridge: Cambridge University Press, 1986), e.g., 10–12. See also Anthony Fletcher, *Outbreak*, xxx.

6. The best known "shocking example" is Stephen Greenblatt's use of the example of the burning town. In a brilliant analysis of Christopher Marlowe's writing, "Marlowe and the Will to Absolute Play," Stephen Greenblatt uses a non-literary text as "a convenient bridge from the world of Edmund Spenser to the world of Christopher Marlowe," thus repeating the marginality of the very text he invites us to "use," or focus on, as a bridge between one canonical and literary text and another. See *Renaissance Self-Fashioning* (Chicago and London: University of Chicago Press, 1980), 193–221.

7. *The Memoirs of Edmund Ludlow*, C.H. Firth, ed., 2 vols. (Oxford: Clarendon Press, 1894), I: 184–5. On Neville in the 1650s, see II: 83–5, 98; and on Marten in 1659, II: 287. An outline of some of the developments of republican thinking can

be found in Perez Zagorin, *History of Political Thought in the English Revolution* (London: Routledge, 1954), 146–63, and in Zera S. Fink, *The Classical Republicans* (Evanston: Northwestern University Press, 1945). Zagorin is unwilling to attribute theorized republican thought to the 1640s, presumably because the republican printed texts emerged in the 1650s, especially after the establishment of the Protectorate and in 1659. However, the way republicans responded to the crisis brought about by the Protectorate suggests that they had been planning possible governments for some time (Zagorin, 148–9). They were obviously a known group before the earliest text he cites, John Wildman's *A Declaration of the Free-born People of England* (1655). Zagorin is of the opinion that *A Copy of a Letter from an Officer of the Army in Ireland* (1656), an anti-Cromwellian and pro-republican pamphlet of disputed authorship, uses Harrington's *The Commonwealth of Oceana* (1656), but may have been published by Neville (150), although it seems equally likely that Neville's thinking might have been incorporated in *Oceana*. See also J.G.A. Pocock, "James Harrington and the Good Old Cause: a Study in the Ideological Context of His Writings," *The Journal of British Studies*, 10:1 (November 1970), 30–48.

8. Henry Neville, *The Isle of Pines* (1668). Reprinted in *The Isle of Pines 1668: An Essay in Bibliography*, Worthington Chauncey Ford, ed. (Boston: The Club of Odd Volumes, 1920). Subsequent references in text are to this reprint.

9. Peter Laslett, ed., *Patriarcha and Other Political Works by Sir Robert Filmer*, (Oxford: Blackwell, 1949). Laslett dates the composition of the *Patriarcha* before the Civil War. He notes (3–7) the extent to which this manuscript was quoted in Filmer's wartime pamphlets.

10. Sir Robert Filmer, *The Anarchy of a Limited or Mixed Monarchy* (1648); *The Necessity of the Absolute Power of all Kings and Especially the King of England By Jean Bodin* (London, 1648). Both are reprinted in Peter Laslett, ed., *Patriarcha and Other Political Works*, and the references are to this volume.

11. See Charles Herle, *An Answer to Doctor Fernes Reply* (London, 1643), quoted by Schochet in *Patriarchalism* (108–9). As Schochet notes, Herle "denies the identity of familial and political authority," arguing "*Allegoryes* are no good *arguments*, they onely illustrate as farre as the likenesse hold. Because a *King* may in some respects be call'd the *Father*, . . . doth it therefore follow because he should govern with the *providence* of a Father, he may therefore governe with the *Arbitrarinesse* of a Father without the consent of his people" (16–17).

12. One of the paradoxical aspects of the implications of Filmer's political programme in relation to the present is that, although all right is determined by history, it has become strangely detached from actual pragmatic politics in the present (285), existing perhaps as something which right-thinking monarchists subscribe to.

13. *A Brief Dialogue Between Zelotopist and Superstition* (1642). The "Antibrownistus" satires are brought together in *Images of English Puritanism: A Collection of Contemporary Sources 1589–1646*, Lawrence A. Sasek, ed. (Baton Rouge: Louisiana State University Press, 1989).

14. John Forster, *The Lives of Eminent British Statesmen* (London: Longman, Brown Green or Spottiswode and Shaw, 1831), 247. See also John Aubrey, *Brief Lives* (Harmondsworth: Penguin, 1972), 265–7.

15. Forster, 247. See also C.M. Williams, "The Anatomy of a Radical Gentleman: Henry Marten," in *Puritans and Revolutionaries*, C. M. Williams, ed. (Oxford: Oxford University Press, 1978), 118–38.

16. Edmund Ludlow, *Memoirs*, I: 66; Forster, 254.

17. *The terrible, horrible monster of the west* (1651), A2r. Other instances of the abuse of Marten can be found in the anti-Rump popular press. One example is an article in *The Man in the Moon* in October 1649. This continues the abuse of Henry Marten and asserts that Rump MPs are given to whoring but are easily deceived by bawds. "A *Bawd*, belonging to the *Mopping School*, was likewise *Carted*, that had Cozened *Harry Marten* and some other members of the *Juncto* in their *Venery*, and sold them *stale-flesh* for *Maids*: which was taken for a high *Contempt* amongst the members

of Parliament, because that *Harry Martyn* is disabled thereby . . . to give any personal attendence in the *House*" (*The Man in the Moon*, newsletter, 10–17 October 1649, 206).

18. *Mr Henry Marten His Speech in the House of Commons Before His Departure Thence* (1648), A2r. Subsequent references in text.

19. David Underdown, *Revel, Riot and Rebellion* (Oxford: Clarendon Press, 1985), 37–40.

20. Henry Parker, *Observations on some of his majesty's late answers and expresses* (London, 1642), in *Revolutionary Prose*, Erskine-Hill and Graham Storey, eds., 35–63; see also 49–50.

21. Thomas Hobbes, *Leviathan, or the Matter, Forme and Power of a Commonwealth Ecclesiatical and Civil* (1651), Michael Oakeshott, ed. (Oxford: Blackwell, 1960), 5. The positive use of Hobbes by republican theorists (as opposed to Harrington's argument with him in *Oceana*) remains, to a large extent, unspoken. However, after the Restoration (when Hobbes's theories were not embraced by the monarchy), his influence can be seen in republican theory, particularly his way of characterizing the commonwealth as non-organic but issuing from the necessity of resolving a war of all against all. Henry Neville uses this aspect of Hobbes's theory of the "artificiality" of the state in *Plato Redivivus*. See *Two English Republican Tracts*, Caroline Robbins, ed. (Cambridge: Cambridge University Press, 1969), 84–5.

22. *The Remonstrance or Declaration of Henry Marten and all the Socity of Levellers* (1648). See also the petitions of Leveller women discussed in this volume in the article by Ann Marie McEntee.

23. *Revolutionary Prose*, extracts from *The Army Debates*, 66.

24. *Coll. Henry Marten's Letters to his Lady of Delight Also Her Kinde Returns With His Rivall H. Pettingalls Heroical Epistles* (London, 1662) and *The King's Cabinet Opened* (1645).

25. Jacques Donzelot suggests this when he notes that the family "consituted a *plexus* of dependent relations that were indissociably private and public . . . integrally affected by the system of obligations, honours . . . [and also] an active participant in the give-and-take of social ties, goods, and actions through the strategies of matrimonial alliance." Donzelot, *The Policing of Families* (London: Hutchinson, 1980), 48.

26. Luce Irigaray, *This Sex Which is Not One*, trans. Catherine Porter with Carolyn Burke (Ithaca: Cornell University Press, 1985, first published 1977), 192. Eve Kosofsky Sedgwick, *Between Men: English Literature and Male Homosexual Desire* (New York: Columbia University Press, 1985), 1–5. Sedgwick writes about "homosocial desire":

> "Homosocial desire," to begin with, is a kind of oxymoron. "Homosocial" is a word occasionally used in history and the social sciences, where it describes social bonds between persons of the same sex; it is a neologism, obviously formed by analogy with "homosexual," and just as obviously meant to be distinguished from "homosexual." In fact it is applied to such activities as "male bonding," which may, as in our society, be characterised by intense homophobia, fear and hatred of homosexuality.(1)

See also Gayle Rubin, "The Traffic in Women: Notes on the 'Political Economy' of Sex," in *Toward an Anthropology of Women*, Rayna R. Reiter, ed. (New York: Monthly Review Press, 1975), 157–210.

27. Examples of the titles of pamphlets from this group are *An Exact Diurnall of the Parliament of Ladyes* (1647), *The Parliament of Ladies* (1647), *The Ladies A Second Time Assembled* (1647) and *Newes From the New Exchange* (1650). There are extensive reprints, adaptations and reworkings of them: this is only a small number of the texts listed in Wing.

28. *The Ladies A Second Time Assembled*, 2.

29. Henry Neville, *Shuffling, Cutting and Dealing in a Game at Pickquet: Being Acted in the Year 1653 to 1658 By O.P. and Others with Great Applause* (1659).

30. W.W., *Antidotum Britannicum* (1681), A2v. See also Henry Neville, *Plato Redivivus* (1680), in Caroline Robbins, ed., *Two English Republican Tracts*.

31. Thomas Goddard wrote, "He would make us believe that he is supporting Our Government, while he endeavours utterly to destroy it: Propounds ruine and slavery in a peaceable way: And disapproves *Civil War* only because he doubts the success." Thomas Goddard, *Plato's Demon* (1681), A4v. For a thorough discussion affirming *Plato Redivivus* as a republican text, see Fink, *The Classical Republicans*, 123–48.

32. Christopher Hill, *Puritanism and Revolution* (London: Secker and Warburg, 1958), 381–2. Hill is discussing Puritan texts which present "a social state which is not bound by inherited conventions" for the working out of individual salvation. He mentions *The Isle of Pines* but it fits very uneasily into his model, sliding as it does between fantasy and political critique. James Holstun, *A Rational Millennium: Puritan Utopias of Seventeenth-Century England and America* (Oxford: Oxford University Press, 1987), 109, 244.

33. Ronald Hutton, *Charles the Second* (Oxford: Clarendon Press, 1989), 247–9.

34. In fact, he finally argues that Filmer's theory could not work because there was no way it could be proved that, after the flood, Shem was decreed a divinely sanctioned and supreme king. See also *The Isle of Pines* (London: T. Cadell, 1768).

35. Roger Thompson, *Unfit For Modest Ears* (London: Macmillan, 1979), 100, 103, *et seq*. Thompson describes the parliaments as "good undergraduate bawdy," and his whole thesis is predicated on the separability of discourse, specifically the removal and isolation of sexual discourse as "bawdy" from all other "serious" discourses such as medical and political.

36. Francis Bacon, "On Plantations," in *The Works of Francis Bacon*, 14 vols., James Spedding, Robert Leslie Ellis and Douglas Denton Heath, eds. (London: Longman, 1890), 6 pt. 2: 457–9, especially 457.

Rational Hunger: Gerrard Winstanley's Hortus Inconclusus

JAMES HOLSTUN

I

Gerrard Winstanley was born in Wigan, Lancashire, probably in 1609. After failing as a London cloth merchant in 1643, he moved to Surrey and found work as a cattle drover. In 1648, he wrote and published three radical religious pamplets. In January 1649, the day before Charles I was sentenced to death, Winstanley completed an astonishing pamphlet titled *The New Law of Righteousness*, which formulates a communist programme for peacefully revolutionizing English society. Winstanley says he heard a divine command for the poor of England to begin communal cultivation of the land: "Work together. Eat bread together; declare this all abroad."[1] With its allusion to Genesis, its communitarian ethic and its parallels between production, consumption and prophecy, this command is a reasonable place to locate the origins of the Digger movement.

During the next 18 months, at least ten Digger communes sprang up in Northamptonshire, Kent, Buckinghamshire, Gloucestershire and Surrey.[2] Winstanley's own commune took shape at George's Hill in Surrey, near London and just outside of Kingston. On Sunday, 1 April 1649, a small group of Diggers broke ground, sowing corn, parsnips, carrots and beans. Winstanley also set to work writing: during the next year he published 14 additional petitions, manifestos, defences and meditations. Six Digger pamphlets by other hands appeared between December 1648 and May 1650. We know little about the fate of the other communes, but Winstanley's folded in April 1650, after a series of gentry-led prosecutions, boycotts and physical attacks on the Diggers' crops, dwellings and persons. Winstanley published his communist utopia, *The Law of Freedom in a Platform*, in 1652. In later life he probably became a Quaker; he died in 1676.

The Digger project forms one of the most important chapters in the agrarian history of early modern Britain, for it presents us with the most important seventeenth-century critique of the enclosure movement from the point of view of its victims – a critique which seventeenth- and twentieth-century depictions of plebeian Englishmen and women as mute traditionalists might lead us to think is all but impossible. The Diggers provide us with the fullest seventeenth-century English vision of a more humane and egalitarian collective life – not despite but because of their focus on daily life at the local level. I will approach Winstanley, the greatest Christian materialist of seventeenth-century England, by way of Ernst Bloch, the twentieth-century Marxist most fascinated by the utopian power of religion and prophecy.

II

The canon of seventeenth-century English literature is opening up to the voices of women and the writers of marginal or non-literary texts, but it seems less interested in the voices of the hungry. Some sorts of deprivation seem to be more audible than others. Erotic deprivation produces the love lament; deprivation of political power, the poem of patronage; both sorts of deprivation, the Petrarchan political sonnet. Deprivation of bodily freedom produces the prison journal or lyric, of political liberty the philippic or manifesto, of virtue the confession or jeremiad. Even deprivation of life produces, through the melodious tear of a bereft swain, the pastoral elegy. But no parallel genre responds to the deprivation of food. The cockaigne poem or narrative, whose avowedly fantastic and whimsical tone tends to deny or naturalize hunger, seems to be a view of hunger from the outside, from the position of the well fed.

This distinction between hunger and other sorts of deprivation holds even if we put "deprivation" into post-structuralist quotation marks and see it as a sort of desire dissolved in language itself rather than the exterior cause of language. As Lacan, Barthes and Derrida argue, language is not simply about sexual desire, but its cause, instrument and object. Foucault argues something similar for the will to power. But hunger does not even begin to lend itself to a talking or writing cure. So far as it suggests a primal existential lack, an absence, a nothingness that produces desire, it brings us dangerously close to an outmoded existentialism. If we dwell too long on it, we risk that indelibly damning epithet, "essentialist humanism." However, we may also hesitate to take the arch-Foucauldian road and call hunger a mere effect of discourse. One way out of the problem is simply to ignore it, and also the mass of poor people (surely the majority of humankind throughout history) who have felt hunger and its threat as primal existential facts.

And this is easy enough to do. For one thing, the hungry and the literate tend to be mutually exclusive groups. Even if hungry people are literate, they tend to be more interested in finding food than in writing about their hunger. And when well-fed literate people record the voices of the hungry, they are typically more interested in hearing their legal testimony, religious confessions, contractual obligations and deferential greetings than in such stark cries as "We want to eat!" – an utterance that provokes embarrassed deafness, not archival attentiveness. Hunger's object of desire, if not exactly a brute fact free of symbolic systems, remains somehow vulgar, material, unworthy of sustained critical reflection or analysis. Remarkably enough, thanks to some of the more florid literary critical appropriations of Bakhtin, we pay more heed to Renaissance repletion, festive gorging, vomiting and defecation than to Renaissance hunger.

A quick explanation for this view of hunger might juxtapose critic and canon – it is only natural that modern critics with more experience of the sex and power drives than of the hunger drive should turn to early modern writers with similar experience. The latter typically invoke hunger as the vehicle for metaphor, as when they speak of the communicant's spiritual hunger for the Eucharist, or the Petrarchan *devoto*'s erotic hunger. When they treat hunger itself, it usually appears as the condition of *the other*, as in that astonishingly cruel Renaissance epithet *starveling*, which almost suggests an elective character type or profession, like the melancholic scholar or the mountebank. In drama and satirical poetry, we see the poor depicted again and again as mouths without brains – perhaps a vision of their actual hunger, perhaps a displacement of guilty, upper-class voraciousness. Even in those works such as More's *Utopia* that register a sort of paternal and humane concern for the hunger of England's displaced and wandering poor, the concern tends to be objective, not subjective: the real terror of hunger is not hunger itself, but the threat that it will breed a mobile, ravenous army. This objectivizing point of view reappears in the modern study of "the vagrancy problem" in early modern England, which might be (but seldom is) more sympathetically described as "the next meal problem."

I want to approach this question through a portion of Ernst Bloch's *The Principle of Hope* – the 1400-page Expressionist prose poem that is his *magnum opus*. Bloch works out a critique of various psychoanalytic theories based on their conceptions of the fundamental human drives. All these drives are regressive in orientation, motivated by some primordial and fixed layer of existence or consciousness:

> The unconscious of psychoanalysis is . . . *never a Not-Yet-Conscious*, an element of progressions; it consists rather of regressions. Accordingly, even the process of making this

unconscious conscious only clarifies What Has Been; i.e., *there is nothing new in the Freudian unconscious*. This became even clearer when C.G. Jung, the psychoanalytic fascist, reduced the libido and its unconscious contents entirely to the primeval.[3]

Bloch goes on to criticize Alfred Adler for his Nietzschean theory of a psychological will-to-power (57). The drives animating these various models of the unconscious – Freud's Oedipal/sexual drives, Jung's frenzy-drive, Adler's power-drive – all face backwards, and Bloch links them with what he calls the "filled emotions (like envy, greed, admiration) . . . whose drive object lies ready, if not in respective individual attainability, then in the already available world" (74).

In the contemporary study of Renaissance culture, we can see versions of these familiar psychological drives at work. After the brief and contained heyday of Frye, polite literary critical society seems to have banished myth criticism as improperly ahistorical and universalist (and perhaps something darker, given the political associations and proclivities of Jung, Eliade and Campbell). But a similar archetypalism – albeit with a distinct *arche* – survives among the more thematic sorts of deconstructive criticism and the critical celebrations of Bakhtinian carnival. Freud's analysis of the sexual/Oedipal drive flourishes, particularly as linguified by structural psychoanalysis and as criticized and adapted by feminist Shakespeareans. Adler's theory of a power drive has had no great impact on literary studies, but its Foucauldian sibling (Nietzsche is the common parent) has certainly proved influential in new historicist and other modes of post-structuralist literary analysis. And the accompanying "filled emotions" of envy, greed and admiration have received sustained critical attentioon in studies of literary patronage, the literary market-place, and theatricality inside the theatre and out.

Bloch's critique of these psychoanalytical drive theories blends historicism and humanism. On the one hand, he insists that human beings and their drives are historically determinate products – that Freud's "libido man lives – together with his dreamed wish-fulfillments – in the bourgeois world a few decades before and a few decades after 1900 (the key year of the secessionist 'liberation of the flesh from the spirit')" (68). At the same time, he proposes an alternative candidate for the primal drive in what he calls "the drive that is always left out of psychoanalytical theory" (64) – the drive to self-preservation, with hunger as its primary expression:

> Very little, all too little has been said so far about hunger. Although this goal also looks very primal or primeval. Because a man dies without nourishment, whereas we can live a little

while longer without the pleasures of love-making. It is all the more possible to live without satisfying our power-drive, all the more possible without returning into the unconscious of our five-hundred-thousand-year-old forefathers. But the unemployed person on the verge of collapse, who has not eaten for days, has really been led to the oldest needy place of our existence and makes it visible. . . . In the late bourgeoisie, to which Freud's psychoanalysis also belongs, hunger was deleted. Or it became a subspecies of the libido, its "oral phase," as it were; subsequently, self-preservation does not occur as an original drive at all. (65, 67)

While the will-to-power (sexual and political) is very much in evidence, the will-to-eat is all but invisible, and hunger seems almost to lie below the threshold of historical visibility.

But at certain striking moments, early modern literature presents hunger more sympathetically as the condition of *the self*: the plebian hunger of *Coriolanus*; the labouring, sweating, hungering and eating cosmos of *Paradise Lost*; the hungry Christ of *Paradise Regained*. The example I want to concentrate on for the moment, however, is less familiar. It is a Digger broadside written in 1650 by nine Northamptonshire starvelings, with a typically verbose seventeenth-century title: *A Declaration of the Grounds and Reasons why we the Poor Inhabitants of the Town of Wellinborrow, in the County of Northampton, have begun and give consent to Dig up, Manure and Sow Corn upon the Common, and Waste Ground, called Bareshanke, Belonging to the Inhabitants of Wellinborrow, by those that have Subscribed, and Hundreds more that give Consent*. The authors note that there are 1,169 receivers of alms in the parish, and that even though the justices at the recent quarter sessions ordered that a stock be established for their relief, charity does not yet reign in Wellinborrow:

We have spent all we have, our trading is decayed, our wives and children cry for bread, our lives are a burden to us, divers of us having 5.6.7.8.9 in family, and we cannot get bread for one of them by our labour; rich men's hearts are hardened, they will not give us if we beg at their doors; if we steal, the law will end our lives, divers of the poor are starved to death already, and it were better for us that are living to die by the sword then by the famine: And now we consider that the earth is our mother, and that God hath given it to the children of men, and that the common and waste grounds belong to the poor, and that we have a right to the common ground both from the law of the land, reason and scriptures; and therefore

> we have begun to bestow our righteous labour upon it, and we shall trust the spirit for a blessing upon our labour. (650)

The indictment-like rhythm of the opening clauses of this passage leads to the painful non-choice of death by famine or death by sword. But a third option appears, as the tenant commoners threaten to take up the patrician sword, only to beat it immediately into the plebeian ploughshare. I particularly like the image of these plebeians, with filial piety, "bestowing" their labour on their mother earth – a bit grandiose, but then, what do any givers have to "bestow," except their own labour, or the appropriated labour of others?

Even more important, this manifesto shows us the hungry poor articulating themselves with utopian force. They aim to end not only their hunger but also the social structure that allows it to exist in the first place. Even in the midst of great physical need, this voice constructs a rational utopian critique of one social totality and a proposal for a humane alternative. This is a rebellion of the belly, which Bacon calls the worst kind, but it is also a rebellion of wounded reason.[4] As E.P. Thompson argues, early modern food riots were not typically spontaneous effusions, but displayed a certain ideological rationale and orderliness in themselves.[5] The Diggers' hunger acquires not only a voice, but a rational revolutionary potentiality, and indeed hunger always has a political potential as well as an existential reality. True, it seems almost purely subjective, focused as it is on the subject's own stomach rather than on the erotic or political object of desire. On the other hand, it implies the irreducibly collective quality of all economic production. It can, in fact, produce consciousness of what the young Marx calls "species being": the fact that human beings are fully human only insofar as they create and recreate themselves through self-conscious collective praxis. At times (and Wellinborrow, 1650, is such a time), it can even help to produce class consciousness and revolutionary action.

Bloch again:

> Hunger cannot help continually renewing itself. But if it increases uninterrupted, satisfied by no certain bread, then it suddenly changes. The body-ego then becomes rebellious, does not go out in search of food merely within the old framework. It seeks to change the situation which has caused its empty stomach, its hanging head. The No to the bad situation which exists, the Yes to the better life that hovers ahead, is incorporated by the deprived into *revolutionary interest*. This interest always begins with hunger, hunger transforms itself, having been taught, into an explosive force against the prison of deprivation. (75)

Hunger has not simply an unconscious, but also a not-yet-conscious; it can produce what Bloch calls the utopian or expectant emotions of anxiety, fear, belief and hope – those emotions "whose drive-intention is long-term, whose drive-object does not yet lie ready, not just in respective individual attainability, but also in the already available world, and therefore still occurs in the doubt about exit or entrance" (74). Hunger is perhaps the central drive in Winstanley's account of human existence. The experience of hunger is the midwife, delivering all from a state of property to a state of community. In his introduction to *Fire in the Bush*, he exhorts his readers, "Be not like the rats and mice, that draws the treasures of the earth into your holes to look upon, whilst your fellow-members, to whom it belongs as well as to you by the law of creation, do starve for want" (448). Those who attempt to maintain private property, and those who steal from the Digger commonwealth, will be punished through a repetition of the anti-collective isolation their actions imply – left to labour and to eat without the benefits and pleasures of community (196–7). Even Winstanley seems to prophesy out of hunger. In his "Preface" to a reissued edition of his first five works, he relates how his own vision of community may be born of hunger – for he forsakes his companions, his ordinary labour, and his food for days at a time in order to write.[6] We will now examine the ways in which the seemingly hopeless suffering generated by the transformations in early modern agriculture helped to generate the communist hope of the Diggers.

III

We might define the moment of the Diggers in 1648–50 as the intersection of two distinct processes moving towards crisis at mid-century. The first process was demographic and natural: the agrarian distress born of the sixteenth- and seventeenth-century growth in population that put increasing pressure on land holdings and led to displacement and vagrancy. This pressure was compounded by a series of bad harvests in early seventeenth-century England. The disastrous harvest of 1648, just before Winstanley's communist inspiration, doubled the price of bread and led to widespread hunger and scattered reports of starvation.[7]

The second process was economic and political: the revolutionary rationalization of early modern English agriculture that has come to be known as the enclosure movement. But the very phrase requires some comment. As Joan Thirsk points out, certain sorts of enclosure were quite traditional, and unobjectionable to all concerned, even the poor. Furthermore, in addition to the generally hated division and enclosure of traditional common lands, this process of agricultural rationalization also included the overstocking of commons by wealthy landowners, the engrossing of scattered small-holdings into contiguous larger ones, the "improvement" of wastes and fens, the development of new agricultural technologies, the conversion of arable land to pasture, the intentional decay of rural dwellings, massive depopulations, new schemes of social welfare and poor relief in response to these depopulations, and new modes of large-scale human suffering consequent on all of these.[8] It might be better to describe these events as a struggle between rival conceptions of the human relationship to the land: between a traditional rights-based model and an emergent property-based model. Property ownership was no invention of early modern improvers, but many areas of England had seen strict property rights limited by a traditional conception of the land as an overdetermined entity crosshatched with multiple and sometimes conflicting rights. Landlords' rights to rents and tithes were at least partially balanced by tenants' rights to common lands, timber, water, fish and game, gleaning, and to a "fair" rent not defined completely by a rack-renting landlord invoking the iron law of the market.

The English Revolution raised the suffering and ideological conflict produced by enclosure to a higher pitch. Among the English poor, the 1640s brought rising expectations of a fundamental social revolution which would produce a true commonwealth by removing not only the great tyrant in Westminster, but the lesser tyrants in the manor, the law court, and the tithe-supported church. In the late 1640s the victorious Parliamentarians had confiscated and sold the bishops' lands, but they still held the lands of other Royalists, dean and chapter lands, crown lands and forests, and it was not yet altogether clear that these lands would pass from one dominant group of the wealthy to another, as they eventually did. We can see evidence of these libertarian expectations in the increase in attacks on enclosures in the early 1640s and in the pamphlets and practices of the Diggers. Again, we may note a period of particular crisis in 1648–49, with the trial and execution of the King, the crushing of the Levellers, and the search for a constitutional settlement.

I want to situate the Diggers' specific response to enclosure by comparing it to two alternatives: the critique of enclosure from the point of view of a half-imagined, half-remembered rural economy of the past, and the utopian advocacy of enclosure by the proponents of agricultural improvement. The first response, paternal nostalgia, has a strong affiliation with the rights-based model of land tenure. One cannot identify it too readily with any particular class or time; a paternalist rhetoric fires an important body of resistance to enclosure among tenants, some landlords, clergy and nobles from at least as early as the fifteenth century to the nineteenth century. Indeed, as Raymond Williams demonstrates in the introduction to *The Country and the City*, where he traces agrarian nostalgia for a golden age ever further backward, there is a sense in which the phenomenon is psychological as well as historical.[9] Frequently, these nostalgic and paternalist writers present their critiques as petitions to an idealized monarch who will set all to rights when made aware of abuses. Reminding their sovereign that feudal tenants' rights also implied feudal obligations, they tie social welfare to national defence. Enclosure, says an anonymous petition of the 1550s to the King's Council and the Lords of Parliament, and the conversion of arable to pasture will weaken the nation, since "shepherds be but ill archers."[10]

The paternalist critique continued throughout the seventeenth century. In *Depopulation Arraigned* (1636), Robert Powell does sanction certain sorts of enclosure, but he condemns depopulation (using the generative language that pervades these debates) as "the strangling or choking of the womb" of the commonwealth.[11] He develops a thoroughly past-centred and traditional concept of a stable economy, in which economic transformation and progress are not even possibilities. After presenting the arguments of his opponents that they may buy as much land as they can and do with it what they will (43), he responds with conservative communitarianism: "Where every man is for himself, *non deus, sed diabolus*, the Devil is for all"(46). He laments the conversion of arable to pasture and the accompanying depopulations, saying that "where hospitable farms, and plentiful fields of corn have been, nothing remains but a champant wilderness for sheep, with a cote, a pastoral boy, his dog, and crook and a pipe" (54–5). Such enclosure will also inevitably lead to idleness and a decay of rents and tithes (32). Depopulating enclosers are tyrannical Nimrods (76), the opposite of benevolent King Charles. Powell concludes with a strong paternalist plea that the King heed earlier examples of paternalist anti-depopulating legislation: "The King shall cover us under the wings of his royal and religious protection, and we shall render to him the dues of our faith and obedience" (118).

We can easily deconstruct this critique of rural decay as a self-deluded yearning for metaphysical presence, or psychoanalyse it as a misremembered recollection of childhood. But, as Williams shows, such fictions conceptualized real social transformations and helped rural people resist real economic and physical violence (12). Furthermore, this paternalist rhetoric frequently found a paternalist response in a series of royal commissions investigating anti-enclosure riots (in 1517 and 1607), and in a series of royal proclamations from the time of Henry VII onwards designed to limit the decay of habitations and the sufferings of rural populations: the Act against Pulling Down of Towns (1489), the Act for the Maintenance of Husbandry and Tillage (1597–98), the Statute of Artificers (1563), the Statute on Cottages (1589), and the Book of Orders (1630–31).

Still social historians as well as Freudians know that *pater*'s helping hand readily clenches into a fist, and here it is important to distinguish between paternalists of different classes: whereas plebian agriculturalists and rural artisans strive primarily to protect their traditional rights to commons, forests, etc., the rural gentry and other non-labouring paternalists work primarily to preserve social order. When the latter attempt to maintain a traditional economy, they easily resort to violence if their efforts are disobeyed or frustrated. We can see this sort of paternalism in the Tudor statutes against vagrancy alongside the statutes against depopulations and the decay of houses.[12]

Indeed, these two paternalisms can come together in a single work, such as the remarkable sermon preached by Robert Wilkinson at Northampton in 1607 in response to the Midlands corn insurrections.[13] Examining Christ's saying, "Men shall not live by bread only," Wilkinson remarks that "two things may be distinctly considered: first, that man liveth by bread, and then secondly that he liveth not by bread alone" (C2r). Noting Satan's temptation to Christ to turn stones into bread, he accuses depopulating enclosures of turning bread into stones (C4r), and he moves on to assume a voice of moving existential sympathy with the poor: "For the belly saith bread must be had, and the soul subscribeth that bread must be had too; and though reason may persuade and authority command, and preachers may exhort with obedience and patience to sustain the want of bread, yet for all that, *venter non habet aures*, in case of extreme hunger men will not be persuaded, but they will have bread" (D3r).

Yet, directly after this first part of the sermon, the writer argues that the corn rioters did wrong, and they should have waited for God to work a miracle (E3v). Preaching to the *aures* of the *venter*, he warns, "Therefore, consider and see I beseech you, whence arise conspiracies, riots, and damnable rebellions; not from want of bread, but through want of faith, yea want of bread doth come by want of faith" (E3r–E4v). At times, in fact, God actually wills the hungry to starve, and they should accept this quietly (E4v). The rioters impiously attempted to turn thrown stones into bread. They failed to "look up to heaven from whence you shall have bread" (E4v). They came forth "like Adam's sons . . . with shovels and spades," then turned into "Tubal-Kain's sons, armed with swords and weapons of iron" (F3v). Most damning of all, they introduced division into the happy paternal harmony of the newly united kingdoms: "Was this a time of all times to disturb the peace of the land; now that king and state were so earnest in hand to unite two kingdoms into one, now to attempt the rending of one kingdom into two?" (F4v). The demands of political order take priority over the unhappy necessity of economic hardship. He concludes by drawing potential rioters' attention to the lesson of previous rioters, hanging from the gallows (F4r). The radical and seemingly unselfconscious contradiction between the two parts of this sermon dramatizes a fundamental weakness in the conservative paternalist case: since it has no way of rationally conceptualizing economic crisis and conflict, no way of envisioning economic crisis save as a moral failing, it can respond with nothing but horror and the gallows.

The second attitude towards enclosure, instrumental improvement, allies itself strongly with the property-based model of land tenure. It sees the early modern countryside and the populations inhabiting it as raw materials subject to pure instrumental reason. This ideology of economic rationalization appears among sixteenth-century improvers, but it comes into its own more in the seventeenth century, when agricultural improvers accelerated their efforts to enclose wastes and put an end to the customary use of them by poor commoners. After distributing plots to the richer sort to compensate them for their lost common privileges, the poor might be maintained by a stock set aside for charity administered by local authorities. The poor commoner exchanges the relative independence of an income supplemented by access to the common and wastes, for the relative dependence of parish charity.[14]

These improvers might best be grouped with early modern utopists, such as More's fictional Raphael Hythloday, Vasco de Quiroga (who tried out More's principles in New Spain), John Eliot, William Petty and James Harrington. All search for the geographic *tabula rasa* of a waste land, a common, or a conquered territory (such as Ireland or North America) that can be surveyed, divided, improved with instrumental reason, and turned into a productive new polity. Similarly, they search for the human raw material of a displaced population (vagrants, the people of Interregnum England, conquered Indians) which can be settled on the land according to a rational and anti-customary new scheme.[15] This sort of instrumental rationality finds its geographical ideal not in a landscape defined by pre-existent customary rights, but in a formless (chaotic or passive) object of rational domination. The anonymous author of *A Consideration of the Cause in Question before the Lords Touching Depopulations* (1607) calls the commons "the nurseries of beggars," a frequent image.[16] "E.G.," the author of *Waste Land's Improvement* (1653), draws an absolute distinction between orderly enclosures and the "wild howling wildernesses" and "deformed chaos" of the wastes. By surveying and dividing them, Parliament will provide work for the poor and keep them from idleness, poverty and crime.[17] And "Pseudonimous," author of a pro-enclosure pamphlet entitled *A Vindication of the Considerations Concerning Common Fields* (1656), preaches that "God is the god of order, and order is the soul of things, the life of a commonwealth; but common fields are the seat of disorder, the seed plot of contention, the nursery of beggary."[18]

These writings typically argue that the only alternative to a society organized to benefit the political and economic interests of a particular ruling class is sheer, primal, chaotic disorder – that the commons are an unmarked *prima materia* that breeds up a population of idle rogues, rather than a space rich in traditions and marked by multiple uses and rights. The most viciously instrumental metaphor of all among the improving instrumentalists is that which compares displaced agricultural tenants to agricultural stock. In his promotional tract of 1609 entitled *A Good Speed to Virginia*, Robert Gray compares a canny prince burdened with an excessive population to a good husbandman; when the latter finds that his grounds "are overcharged with cattle, he removes them from one ground to another, and so he provideth well both for his cattle and for his grounds."[19] This is a particularly tortuous and vicious simile. One of the prime causes of rural distress was the overstocking of common land by wealthy landlords, which thus produced a "surplus" of people trying to support themselves on the commons; the sheep turn the impoverished tenants into human sheep, who are to be encouraged (or ordered) to graze elsewhere. One sort of superfluous commoner (displaced English tenants) will be used to displace another (Native American pastoral agriculturalists). This is the carcinogenic logic of enclosure.

When criticizing this opposition of order and disorder, we can usefully move beyond the deconstructive critique of primitivism (which might simply note the recurrent Western binary of *techne* and *physis*), to a key insight formulated by Adorno and Horkheimer: the encounter between "culture" and "nature" is – not occasionally or incidentally, but always and essentially – a displaced version of an encounter between dominant culture and subordinate culture.[20] Outside of Antarctica and some alpine regions, there are no wildernesses.

American historians of ideas are still too fond of concepts such as "frontier," "wilderness," and "expansion"; any account of American history resting on them is a self-deluded recoding of the genocidal origins of the American nation. Similarly, British historians follow their seventeenth-century utopian forebears in juxtaposing "order" and "disorder," as if conflicts between two social groups could be explained as a conflict between form and matter.[21] "Nature" is always already worked over in some measure by an indigenous human population. Ideologists of dominant culture designate some area as "wilderness" as either a prelude or an epilogue to the eviction and murder of its inhabitants.

At a few striking moments, even the improving instrumentalists acknowledge the ideological quality of the opposition between order and disorder, civility and nature. "E.G.", for example, simultaneously denies and admits the present-day usage of "waste" lands. Parliament should maintain control of the lands it has seized, not sell them, since "in letting there might be such consideration had, and such allowances made unto the said persons, as might be proportionable and answerable unto their right and interest, and would give them full (yea, better) satisfaction than their lying waste (notwithstanding their common benefit) as they now do." The reason for this – he observes in a sprightly *jeu d'esprit* – is that the commoners would rather pay substantial rents for enclosed and "improved" land than "enjoy the present privilege and immunity of commoners upon the said land."[22] Surely we need to move beyond formal literary pastoral when discussing the mythopoeic power of the seventeenth-century topographical imagination.

The ideology of improvement prevailed over paternalism for a number of reasons. To begin with, its techniques – engrossment, enclosure, decay of dwellings, etc. – tend to be one-way processes. Despite legislative attempts to restore arable land and dwellings, such regressions were infrequent and short-lived. Second, utopian improvers could adopt a religious rhetoric of their own – though one anchored more in the prophetic books than in the gospels. They were generally better attuned to the "progressive" and millennial advancement of learning much beloved by Puritan intellectuals in the seventeenth century.[23] Utopian improvement also adapted itself more readily to the imperial conquests and transformations of the "dark corners of the land" in Ireland, Celtic Britain and the New World.[24] Finally, utopian improvers were able to assimilate effectively the powerful social rhetoric of the conservative paternalists, with whom they shared an overriding concern for social order. Indeed, as Buchanan Sharp notes, the critique of socially-produced vagrancy, one of the prime arguments against enclosure in the sixteenth century, became one of the prime arguments for it in the seventeenth, when proponents of enclosure proposed to limit vagrancy by enclosing common land and setting up regular charity stocks with the rents derived from them.[25]

For example, in *The English Improver Improved* (1652), William Blithe sees the cure for rural suffering not in the imagined past of the nostalgic paternalists, not in some revolutionary future, but in a technologically-improved version of his own hierarchical England.[26] On the one hand, the body of Blithe's book promises a revolution in agricultural technology through improved implements, planting techniques, procedures for draining and enriching soils, for transforming waste lands into arable, etc. On the other hand, the book's introductory matter presents the English class structure as an immutable given – a second nature less transformable than the first. Blithe addresses a separate epistle to each appropriate class, "to each a portion as I conceived most suitable to work their spirits into a flexibleness of practice and acceptance," with one epistle to Cromwell and the Council of State, and others to the "industrious reader" (presumably the wealthy landowner looking for a higher rate of return on his land), the nobles and gentry, the army, the "husbandman, farmer, or tenant." Finally, he addresses "the cottager, labourer, or meanest commoner," counselling him to remain quiescent in the face of expropriation and the temporary hardships wrought by a programme of improvement.

Interestingly enough, Blithe's primary antagonists in this work are not the paternalists (whose cause seems to be fading by mid-century), but the Diggers – specifically Winstanley's commune in Surrey, long since rooted out:

> I am neither of the Diggers' mind, nor shall I imitate their practice, for though the poor are or ought to have advantage upon the commons, yet I question whether they as a society gathered together from all parts of the nation could claim a right to any particular common: and for their practice, if there be not thousands of places more capable of improvement than theirs, and that by many easier ways, and to far greater advantage, I will lay down the bucklers.

He goes on to attack their social communism, which he says will ultimately fail, "unless they bring us to the New Jerusalem, or bring it down to us."[27]

But the Diggers' New Jerusalem need not be brought down from above. In *The Law of Freedom*, Winstanley prophesies the agrarian birth of "commonwealth government" which, like Milton's tawny lion, will "arise from under the clods, under which as yet it is buried, and covered with deformity" (533). The Diggers' revolutionary project is precisely a mundane one that envisions commoners as a national class, not a local group; brings them together in a non-hierarchical agrarian communal praxis, not imposed wage labour; and encourages them to create themselves anew, not remain the passive object of instrumental reason. Blithe's anti-communist calumny attempts to divert attention from the perpetually deferred and exponentially more fantastic capitalist dream of a world improved for all persons and all classes by technical means alone. In his epistle to the "cottager, labourer, or meanest commoner," Blithe protests that he is not out to level all classes and achieve social parity like the Diggers, but only "to make the poor rich, and the rich richer." This is the capitalist New Jerusalem, which always glimmers just beyond that pile of groaning rags; its prophets still walk the earth.

IV

The Diggers propose a progressive and dialectical response to the misery and dislocation born of enclosure: not the paternalists' mythical past, not the improvers' enriched version of present-day social relations, but a revolutionary transformation of those relations and creation of a genuinely distinct future. In this section, I will contrast the Diggers with the paternalists, dealing first with space (the relation between the local community and the nation), then with time (the role of historical nostalgia); in the next section, I will turn to the Diggers' engagement with the improvers.

The revisionist champions of local history have produced a renaissance of conservative paternalism; the great progenitor here might well be Peter Laslett's *The World We Have Lost*, with its portrait of early modern England as a one-class society. Historians such as Alan Everitt have followed, setting the local against the national, by saying that the English Revolution did not really trouble the stolid *gemeinschaft* of the county communities. The revisionists "see local society as basically settled and harmonious, with vertical links binding together the different social groupings and a general acceptance of the authority and leadership of the gentry."[28] In this argument, the counties become the rooty rural site of proto-Burkean customary resistance to the deracinated proto-Jacobin ideologies of the urban centre. Fletcher and Stevenson define plebeian consciousness by a certain plucky resilience – certainly not by any rational reflection on matters of national importance. As a result, plebeians become almost plantlike, "rooted in the sense of belonging to a local environment." So far as the rural lower classes have an ideology at all, it is an unreflective one defined almost entirely by local traditions, rituals, festivities, rural sports, etc. For instance, "Music, the most accessible, public and democratic of the arts, lifted men's spirits at work and play" (10); Americans familiar with paternalist reconstructions of slave culture may hear a disturbing echo, with banjo obbligato.

Neo-paternalist theory relies heavily on the concept of deference – that hoary but hardy civil offshoot of the Great Chain of Being. Fletcher and Stevenson observe that "The traditional concept of order was suited to a localised society in which hierarchy, together with obligation to those below and deference to those above, made sense of people's lives" (2–3). It seems to me an inadequate updating of this idea to say, as Fletcher and Stevenson do, that it is under attack and modification in the early modern period. Such a modification underestimates the explicit rejections of deference in the pre-modern and early modern world (witness the Lollards, the Anabaptists of Meunster and the Marian martyrs) and the pervasiveness of deferential behaviour in the modern world (witness human behaviour in any "rational" bureaucracy – a corporation, say, or a university). Too often, we simply assume deferential plebeian consciousness or derive it automatically from deferential actions. However much we may agree that deference is an important mode of organizing seventeenth-century social life, it is perhaps less an instinctive, universally-experienced and never-conceptualized *mentalité* than a site for uneasy compromise, unrest and even open contestation. We might reasonably apply to illiterate plebeian culture the same scepticism we apply to elite literate patronage culture, in which deferential public statements coexist with resentful and satiric statements made via the privacy of a diary, the retrospective insulation of a memoir, or the protective alias afforded by poetry and drama.

And the Diggers show that the theory of a plebeian critique of deference need not be altogether speculative. Their pamphlets are the signal seventeenth-century instance of local plebeian experience forming the basis for a theory of national political life, and a programme for changing it. In *A Mite Cast into the Common Treasury*, Robert Coster inverts the idyllic but ideologically partial view of manorial life with a tenant's-eye view of patriarchal ritual:

> If the Lords of Manors, and other gentlemen who covet after so much land, could not let it out by parcels, but must be constrained to keep it in their own hands, then would they want those great bags of money (which do maintain pride, idleness, and fulness of bread), which are carried unto them by their tenants, who go in as

slavish a posture as may be; namely, with cap in hand and bended knee, crouching and creeping from corner to corner, while his Lord (rather tyrant) walks up and down the room with his proud looks, and with great swelling words questions him about his holding. If the lords of manors, and other gentlemen, had not those great bags of money brought before them, then down would fall the lordliness of their spirits, and then poor men might speak to them; then there might be an acknowledging of one another to be fellow creatures. (657)

Here we see not a desire for continued patriarchal charity, but the Digger programme for abolishing the landlord/tenant distinction through a programme of labour withdrawal. We also see the destruction of a deferential verbal economy which moves us from one-sided domineering questioning, towards reciprocal speech between "fellow creatures" (a favourite Ranter phrase). This dialogue itself seems to be the first sign of a classless society – a revolutionary transformation quite distinct from carnivalesque inversion, which preserves the categories of ruler and ruled. If the typical mode of the courtly lyric is a deferential indirect address to patron, then the typical mode of the Digger pamphlet is the behatted, face-to-face address from one fellow creature to another.

The anonymous author of *Light Shining in Buckinghamshire* (a Digger or near-Digger pamphlet published by December 1648, before Charles's execution) insists on bringing an anti-deferential attitude home from court: in addition to kings as such, he attacks what he calls "petty kings" (earls, dukes, marquesses, viscounts), "vice kings" (deputies and mayors), kings of patents and, most hated of all, "hedge kings, viz. those called lords of the manors, those fellows that can keep a court-leet, and enslave all within their territory" (636). He presents us with a more hard-edged satire of the deferential universe, calling tenantry another name for slavery, and attacking "the chief encloser, called the Lord of the Manor, or some wretch as cruel as he," for enclosing the land and forbidding rights to timber, common lands, game and fish. His railing satire of a civic processional shows the Diggers' capacity to distance themselves from the rituals of public order: the processional begins with a "Major" followed by "a Just-ass of Peace and Coram" and

twelve Aldermen following after in their Cunnie skin gowns, as so many fools in a midsummer ale, and those petty-tyrants shall domineer over the inhabitants by virtue of their patent, and enclose all, letting and setting of the poor's lands too, and moneys, stocks of moneys to their own use . . . so that you see all tyranny shelters itself under the king's wings: is it not time then to throw down the king, and bring his person to his answer: these patents and charters is the main wheel and prop that upholds the king's tyranny. (620)

He also says that the head tyrant (the king) tyrannizes over his sub-tyrants like "the subtle nasty fox with his dirty tail" – transferring a favourite Reformation image (cf. Duessa in *Faerie Queene* 1.12) to a primarily political and economic context. He continues:

> And because the Lord Keeper, Privy Seal, and Treasurers long tails should not daggle in the dirt, they must have each another sycophant slave apiece to carry up for them with their hats off doing homage to their breech. Oh height of all baseness! Why, oh, his majesty's breath of honour it may be blows out there, and therefore he holds up his gown that it might blow him that holds it up, and makes him be called Sir. (618)

This satire is not, I think, a Rabelaisian/Bakhtinian carnivalesque celebration of the body's lower functions, nor even a trace of psychoanalytic spore in a seventeenth-century context, but an exercise in excremental levelling.

The revisionist appeal to social life structured by status groups and deference attempts to replace a rival explanation of social life focusing on social classes and conflict, including class struggle. In *The Politics of Landscape*, James Turner says that fears of class war grew through the 1630s and 1640s, and that "both sides saw the conflict as economic, and recognized that status depended on the means of producing wealth."[29] The local gentry fear the Diggers precisely because they attempt to connect the localities and the nation by publishing epistles to the army, Parliament, London, other disaffected tenants; forming correspondence societies of a sort linking the scattered Digger communes; and developing a revolutionary programme for transforming the nation. The spectre of this new sort of collectivity emerging from the localities – a beast with many heads but one mind – may explain the seemingly disproportionate anxiety of the Council of State, which at least twice ordered General Thomas Fairfax to disperse the Diggers. John Bradshaw, regicide and President of the Council, wrote to Fairfax in April 1649, directing him to take a troop of horse and disperse "that tumultuous sort of people assembling themselves together not far from Oatlands, at a place called St George's Hill; and although the pretence of their being there by them avowed may seem very ridiculous, yet that conflux of people may be a beginning whence things of a greater and more dangerous consequence may grow, to the disturbing of the peace and quiet of the Commonwealth."[30]

The Diggers substitute the deracinating power of natural law theory for place-bound paternalism. Like the paternalists, they attack the depredations of present-day enclosures with an explicitly moralistic rhetoric, but they resist characterizing them as a decline from some golden age that can be restored by a conservative religion and politics. Rather, the Diggers' analysis of economic enclosure becomes the model for a full-scale critical theory of society, and the beginning of a utopian social programme. Digger history conjures up no mythically virtuous reign of a Protestant godly prince (whether Oliver, young Charles, Prince Henry, Elizabeth, or King Edward), no ancient constitution preserving Saxon liberties, no medieval era of idyllic housekeeping before the onslaught of the flocks. Winstanley even avoids the almost instinctive Protestant description of an early Christian era of religious purity sullied by antichristian Romish innovation. Despite some predictable sympathy for the apostolic communism of the first Christian community described in the Book of Acts (184), he seems not to be terribly interested in the history of the early Church, or in denouncing the doctrinal lapses of the various Roman and Anglican Antichrists.

True, Winstanley's pamphlets are populated by villainous "Norman" freeholders, gentry and even toll-takers (506). But his anti-Normanism never becomes philo-Saxonism.[31] In his *Appeal to the House of Commons*, he undercuts any image of a pre-Norman paradise when he says that William the Conqueror "took the land from the English, both the enclosures from the gentry, and the commons and waste lands from the common people, and gave our land to his Norman Soldiers" (304). In *A Letter to the Lord Fairfax*, he makes the same claim. The Norman conqueror

> took freedom from every one, and became the disposer of both enclosures and commons . . . When the enemy conquered England, he took the land for his own, and called that his freedom; even so, seeing all sorts of people have given assistance to recover England from under the Norman Yoke, surely all sorts, both gentry in their inclosures, commonality in their commons, ought to have their freedom, not compelling one to work for wages for another. (287)

In this strategically confused account of the Norman Yoke, Winstanley shifts the definition of freedom from a national and political to an economic base. He begins with an admission that pre-Norman England included both commons and enclosures, and that the enemy established his "freedom" or political power by redistributing these lands. Winstanley's solution – restoring to all classes the freedom to do what they will with their rightful property – seems at first quite accommodating to the gentry. But then, in the last phrase, we find that freedom must be economic as well as political: since (as we will see) Winstanley feels that enclosures cannot exist without wage labour, then limits on those social forces that compel wage labour will destroy the enclosures and, by extension, the gentry. Winstanley attacks the Saxon as well as the Norman Yoke, proposing to "restore" a gentry-free egalitarian state that never existed before.

In other words, Winstanley moves from a historical rhetoric to a natural rights rhetoric, following a path taken by many mid-century radicals, including Henry Marten and many Levellers. Winstanley's only true utopia is the unalienated communal life which *The New Law* locates variously in Eden, where "the whole creation lived in man, and man lived in his maker, the spirit of righteousness and peace, for every creature walked evenly with man, and delighted in man" (155), or during the reign of Christ, when "there was a sweet community of love between all members of that humane body"(204). But Winstanley spends relatively little time locating this state in history or elaborating on its historical specificity. In *The New Law*, he even constructs a half-attack on the historicity of Adam (176) and of Christ, warning against the "Fleshly wisdom and learning" that "teaches you to look altogether upon a history without you, of things that were done 6000 years ago, and of things that were done 1649 years ago" (212). With a stretch, we could read this as orthodox Christianity insisting on bringing Scripture lessons home in the present, but when we combine his argument here with his recurrent attack on the idea of a physical hell and heaven (219), we see him pushing away from a theory of positive law and biblical history towards a theory of natural law and utopia.

Winstanley's local critique of enclosure allows him to break down a periodized account of human history and remove its power to tyrannize the present. Communal agricultural labour is by no means a consequence of the Fall, as Winstanley insists with georgic fundamentalism. Quoting God's prelapsarian exordium in Genesis I to subdue the earth, he comments, "And this implies ploughing, digging, and all kinds of manuring. So then observe. That bare and simple working in the earth, according to the freedom of the Creation, though it be the sweat of men's brows, is not the curse" (423). Similarly, enclosure and the tenant/landlord relation are not the punitive consequence of the Fall, but the Fall itself: "But when mankind began to quarrel about the earth; and some would have all, and shut out others, forcing them to be servants; this was man's fall, it is the ruling of the curse, and it

is the cause of all divisions, wars, and pluckings up" (424). Enclosure
continues throughout history. The author of *Light Shining* says that
Nimrod, that archetypal political despot, and his successors strove to
see who could be "the greatest encloser and tyrant" (628–9). In *The
Law of Freedom*, Winstanley uses enclosure to link religious history and
politics when he identifies the traditional law of kings with "the soldier,
who cut Christ's garment into pieces, which was to have remained uncut
and without seam; this law moves the people to fight one against another
for those pieces, viz., for the several enclosures of the earth, who shall
possess the earth, and who shall be the ruler over others" (589). In *Fire
in the Bush*, Winstanley calls the Calvinist gathered churches religious
enclosures: "For all your particular churches are like the enclosures of
land which hedges in some to be the heirs of life, and hedges out
others; one saying Christ is here with them; another saying no: but
he is there with them" (445–6). Indeed, given the foundation of
the state Church in a system of tithing, this is something more than
an analogy. The kingdom of heaven itself will consist of communal
agriculture without enclosure. Winstanley adapts Matthew 22:30, which
depicts a heaven where the saints "neither marry, nor are given in
marriage, but are as the angels of God in heaven," to a programme
for agrarian revolution: "But in the time of Israel's restoration, now
beginning, when the king of righteousness himself shall be governor
in every man; none then shall work for hire, neither shall any give
hire, but every one shall work in love, one with, and for another; and
eat bread together, as being members of one household" (190–1). In
place of this ascetic heaven of Scripture and the enclosed gardens of
aristocratic *otium*, Winstanley envisions a paradise of communal love
and labour.

V

In *The Great Instauration*, Charles Webster links Winstanley to the
seventeenth-century Puritan Enlightenment that combined the Baconian
advancement of learning and millenarian theories of progress (367–8).
But the majority of Bacon's followers work according to what I
have called the instrumental ideology of utopian improvement. Their
programmes and proposals reveal the disquietingly authoritarian tendency of Baconian reason to turn its geographical and human objects
of inquiry into pure objects of spatial and political domination. The
proponents of improvement characteristically present their schemes
as the encounter of an eschatologically-tinged absolute reason with a
neutral or recalcitrant subject matter – waste land, commons, fens,

forests, the New World. This encounter is always also a masked attempt to dominate the human populations supporting and creating themselves through the rational use of these lands. Bacon's own writings, particularly his technological utopia, *The New Atlantis*, conjure up a dream of universal "improvement," which will allow those possessed of the new science to assume a godlike relation to nature and human nature. In Bacon, at least, and his improving descendants, we see stark examples of the will-to-power that Adorno and Horkheimer see at the heart of all Western enlightenment: "What men want to learn from nature is how to use it in order wholly to dominate it and other men" (4).

Like many of the utopian improvers, Winstanley is an agrarian millennialist. As early as *The New Law*, he suggests that the communal cultivation of the soil will lift the Adamic curse and make the earth more fruitful (153, 199). And in *The Law of Freedom*, he sets out a programme of scientific inquiry that is not worlds away from the one pursued by the projectors in Bacon's Salomon's House. Winstanley's utopians will attend public speeches "of all arts and sciences, some one day, some another; as in physic, chirurgery, astrology, astronomy, navigation, husbandry, and such like" (563). Yet Winstanley's writings lack the technocratic spirit that pervades Bacon's. He pursues what we might call a "Green Millennialism" – a pantheistic materialism that denies any radical distinction between spirit and matter, between God, humans and nature. Just as Winstanley rejects the paternalist critique of enclosure for a radical and egalitarian theory founded in natural law, so he rejects the instrumental ideology of utopian improvement for a humanized programme of collective self-fashioning through agrarian praxis.

Winstanley's corporate ideal distinguishes itself by its egalitarianism, its emphasis on common preservation rather than oppressive order, and its basis in an agrarian praxis simultaneously sensuous and rational. We see Winstanley's egalitarian impulse even when he employs some of the older corporate metaphors, as when he tells the city of London that "whole mankind was made equal, and knit into one body by one spirit of love, which is Christ in you, the hope of glory, even as all members of man's body, called the little world, are united into equality of love, to preserve the whole body" (323). Winstanley pushes the medieval corporate metaphor in an egalitarian direction by emphasizing the connectedness rather than the hierarchical differentiation of the parts, and by omitting the traditional head.

Winstanley's corporate ideal stresses common preservation over the various order-based ideals favoured by dominant culture, such as the

hierarchical body politic, the episcopal church, the single-minded body
of the disciplined army, the separated community of the visible saints.
Even in his pre-communist pamphlet, *Truth Lifting Up Its Head*,
Winstanley formulates a monist metaphysics of corporate preservation:
"The spirit of the father is pure reason: which as he made, so he knits
the whole creation together into a oneness of life and moderation;
every creature sweetly in love lending their hands to preserve each
other, and so upholds the whole fabric" (108). In *The New Law*,
he extends this into a theory of subjectivity, whereby "all the glory
and content that man takes in other creatures of the earth, it is but
a rejoicing in himself" (169). The new heaven and new earth will
exist when "a man shall be made to see Christ in other creatures,
as well as in himself, every one rejoicing each in other, and all
rejoicing in their king" (170). In *The Law of Freedom*, Winstanley
contrasts the original impulse to "common preservation," which is "a
principle in every one to seek the good of others, as himself, without
respecting persons," with "self preservation," which has no regard for
"the peace, freedom, and preservation of the weak and foolish among
brethren" (537). This emphasis extends even to Winstanley's theory
of sexuality. In *A Vindication*, he criticizes the Ranters not for their
sinful disorderliness, but for practising a predatory love that creates
bondage instead of "the universal love," which "seeks the preservation
of others as of one self" (401); consistently enough, he concludes this
critique by warning, "Let none go about to suppress that ranting power
by their punishing hand" (402). Winstanley's rationale for the sabbath
derives not from the conservative Puritan ideal of order, but from
an egalitarian combination of bodily rest, rational inquiry (it will
be an occasion not for preaching but for public lectures on natural
and moral philosophy) and communitarian fellowship: "the people
in such a parish may generally meet together to see one another's
faces, and beget or preserve fellowship in friendly love" (562–3).
In focusing on this collective quality of human being, Winstanley's
corporate ideal resembles more than anything else the republican
theory of the *vivere civile*, of which he seems to have had almost no
knowledge.

But what truly distinguishes Winstanley's corporate ideal, even from
republicanism, is that he bases it in the agrarian labour which was itself
the actual foundation of the British economy, thus moving away from
those various repressive corporate ideals which instrumentalize this
labour and degrade those who practise it. In *The Agrarian History of
England and Wales*, Joan Thirsk comments, "After enclosure, when
every man could fence his own piece of territory and warn his neighbors

off, the discipline of sharing things fairly with one's neighbors was relaxed, and every household became an island unto itself." She wonders why the opponents of enclosure never availed themselves of their most forceful argument: that enclosure and strict property rights would destroy the vigorous, communal, and co-operative spirit preserved in the practice of traditional agriculture in small holdings and common fields.[32] But Winstanley derives his utopian programme from precisely this experience of communal agricultural praxis, and of hunger when it is hampered. In *Truth Lifting Up Its Head*, Winstanley imagines the question, "What is prayer?" and answers, "Till the ground according to reason" (136–7). In *The Law of Freedom*, he praises labour not only because it supports the commonwealth and tames pride, but because "it is for the health of their bodies, it is a pleasure to the mind, to be free in labours one with another" (593). Again and again, dominant culture characterizes radical culture as a vengeful inversion: tenants wish to turn the tables and make their lords labour for them. Winstanley, on the other hand, points towards a new system based in humane collective agrarian praxis. In Sartre's terms, the fused group of agrarian labourers becomes the model for the fused group of the commonwealth, which will help stabilize the heretofore only serial group of the anti-monarchists.

Creator and creature merge easily in *The Law of Freedom* – not just through the incarnation, or through moments of special grace, or in the New Jerusalem, but in the present: "For if the creation in all its dimensions be the fullness of him, that fills all with himself, and if you yourself be part of this creation, where can you find God but in that line or station wherein you stand?" The attempt "to reach God beyond the Creation, or to know what he will be to a man, after the man is dead, if any otherwise, then to scatter him into his essences of fire, water, earth and air, of which he is compounded, is a knowledge beyond the line, or capacity of man to attain to while he lives in his compounded body." Anyone attempting such an inquiry "doth as the proverb saith, build castles in the air, or tells us of a world beyond the Moon, and beyond the Sun, merely to blind the reason of man" (565). The Diggers no longer lay claim to a God beyond the Creation, and so lose the Baconian claim to a godlike power over neutral physical or human nature.

As Sabine suggests, Winstanley adopts "Reason" as a synonym for God "because the latter suggests a being apart from nature and from man" (40). The nature of reason, Winstanley says in *Truth Lifting Up Its Head*, is "not to preserve a part, but the whole creation" (105). In *The New Law*, Winstanley's very syntax fuses God and human:

> As it is said, that the king of righteousness takes delight in nothing, but what is within himself, and what proceeds out of himself: so the heaven of an enlivened heart is not a local place of glory at a distance from him, but the seeing and feeling the Father within, dwelling and ruling there; and to behold the glory of that power proceeding forth of himself, to which he is made subject, through which he walks righteously in the Creation, and in which he rests in peace. (217)

The first sentence presents God as container and thing contained; the second sentence likewise presents the heart as the container of heaven and God, and as ruled by them. And the last long prepositional phrase is strategically confused – presumably the "beholder" is a human, who is "made subject" to a power. But like God in the first sentence, he sees that power "proceeding forth of himself," and he "walks righteously in the Creation" as the God of Genesis walks in the Garden. The effect of this passage is like the effect of Winstanley's prose more generally: its half-parallelisms and confusions lie halfway between mere syntactic awkwardness and an effort to break down the relations of domination and hierarchy in received theology.

Similarly, the Diggers' earth is never a neutral raw material, but a living substance marked by and interwoven with divinity and human praxis. Whereas the utopian improvers personify the common as a bad mother, the "nursery of beggars," Winstanley describes the ideal common earth in *The True Levellers Standard* as a good mother "that brought us all forth: that as a true mother, loves all her children. Therefore do not thou hinder the mother earth, from giving all her children suck, by thy enclosing it into particular hands" (265). In *Truth Lifting Up Its Head*, Winstanley presents an evocative and metaphoric version of this agrarian monism. Much of the pamphlet is a dialogue between a relatively orthodox questioner and a Winstanleyesque respondent. Attempting to hold Winstanley to Nicene fundamentals and a rigorous distinction between earth and heaven, body and spirit, the questioner asks whether Christ died and ascended into heaven. Winstanley responds that he descended into the earth and stayed there – as a sort of divine manure: "Now the body of Christ is where the Father is, in the earth, purifying the earth; and his spirit is entered into the whole creation, which is the heavenly glory, where the Father dwells; which is a glory above the flesh" (112–13).

Winstanley's monistic metaphysics turns into a rational physiocratic sociology when he begins discussing the motivation for social conflict. In *A New-Yeers Gift* he says that "All this falling out or quarrelling among mankind, is about the earth who shall, and who shall not enjoy it" (380). He develops this idea most fully in *The Law of Freedom*. At the beginning of the first chapter, he acknowledges rival definitions of freedom: freedom of trade (which is only "freedom under the will of a conqueror"), freedom of religion (but this is "an unsettled freedom"), the Ranters' sexual freedom (which is "the freedom of wanton unreasonable beasts"), and the freedom of the elder brother to be a landlord of all the earth (which is "but a half freedom, and begets murmurings, wars, and quarrels"). True freedom, he says,

> lies where a man receives his nourishment and preservation, and that is in the use of the earth. . . . Do not the ministers preach for maintenance in the Earth? the lawyers plead causes to get the possessions of the earth? Doth not the Soldier fight for the Earth? And doth not the landlord require rent, that he may live in the fullness of the earth by the labour of his tenants? And so, from the thief upon the highway to the king who sits upon the throne, do not every one strive, either by force of arms, or secret cheats, to get the possessions of the earth from one another, because they see their freedom lies in plenty, and their bondage lies in poverty? (519, 520)

Later in that work, an imagined "zealous, but ignorant professor" objects that Winstanley's focus on the things of the earth is a "low and carnal ministry indeed, this leads men to know nothing, but the knowledge of the earth, and the secrets of nature, but we are to look after spiritual and heavenly things." Winstanley responds with a materialist catechism, asking again if all zealous professors, as well as ministers, soldiers and lawyers, do not struggle to enjoy the earth, concluding, "Why do you heap up riches, why do you eat and drink, and wear clothes? Why do you take a woman, and lie with her to beget children? Are not all these carnal and low things of the Earth? and do you not live in them, and covet them as much as any? nay more than many which you call men of the world?" (555–6). The tone here is important, I think – partly a traditional Christian condemnation of hypocrisy, but partly an almost Ranterish attempt to seduce his readers into acknowledging and embracing the carnal desires underlying their spiritual pretension.

The first thing that may strike us about the Diggers' characterization of the English poor is its similarity in tone to the moral polemics of the paternalists – the poor are victims of an inhuman process of enclosure. None the less, the solution he offers brings him surprisingly close to the instrumental improvers. Rather than proposing that displaced tenants be resettled on the land in paternalist fashion, he proposes to accelerate the process of depopulation through a programme of voluntary labour withdrawal. In *The New Law*, directly after the voice in his trance tells him to "Work together. Eat bread together; declare this all abroad," it goes on to give him some more practical advice for accomplishing this: "'Whosoever it is that labours in the earth, for any person or persons, that lifts up themselves as lord and rulers over others, and that doth not look upon themselves equal to others in the creation, the hand of the Lord shall be upon that labourer: I the Lord have spoke it and I will do it'; Declare this all abroad" (190). A bit later, he elaborates, saying that anyone who lays sole claim to any piece of land, "let such an one labour that parcel of land by his own hands, none helping him" (195). This programme is modest in the short term, but revolutionary in the long. It differs markedly from the deferential patience that simply waits on God's will, which is a ruse of the "tithing priest" (388–9). But neither is it a simple exercise of force, whose capacity for perpetuating economic tyranny has been underscored in the recent Civil War: "For this is the fruit of war from the beginning, for it removes property out of a weaker into a stronger hand, but still upholds the curse of bondage" (355). Rather, in this proposal for labour withdrawal, Winstanley tries to envision a new, pacific use of power. Unlike earlier anti-enclosure rioters, who attacked hedges and other creatures of enclosure, the Diggers attack the system of landlordage and tenantage that creates them. They propose a quantitative increase in anti-paternalist depopulation which will lead dialectically to a qualitative change in land tenure: when enough tenants leave their landlords behind, the landlords will have to work their own fields, and the distinction between landlord and tenant, between enclosure and common field, will disappear.

Like other Renaissance utopists, Winstanley sees the positive revolutionary potential in the negative social process of depopulation and sectarianism: "Before you live you must die, and before you be bound up into one universal body, all your particular bodies and societies must be torn to pieces" (445). A dialectic of bodily displacement and placement characterizes early modern utopias in general. For instance, the fear of ungoverned vagrancy in Book 1 of *Utopia* leads in Book 2 not to reactionary paternalism, but to an accelerated and rationalized movement of bodies in the Utopian state: between one household and another, one city and another, the country and the city, the homeland and the colonies – all carefully regulated according to the totalizing reason of the Utopian state. Similarly, John Eliot constructs his utopian "praying towns" out of the remnants of Algonquian culture, traumatized and decimated by European disease and conquest (notably smallpox and the Pequot War), then proposes his experiment in civility as a model for a political settlement in war-torn England.[33]

But Winstanley's programme resists the moment of military force that lies at most utopian origins – his vague threat of the "hand of the lord" rising against adamant wage labourers is about as close as he ever comes to violence (190, 195). For Winstanley, the English people are the subjects, not the objects, of the English Revolution, as he reminds Cromwell and his grandees again and again: "We do claim this our privilege [freedom of the common lands], to be quietly given us, out of the hands of tyrant-government, as our bargain and contract with them; for the parliament promised, if we would pay taxes, and give free quarter, and adventure our lives against Charles and his party, whom they called the common enemy, they would make us a free people" (276). In their elective displacement, the Digger communes resemble more closely the communities of the Separatist and Independent *émigrés*, with the advantage that their claim to the English commons is more legitimate than the Puritans' claim to Algonquian Massachusetts. Indeed, just as Winstanley's programme of labour withdrawal encourages tenants to break with manorial discipline, so too his anti-clericalism (which is the underlying social motive of his attack on exterior and imposed interpretation) is a deracinating imperative designed to free prospective Diggers from parish discipline. If paternalism aims to put displaced people back into their old place, and if utopian improvement aims to displace them from this old place and fix them fast in a new one, then the Diggers encourage them to withdraw from an old place and create a new place by electing it as their own.

Winstanley's green millennialism also distinguishes him from James Harrington, the other great materialist political theorist of the English Revolution, who also envisions the kingdom of God as the product of agrarian reform.[34] Harrington's theory of history as a series of conflicts between the "superstructures" and the "foundation" – between governmental forms and the capacity to make war based on the distribution of property – is a remarkable achievement in the history of materialist thought. But as Christopher Hill notes, Harrington "was what Marxists call an economic determinist: he conceived of economic change as a blind impersonal force which somehow produced political change of its own accord, without the lever of mass political action."[35] For Harrington, land is important primarily for its ability to generate rent income, and so to support a militia; his agrarian reform will limit property inheritance, while leaving traditional landlord/tenant relations untouched. Harrington's ideal polity will be instituted through the anti-monarchical but authoritarian imposition of will from above –

the legislative fiat of the Lord Archon Olphaus Megaletor, his fanciful amalgam of the Lord Protector and Lycurgus.

Winstanley, on the other hand, writes not primarily to convince a dictator prince, but to win over a rural proletariat (and other sympathetic groups) to a programme of mass political action. He is painfully aware of the necessity for, and yet the difficulty of, this action. Furthermore, he emphasizes much more than Harrington the existential quality of the human connection to the earth – the way in which human identity is interwoven with collective agrarian praxis. Far from being a mechanical materialist, Winstanley preserves a keen sense of the way in which various levels of social power are distinct from and yet work to reinforce and define each other. In the third chapter of *Fire in the Bush*, Winstanley tries his hand at an extended piece of allegorical exegesis and, as usual, he is less than a resounding success. But his failure (if we can call it that) takes him some distance towards Gramsci's theory of hegemony. He calls the antagonist of Christ "a fourfold power, much idolized" (463), comparing it to the four visionary beasts of Daniel 7. The first power (indeterminate in species, but with iron teeth) is "the imaginary, teaching power" associated with the universities and the ministry. The second power, like a lion with eagle's wings and standing like a man, is "the imaginary judicature" associated with the courts and their laws. The fourth, leopard-like power is the "imaginary art" of "buying and selling the earth." In other words, religion, civil politics, the law and economics.

But matters get more complicated. Continuing to follow Daniel, he remarks that the leopard of buying and selling has four heads: "the power of the sword," "the power of the law," "the power of the covetous imaginary clergy," and "the power of a blind deceived heart, over-awed with fear of men." In other words, the economic level is inseparable from the levels of civil political rule, the law and the clergy – and from the human internalization of all these oppressive powers. Winstanley continues, saying that "all these beasts, they differ in shape, and yet they agree all in one oppressing power, supporting one another; one cannot live without another; and yet they seem to persecute one another; and if one truly die, all dies." Similarly, the imaginary teaching power of the clergy, Winstanley remarks, "though he come last, yet indeed he is the father, that begot the other" (466).

From the standpoint of a mechanistic materialism, or its equally mechanistic anti-dialectical critique, it is simply absurd to claim that these strata of society are both distinct from and contained within each other, that clergy power is both product and producer of legal, political and economic power. But this is precisely the point at which Winstanley's green millennialism comes to resemble twentieth-century cultural materialism, which also tries to find some alternative to characterizing social spheres as utterly determined or utterly independent, which also attempts to shift focus from questions of priority (clergy first or politics first?) to questions of concrete social interrelation (how do the clergy and civil rulers differ from each other and reinforce each other?). To the anxious "No priest, no king" of James Stuart, Winstanley responds hopefully and more complexly, "No priest, no king, no judge, no landlord." Whereas the university-trained gentry humanist, James Harrington, and the utopian improvers produce a mechanistic materialism that turns people and the lands they inhabit into objects of domination, the plebeian autodidact, Winstanley, produces a sophisticated cultural materialism that proposes to turn people into the guiding rational subjects of the history they will make for themselves on the land.

VI

I will conclude by contextualizing the Digger project in two ways: in this section, by contrasting it to the dominant and canonical genre focusing on the early modern countryside, and in the next, by tying it to the continuing tradition of agrarian socialism.

As the Jonsonian city comedy dominates our literary vision of seventeenth-century city life, so the Jonsonian country house poem dominates our vision of the countryside. For this remarkably coherent group of poems we might begin with the generic touchstone of Jonson's "To Penshurst," and move on to Carew's "To Saxham" and "To My Friend G.N., from Wrest," Herrick's "The Country Life," "A Panegyrick" and "The Hock Cart, or Harvest Home," and Marvell's mutation of the genre in "Upon Appleton House." Country house conventions also appear in adjacent aristocratic genres: pastoral romances such as Sidney's *Arcadia* (with its idealizing portrait of Kalander's House), fairy poems and celebrations of rural sports and festivals such as we see prominently in Herrick, topographical poetry such as Denham's "Cooper's Hill," and aristocratic epithalamiums from Spenser to Jonson to Donne to Marvell.[36] In the opening of *The Country and the City*, Raymond Williams wrote the watershed critical analysis of the seventeenth-century country house poem, and it takes us at least halfway to the Diggers. In a later interview looking back on that book, Williams comments, "I found it necessary to say in the crudest way that these houses were primarily sites of exploitation and robbery and fraud."[37] He argues that the country house poem, like an aristocratic version of pastoral more generally, does significant ideological work by constructing a myth of the pastoral golden age that extracts the lapsarian curse of agrarian labour:

> What is really happening, in Jonson and Carew's celebrations of a
> rural order, is an extraction of just this curse, by the power of art,
> a magical recreation of what can be seen as a natural bounty and
> then a willing charity: both serving to ratify and bless the country
> landowner, or, by a characteristic reification, his house. Yet this
> magical extraction of the curse of labour is in fact achieved by a
> simple extraction of the existence of labourers. (32)

Throughout *The Country and the City*, Williams resists the tendency
to reduce agrarian unrest to a timeless struggle between tenants and
landlords, the poor and the rich; he insists that classes are dynamic and
malleable relationships, not fixed topographical sites. But he also insists
that any morally responsible criticism should maintain an imaginative
sympathy with the extracted labourers.

Williams's Left Leavisism has brought him charges of anachronistic
and ahistorical moralism – from anti-Marxist critics at first, but also,
more surprisingly, from poststructuralist critics who share his cultural
materialist assumptions about the worldliness of literature and literary
criticism.[38] These critics have defended the country house poets by
arguing that they do, in fact, display an awareness of and a sympathy
with agrarian labourers, or that such a sympathy was not conceptually
available to them.

These defences (which are mildly contradictory) do not seem very
persuasive to me. The worst sort of anachronism is not the sort that
moralizes, but the sort that purges an earlier epoch of those social
contradictions within it that create its own temporality and (through
their dialectical working-out) their connection to us. In the name of a
rigorous historicism, earlier periods become single beings, thinking a
green thought in a green shade. Not surprisingly, the thoughts and the
thinkers that remain tend to be those of dominant culture.

Still, in a sense, Williams's discussion of the country house poem
invites such criticism. Any avowedly "moralistic" criticism that wishes
to avoid the charge of projecting an anachronistic moral posture
should show the oppositional voices that inhabit the era in question
and, unfortunately, Williams's discussion of the earlier seventeenth
century lacks such voices as those of Duck, Goldsmith, Crabbe and
Cobbett which he examines in later eras. Here, the Diggers provide
a crucial seventeenth-century supplement: the most powerful country-
born critique of the seventeenth-century manorial economy which finds
its acme (paternalist, improving, or both) in the country house poem.
The Digger pamphlets present both a temporal and practical critique

of the spatial and iconographic fetishism of the country house poem.

Like the patronage poet's presentation of deferential clients on a higher social plain, the country house poets' presentation of deferential tenants dissimulates the existence of an economy.[39] Williams focuses on this recoding, looking at the way in which country house poems practise a pre-capitalist or early capitalist version of commodity fetishism: that functional process of capitalist mystification which detaches commodities from the workers who produce them, constructing for the commodities an exalted and almost human independence, and for the workers a degraded and almost thing-like impotence. With great *sprezzatura*, country house poets turn feeding tenants and eating lords into feeding lords and eating tenants. Not only do landlords wish to extract surplus labour value from their tenants, they also wish to recode that very extraction as a virtuous donation. The country house poem, Williams says, effaces the practical reality of agrarian labour by substituting for it an image of endless effortless feasting, offering as compensation for a perpetually denied charity of production a periodic charity of consumption:

> A charity of production – of loving relations between men actually working and producing what is ultimately, in whatever proportions, to be shared – was neglected, not seen, and at times suppressed, by this habitual reference to a charity of consumption, an eating and drinking communion, which when applied to ordinary working societies was inevitably a mystification. All uncharity at work, it was readily assumed, could be redeemed by the charity of the consequent feast. (31)

"To Saxham" gives us the most striking example of this mystification. Rather than the tenants' labour preserving the lord throughout the year, we find the charity of his table preserving them; in return, they bless his table with their prayers. Mildmay Fane, the Earl of Westmorland, gives us a splendid example of this dissimulation in "To Retiredness," where he calls a personified "Retiredness" the "Great patron of my liberty." Thanks to this tautology, he is able to turn his "hinds" and their labour – the true patrons of his liberty – into mere objects for pastoral contemplation:

> Then turning over nature's leaf,
> I mark the glory of the sheaf,
> For every field's a several page
> Deciphering the Golden Age. (lines 31–4)

This is one of the starkest and most unselfconscious transformations of the site of plebeian georgic labour into aristocratic pastoral contemplation. And indeed, the transformation of a productive terrain into an object of aesthetic contemplation – into a landscape – is a classic technique of ruling class pastoral, from the Renaissance to the present.

Beginning with Williams, and continuing into some of the more methodologically sophisticated recent sorts of political and literary analysis, critics of the seventeenth-century country house poem have typically employed an immanent critique, focusing on the gaps and fissures and moments of ideological bad conscience revealed in the poems themselves. But an immanent critique cannot finally reveal the sort of critical consciousness we see in the following account of a different sort of country house, drawn from a letter of 1649 written by seven Diggers to the Council of War and General Thomas Fairfax – who would resign his commission and retire to Appleton House the following year:

> But now sirs, this last week upon the 28th of November, there came a party of soldiers commanded by a cornet, and some of them of your own regiment, and by their threatening words forced three labouring men to help them pull down our two houses, and carried away the wood in a cart to a gentleman's house who hath been a cavalier all our time of wars, and cast two or three old people out who lived in those houses to lie in the open field this cold weather. (344)

The habitations of the rural poor are less familiar to us than the aristocratic great houses, even though they were much more numerous. This is partly because they tend not to exist any longer, partly because canonical poets seldom took notice of them. But, of course, they did exist – indeed, if they had not, the great houses would not have either. First a parallel. This account of eviction, demolition and property transfer suggests Marvell's account in "Upon Appleton House," which tells how one of Thomas Fairfax's progenitors (William Fairfax) abducted another (Isabel Thwaites) from a nunnery and married her, how their sons made that nunnery a quarry for renovations to the family estate after the dissolution of the religious houses by Henry VIII. Moving out of Marvell's poem into the later marriage of Maria Fairfax, we might note that, just as Fairfax's troops transfer the property of their poor former allies to their wealthy former enemies, so he married his daughter Maria to George Villiers, second Duke of Buckingham. What pushes the parallel beyond abstract formality is the reconciliatory and exclusionary logic of real property.

But, finally, the contrasts dominate. For the eternal present of the country house poem, we have the juridical specificity of 28 November

1649. For the easy comestible cosmos of Penshurst, we have a world of commands, threats and force. For Saxham's happy eaters welcomed to the fireside, we have "labouring men" constrained to destroy two houses and cast old people out in a field. What finally strikes us is the grinding quotidian familiarity of these rural brute facts: that force wins out over need, that poor people get evicted, that their houses are rather fragile things that can simply be pulled down.

Of course, the Diggers' account is not much of a country house poem, and we should not look to see it anthologized soon alongside "Penshurst." But if we simply classify it as "non-literary," then we miss the critical engagement between the aristocratic and spatial imagination of country house pastoral, and the egalitarian and temporal imagination of Digger georgic. Where the country house poem presents the occasional charity of consumption as compensation for the perpetual absence of a charity of production, the Digger pamphlets present us with a social vision integrating working, labouring, talking: "Work together. Eat bread together; declare this all abroad" (190). Where the country house poem attempts to reduce lived human praxis to icons or emblems, time to space, conflict to order, the Digger pamphlet attempts to restore an awareness of agricultural praxis, showing how the conflict between the relations and the conditions of agrarian production could open the door to a revolutionary and egalitarian future.

Country house poems operate according to a fundamentally spatial vision, which consistently attempts to reduce lived human processes to iconic or topographical artifacts. They richly reward examination inside the tradition of contemporary landscape painting, for they present the houses, the surrounding landscape and the local tenants through an iconic imagination that effaces the reality of rural production and, indeed, of time itself. The terrain is a landscape, something seen. Topography figures a fantasy of uncreated wealth and dynasty; again and again, we see the country houses described as "piles" of native stone increate that have emerged, as if by themselves, from the soil. Trees are dynastic emblems: the oaks of Sir Philip Sidney and Lady Leicester and the copse of Gamage in "To Penshurst," and in "Upon Appleton House," the dynastic "Fairfacian Oak" (line 740), dangerously doubled by the emblematic Caroline oak, which seems to be infected by a Villiersesque traitor worm and felled by a Cromwellian hewel (lines 537–60). The tenants, too, are typically presented iconically. In "To Penshurst," they are the bashful bearers of gifts, "emblems of themselves" (line 56) to the Sidney family, and in "Appleton House," they are a "stately frontispiece of poor" (line 65). In Herrick's striking partial demystification of the genre, we see tenants most thoroughly instrumentalized:

> Come, sons of summer, by whose toil
> We are the lords of wine and oil;
> By whose tough labours and rough hands
> We rip up first, then reap our lands. (lines 1–4)

Just as country house poets efface agrarian praxis, so they retreat from the chaotic military praxis of Civil War England. The year after receiving the Diggers' petition, Fairfax resigned his command of the parliamentary armies because of his reluctance to invade Scotland, but he still enjoys a floralized enclosed simulacrum of the battlefield in "Appleton House," where the bees "fire fragrant volleys" and "the gardener had the soldier's place" (298, 336). Mildmay Fane, who had supported the King in the early phases of the Civil War, and suffered as a result two sorts of non-pastoral enclosure (in the Tower, and then restriction to an area near London), retreated to Apthorpe in 1644, where he rested "out of fears or noise of war," and where he heard no other contest than his tenants' whimsically presented attempts to "make the tenth [their tithes] go less" ("To Retiredness," lines 61, 50).

The Digger pamphlets, on the other hand, present us with a plebeian georgic, where the agrarian plain, subject to communal labour, prophesies a relatively egalitarian future. For the Diggers, land is never a contemplative landscape, but a site of human praxis; it is always already fought over, worked, bled into, manured, subject to the struggle between Norman landlord and freeborn Briton. Trees are objects of cultivation, and the site of a battle for rights. In *A Declaration from the Poor Oppressed People of England*, the Diggers stake a claim to "lay hold upon, and as we stand in need, to cut and fell, and make the best advantage we can of the woods and trees, that grow upon the Commons" (272). This concrete struggle adds a material resonance to the following characterization of tyrannicide in *A New-Yeers Gift*:

> For kingly power is like a great spread tree, if you lop the head or top-bow, and let the other branches and root stand, it will grow again and recover fresher strength. . . . But alas oppression is a great tree still, and keeps off the sun of freedom from the poor commons still, he hath many branches and great roots which must be grubbed up, before every one can sing Sion's songs, in peace. (353, 357)

This is truly a georgic millennialism, which has broken out of the paternalist cycle of extorted labour and carnival, the improving dialectic of enclosure, displacement and improvement. Most important, the poor are no longer topoi in a landscape, but literate authors or rational, illiterate subscribers – speakers in their own voices about themselves and their practical activity.

The Diggers see not an opposition but a fundamental continuity between military praxis, which has overthrown the king, and communal agrarian praxis, which will overthrow the hedge kings and the tithe-fed tyrants of a state church. In *The Law of Freedom*, echoing John the Baptist's echo in Luke 3 of Isaiah 40, Winstanley submits the alpine imagination of courtly and monarchical pastoral to the levelling georgic imagination of Digger prophecy:

> A Monarchical army lifts up mountains, makes valleys, viz., advances tyrants, and treads the oppressed in the barren lanes of poverty. But a commonwealth's army is like John Baptist, who levels the mountains to the valleys, pulls down the tyrant, and lifts up the oppressed: and so makes way for the spirit of peace and freedom to come into rule and inherit the earth. (575)

If the enclosed gardens and fields of Mildmay Fane and Thomas Fairfax suggest a poetic attempt to return to Eden through pastoral nostalgia and utopian improvement, then the disenclosed fields of the Digger pamphlets suggest an attempt to recreate Eden through communal agricultural praxis.

Bloch remarks that "All emotions refer to the horizon of time, because they are highly intentioned emotions, but the expectant emotions open out entirely into this horizon" (74); if we follow Bloch in speaking of filled and expectant emotions, then perhaps we should also speak of filled or sated genres such as the country house poem, and expectant or hungry ones such as the Digger pamphlet. The country house poem is at home in its own present. The filled aristocratic pastorals of the country house poets move unremittingly towards a model of the present as a plenitude – a temporally as well as spatially enclosed landscape. When the future does appear in the country house poem, it appears as the future of the same – the fantasy of pure dynastic replication through primogeniture, entailment and the genial infusion of paternal virtue, which will help find "a Fairfax for our Thwaites," in the strangely incestuous phrase of "Upon Appleton House" (line 748). This filled or closed quality finds a topographical correlative in the enclosed landscape of the landlord's fields and garden, and a discursive one in the closed couplets most favoured by the poets and Marvell's foursquare stanzas comprising eight lines of eight syllables.

The Digger pamphlets, on the other hand, are ill at ease in their own present, which they submit to the transformative revolutionary praxis of communal agriculture and radical prophecy. In the Digger pamphlets, we see a deeply felt experience of what Ernst Bloch calls "non-synchronism" – the way in which a single historical moment may be inhabited by several contradictory times.[40] The Digger "now" defined by the chafing of the Norman Yoke is a radically different "now" from that of the country house's Golden Age. This sense of temporal unevenness in the present seeks out scriptural analogues. Winstanley is as enamoured as any millennialist of the cryptic "time and times and half a times" of the Old and New Testament apocalyptic books. In *Fire in the Bush*, he says that "Time shall dash against times, and times shall dash against the dividing of time; and the divisions in the dividing of time shall destroy him; till the Creation be cleansed of all these plagues. . . . And this makes way for Christ, the universal love, to take the kingdom, and the dominion of the whole earth" (467). More specifically, he says the "dividing of time" in England may be seen in "the variety of Churches, and differences in religion, that is amongst men; every one pleading his privilege, or else it is called the dividing of time, in regard the government of the land is taken out of the hands of one man, and put into the hands of many" (485). The pamphlet form itself, with its public subject matter, its semi-structured quality and its desire for a response, opens itself up into a future.

Country house poems have attracted considerably more critical attention than the Digger pamphlets, for they lend themselves much more readily to the spatially-oriented hermeneutics of modernism. A conventional account of aesthetic and critical modernism, frequently associated with Lukács, is that it privileges space over time, or spatializes and reifies temporality itself by turning it into a purely interior or subjective experience. I think that this account retains a good deal of explanatory force – not only for modernism, but for its semi-detached heir, aesthetic and critical postmodernism. One of the more interesting phenomena in recent Renaissance studies has been the evaporation of temporality as a category of critical analysis, along with the allied concepts of intention, utopia, consciousness and revolution. Neither anti-modernist historical revisionism (with its contempt for "Whig" history and its model of a deferential social system), nor modernist New Criticism (with its refutation of the intentional fallacy and its emphasis on the verbal icon), nor post-modernist deconstruction (with its critique of phenomenology and its claim that temporality is a matter of spacing and endlessly deferred presence), nor new historicism (with its focus on emblematic set pieces, the systemic play of power, and synchronic cultural snapshots), has shown much interest in the temporality of Renaissance literature.[41] But questions of method are inextricably tied to questions of canon, and no attempt to argue for spatial form and the literary system which simply ignores oppositional prophetic writing like Winstanley's can prove convincing.

Unquestionably, the seventeenth century presents us with a number of fascinating courtier poets focused on the patronage system and the aristocratic landscape; it also presents us with a number of equally fascinating farmer prophets focused on their fields and the future. The dominant cultures of early modern Britain see the violent clashing of times and peoples in the English Revolution and either attack it as an irrational chaotic Babel,[42] or retreat from it into the filled *hortus conclusus* of a country house or some analogous meditative site. The Diggers, on the other hand, see it pregnant with utopia. Their expectant *hortus inconclusus* opens up into the socialist future.

VII

This is not to say that this opening up has gone unnoticed and unchallenged. Four main anti-socialist strategies have emerged for detaching the Diggers from their future. We might characterize them briefly as snubbing, sneering, periodizing and Stalinizing. The first technique is a mode of strategic avoidance. In her massive *Agrarian History of Britain and Wales*, Joan Thirsk spares the Diggers barely a page. There, she agrees with the Diggers' gentry opponents that their communal project constituted a gross affront to local landowners, and that the land they cultivated was poorly chosen anyway – as if the gentry would have found a better-situated commune less provocative. Of their theory of agrarian praxis, she says nothing. Similarly, Kevin Sharpe laments the "disproportionately large number of pages" historians have spent in analysing "minor sects and crackpots," given that "Land and liberty never became the slogan of the English Revolution; radical millenarianism never infected the poor; the radical groups, especially the most important, never appealed to the poor." Never, never, and especially never; except, of course, when they did. So long as raillery and brisk impatience can pass for sober historical judgment, the Diggers will have a hard time assuming their true historical importance in our understanding of the seventeenth century.[43]

In a second technique, revisionist historians have tried to enclose Winstanley in an eternal present, in which his prophetic socialism is a mere alibi for his non-ideological pursuit of personal gain and revenge inside a fixed social system. Richard T. Vann led the way by examining Winstanley's pre- and post-Digger career and constructing a psychological explanation for the Digger movement: "The experiment in Digger communism would seem to have come between the ruin of a career as a Merchant Tailor and the scarcely propitious beginning of one as a steward and corn-trader. These few facts about his life seem to invite the interpretation of the radical as one who turns on a system in which he personally has failed." James Alsop has followed up on Vann, investigating Winstanley's business dealings with the dogged ferocity of a delinquent accounts collector. Winstanley's early inability to succeed in the business world led to his resentful radicalism with a sort of fumy necessity, while his later small success in that world confirms with stunning force the insincerity of his Digger days.[44] This seems an unusually coarse example of the genetic or "Whig" history that revisionists claim to find offensive in socialist historians. And it may seem less than generous to fault a poor man for seeking wage labour and some measure of financial security in the 1650s and 1660s; Winstanley's alternative was not a continuation of Digging (the violence of the gentry had made that impossible), but poverty, isolation and starvation.

The third technique encloses the Diggers in a pre-modern past with some such claim as, "Winstanley is a religious thinker, not a social revolutionary."[45] This is a peculiar binary opposition that can survive only inside a hermetic version of the history of ideas. Inside the sociology of religion (or the history of political languages, or social history), however, religion is simply one mode of social practice among others, so a rigorous distinction between religion and society makes about as much sense as one between apples and fruit. Of course, the sociology of religion can and does talk about spheres of religious experience and institutional life within a social totality, but it seems particularly unhelpful to attribute faith in a closed religious sphere to the Diggers, given that they spend so much time attacking the social institutions that made that sphere possible in mid-seventeenth-century England (tithing, the universities, a caste of professional clerics), and also the conceptual oppositions (between spirit and matter, clergy and laity, heaven and earth, contemplation and labour, the millennium and human history) that help to justify and reproduce this sphere. These historians of ideas have been unable to assimilate Sabine's 50-year-old insight: "By what may seem at first sight a paradox, the very universality of religious experience in the life of the saint gives to Winstanley's personal philosophy a tone of secularism. . . . In short, religion was for him a way of life, not a ceremonial, a profession, or a metaphysic" (48).

The fourth technique is the invention of J.C. Davis in *Utopia and the Ideal Society*. Davis attacks socialist partisans of Winstanley not by denying their connection to him, but by insisting on it – with a twist.[46] Particularly in *The Law of Freedom*, he argues, Winstanley reveals an authoritarianism endemic to all socialism; scratch a socialist and find a Stalinist. Davis develops this thesis through two primary distortions. First, he exaggerates the severity of the Digger disciplinary mechanism, saying (with no apparent evidence) that *The New Law* advocates "slavery" for all those who resist Digger discipline, and that *The Law of Freedom* threatens them with "judicial slavery" – a rather scary name for the rather familiar phenomenon of penal correction (180, 196). Second, Davis plays down the extent to which Winstanley's indubitable movement towards disciplinary severity in his final work simply responded to the systematic and violent harassment of the Digger colony from its inception to its demise a year later. The Diggers were subjected to economic boycotts, threats, lawsuits, pullings-down of houses, trampling of crops, and vicious beatings – as a result of which one Digger miscarried (433), while another almost died (295). In what Winstanley calls the "pitched battle between the lamb and the dragon" (281), Davis hears only the bleating of the lamb, while the customary coercion practised by English property owners remains silent, natural, part of a picturesque landscape. Jumping the English Channel and 140 years, we might compare Davis to the French revisionists, whose bicentennial paroxysms over the Terror drowned out the far greater economic and political violence of the *ancien régime* and counter-revolutionary Europe.

It seems to me that the Diggers' *hortus inconclusus* opens up more readily into contexts other than that of twentieth-century totalitarianism – notably, into the traditions of Quakerism and communist sectarianism, English prophetic literature (Milton, Bunyan, Blake, Whitman), and social utopianism (Bellers, Plockhoy, Fourier, Marx, Morris). Here, I will concentrate on the context of continuing resistance to agrarian enclosure. If large-scale resistance tended to disappear in England after the Restoration, then conflicts between rights-based and property-based conceptions of the forests certainly did not, as E.P. Thompson has shown in *Whigs and Hunters*.[47] In Scotland, the disruption of traditional agriculture by improving enclosure did not reach its height until the Highland Clearances of the eighteenth and early nineteenth centuries; in *Capital*, Marx traces this process as part of the continuing narrative of primitive accumulation. The Clearances disrupted the patriarchal economies of the clans, as scientific improvers (many of them English or Lowlanders, but working in tandem with Highland nobility and landowners) brutally evicted the crofters and converted their communal small-holdings into pasture land and deer parks. This conflict continued almost into the twentieth century, with the Crofters' War and the Battle of the Braes on the Isle of Skye in 1882. The cult of Scots picturesque, built on bleak landscapes and ruined crofts, shows that aestheticization is the last phase of capitalist genocide.

The seventeenth-, eighteenth- and nineteenth-century invaders of North America presented their genocidal clearing and enclosure of the indigenous common lands as a programme of providentially-sanctioned and rational improvement. Something like a country house ethic re-appears among North American environmentalists working in the tradition of John Muir, for whom national parks are nature reserves rather than monuments to exterminated social ecologies. For instance, what is now Yosemite Park was, at the beginning of the nineteenth century, part of the Miwok nation of "Digger" Indians (so called because of their harvesting of tubers), who "were the most numerous native tribe in North America. . . . Their complex systems of land use, land tenure and land management had modified a diversity of California landscapes, and supported the greatest human population density found in the Americas north of Mexico."[48] They were decimated by disease in the 1830s and by military attacks throughout the nineteenth century.

We can see an even more striking and contemporary version of the controversy over the commons in South America. An aestheticized environmentalism has led most Americans and Europeans to see the struggle over the rain forest as a battle between tree and bulldozer rather than one between two economies: between the destructive economy practised by ranchers and log-harvesters, and the renewable economy of petty extraction (rubber tapping, small farming, nut gathering) practised by the two million forest people – Indians, river bank peoples and rubber tappers. Hecht and Cockburn point out that "The extinction is not only of nature but of socialized nature: what is also being exterminated in the Amazon is civilization" (62). The last 30 years have proved particularly devastating to the forest peoples: "From the sixties until today the entire Amazon has been convulsed by an enormous enclosure movement easily rivaling the conversion of public land to private property in early modern Europe. . . . Indeed, the Amazon is the site of one of the most rapid and large-scale enclosure movements in history as more than 100 million acres pass from public to private ownership."[49]

This process has provoked responses analogous to those of European peasants resisting enclosure, including the Diggers: the formation of new political collectives such as unions of rural workers, the emergence of a group of self-educated organic intellectuals such as the late Chico Mendes (who was murdered by a landowner in 1988), and the development of techniques of non-violent resistance to enclosure such as the *empate*, the sit-down strikes of forest peoples resisting workers with chainsaws employed by the great landowners.[50] We might also compare the green millennialism of the Digger pamphlets with the *Forest Peoples' Manifesto* of 1985 and 1989, which proposes an end to the division of the forest into lots for colonists, a new technology that will benefit the people of the forest, the establishment of extractive reserves, and "Administration and control of reserves directly by the extractive workers and their organizations".[51]

These extractive reserves of rubber and brazil nut trees, which envision a new/old variety of collective life on the land, resonate strongly with the Digger utopia. Ailton Krenak, a self-educated Krenak Indian, describes them in terms that Winstanley would find striking:

> Extractive reserves bring into play part of the population which came to the Amazon to "civilize" it along with the Indians, but who instead learn from them a new way of living with nature. Rubber tappers learn how to humanize nature and themselves. Thus the reserve brings a new form of social culture, and economic character. Migrants to this region came in search of land, but the property of the people cannot be commercialized. An extractive reserve is not an exchange item, and it isn't property. It is a good that belongs to the Brazilian nation, and people will live in these reserves with the expectation of preserving them for future generations. This is tremendously innovative.[52]

Here, we might compare the Digger declaration from Iver, which sets the mark of Cain on what it calls "Earthmongers," saying that "we affirm that they have no righteous power to sell or give away the earth, unless they could make the earth likewise, which none can do but God the eternal spirit" (129). Refusal to sell the land is a pledge with the future.

Of course, the projects of the Diggers and the forest peoples are radically diverse and subject to their proper dynamics. The political contexts are quite distinct: a national revolution with strong but stifled egalitarian elements on the one hand, a Fascist military government moving towards an ostensibly democratic one on the other. In place of the long-term history of religious conflict in Winstanley's England, we have a long-term ethnic conflict in Brazil, where developers have sent flu-infected settlers into Indian lands in order to infect and exterminate them – a primitive but effective mode of genocidal germ warfare. Furthermore, the process of enclosure has proceeded much more rapidly in the Amazon, and the conversion of Brazilian rain forest to pasture (and rapidly thereafter, to wasteland) is even less reversible and more devastating than the conversion of English arable to pasture or common lands to private holdings.

But these differences should not blind us to the process tying the two times and places together, for the Diggers and the forest people respond to the same phenomenon: global capitalism in the phase of primitive accumulation. Primitive accumulation, as Marx discusses it in *Capital*, is that early- or pre-capitalist phase that divorces producers from the means of production, and prepares them to become mere sellers of their labour power.[53] To link early modern England and contemporary Brazil in this fashion is not to venture into anachronism, since capitalism is not a system, not even a mechanical sequence of systems (early, middle, late), but a complex, non-synchronous narrative. A single "phase" like primitive accumulation may appear again and again in different places. Conversely, any given historical moment incorporates more than one "time," more than one mode of production. Winstanley's England, for instance, contained the remnants of a feudal agriculture, an early capitalist and possessive individualist agriculture driven by a dynamic of improvement and primitive accumulation, and (among the Diggers) a small-scale practice of communism. Our own historical moment includes the primitive communism of a few uncolonized aboriginal peoples, primitive accumulation in the industrializing Third World nations, early capitalism to rival Engels' Manchester in the industrialized Third World (and in the un-unionized and environmentally degraded First and Second), and even the plausible spectre of a post-industrial "information order" in some ruling class ambients around the world.[54]

It is crucial to remain sensitive to these different times within a single historical moment, since critical and utopian consciousness resides precisely in the lived experience of and critical reflection on this non-synchronous dissonance – the clashing of time, and times, and half a time that pervades everyday life. Given the tendency of many contemporary historicisms to equate history with a rigorous periodization, which carries us along from one dominant mode to another, it is particularly important to note these moments of rational hunger, like that of the Diggers', that reveal critical dissonance with a dominant mode, affiliative resonance with a far-distant moment. When the Diggers cultivate George's Hill, the broken enclosures open up into the rain forest, and we see the common human desire of Diggers and Forest People to create themselves freely through collective praxis on the land. The Diggers' Eden on George's Hill and Winstanley's prophetic writings are certainly of the seventeenth century, and he certainly was not a seventeenth-century Marxist (as periodizing, anti-socialist historians never tire of pointing out). Yet his vision of a once-and-future human relationship to the land, based on common preservation rather than enclosure and rigorously divided ownership, remains non-identical to the oppressive dominant culture of his present, and affiliates itself with distant visions such as Ailton Krenak's of a once-and-future Amazon: "It is for this that the region is so beautiful, because it is a piece of the planet that maintains the inheritance of the creation of the world. Christians have a myth of the garden of Eden. Our people have a reality where the first man created by god continues to be free. We want to impregnate humanity with the memory of the creation of the world."[55] In Bloch's phrase, this memory of a humane socialist future is the Diggers' not-yet-conscious, and might be ours.

NOTES

I am grateful to Joanna Tinker for her comments on a draft of this article.

1. Unless otherwise indicated, I will quote all Digger writings from George Sabine's edition of works by Winstanley and others, modernizing spelling but maintaining original punctuation. Sabine's edition is comprehensive, with these exceptions: Winstanley's *Englands Spirit Unfoulded* (discovered and reprinted by G.E. Aylmer), the Digger *Declaration from Iver* (discovered and reprinted by Keith Thomas as "Another Digger Broadside"), both reprinted in Charles Webster, ed., *The Intellectual Revolution of the Seventeenth-Century* (London: Routledge and Kegan Paul, 1974); Winstanley's two earliest pamphlets, *The Mysterie of God* and *The Breaking of the Day of God* (both summarized in Sabine); Winstanley's Preface to a 1649 collection of his first five pamphlets entitled *Several Pieces Gathered in one Volume* and a number of Digger songs dropped by Sabine, all reprinted in Christopher Hill, ed., *The Law of Freedom and Other Writings* (Harmondsworth: Penguin, 1973); and a letter Winstanley wrote to his landlady, Lady Eleanor Davies/Douglas, discovered and published by Paul Hardacre as "Gerrard Winstanley in 1650," *Huntington Library Quarterly*, 22 (1958–59), 345–9. Sabine's Introduction is the best short guide to Winstanley's life and work; Christopher Hill's "The Religion of Gerrard Winstanley," an impassioned anti-revisionist argument for Winstanley's continuing importance, is collected in Volume Two of *The Collected Essays of Christopher Hill* (Amherst: University of Massachusetts Press, 1986), 185–252. Other major studies of Winstanley include Lewis H. Berens, *The Digger Movement in the Days of the Commonwealth* (1901; reprinted London: Holland Press and Merlin Press, 1961); David Petegorsky, *Left-Wing Democracy in the English Civil War* (London: Gollancz, 1940); Olivier Lutaud, *Winstanley: Socialisme et Christianisme sous Cromwell* (Paris: Didier, 1976); T. Wilson Hayes, *Winstanley the Digger* (Cambridge: Harvard University Press, 1979); Timothy Kenyon, *Utopian Communism and Political Thought in Early Modern England* (London: Pinter, 1989); and George M. Shulman, *Radicalism and Reverence: The Political Thought of Gerrard Winstanley* (Berkeley: University of California Press, 1989).
2. Thomas, "Another Digger Broadside," 58–9.
3. Ernst Bloch, *The Principle of Hope*, 3 vols., trans. Neville Plaice, Stephen Plaice and Paul Knight (Cambridge, Mass.: MIT Press, 1986), 56.
4. Francis Bacon, "Of Sedition," *The Works of Francis Bacon*, Vol. 4, James Spedding *et al.*, eds. (Boston: Brown and Taggard, 1862), 12: 126.
5. E.P. Thompson, "The Moral Economy of the English Crowd in the Eighteenth Century," *Past and Present*, 50 (1971), 76–136.
6. Hill, *The Law of Freedom*, 155–6.
7. Hill, *The Law of Freedom*, 22.
8. Joan Thirsk, ed., *The Agrarian History of England and Wales, Volume 4: 1500–1640* (Cambridge: Cambridge University Press, 1967), 200–55.

9. Raymond Williams, *The Country and the City* (New York: Oxford University Press, 1973), 12.
10. R.H. Tawney and Eileen Powers, eds., *Tudor Economic Documents*, 3 vols. (London: Longman, 1924), 1: 55.
11. Robert Powell, *Depopulation Arraigned* (London, 1636; reprinted Amsterdam: Theatrum Orbis Terrarum, and Norwood, New Jersey: Walter J. Jonson, 1976), 4.
12. Tawney and Powers, *Tudor Economic Documents*, 2: 296–369.
13. Robert Wilkinson, *A Sermon Preached at North-Hampton* (London, 1607).
14. Buchanan Sharp, "Common Rights, Charities and the Disorderly Poor," in Geoff Eley and William Hunt, eds., *Reviving the English Revolution: Reflections and Elaborations on the Work of Christopher Hill* (London: Verso, 1988), 107–38, ref. to 129–30.
15. James Holstun, *A Rational Millennium: Puritan Utopias of Seventeenth-Century England and America* (New York: Oxford University Press, 1987), 34–48.
16. Joan Thirsk and J.P. Cooper, *Seventeenth-Century Economic Documents* (Oxford: Clarendon Press, 1972), 107.
17. Ibid., 135.
18. Ibid., 144.
19. Ibid., 758.
20. Max Horkheimer and Theodor W. Adorno, *Dialectic of Enlightenment*, trans. John Cumming (New York: Seabury, 1972).
21. Anthony Fletcher and John Stevenson, eds., *Order and Disorder in Early Modern England* (Cambridge: Cambridge University Press, 1985).
22. Thirsk and Cooper, *Seventeenth-Century Economic Documents*, 137–8.
23. Charles Webster, *The Great Instauration: Science, Medicine and Reform, 1626–1660* (London: Duckworth, 1975).
24. Christopher Hill, "Puritans and 'the Dark Corners of the Land'," *Change and Continuity in Seventeenth-Century England* (Cambridge: Harvard University Press, 1975), 3–47.
25. Sharp, "Common Rights," 133.
26. William Blithe, *The English Improver Improved*, third impression (London, 1652).
27. Blithe, *The English Improver Improved*, "Epistle to the Industrious Reader."
28. Peter Laslett, *The World We Have Lost*, second edn. (n.p.: Scribner, 1971); Alan Everitt, *The Community of Kent and the Great Rebellion, 1640–1660* (Leicester, 1966); quotation from Richard Cust and Ann Hughes, *Conflict in Early Stuart England, Studies in Religion and Politics 1603–1642* (London: Longman, 1989), 5. We might even say that the last two decades have witnessed an interdisciplinary renaissance of local studies – not only among revisionist historians, but also in the *histoire des mentalités*, in Clifford Geertz's proposal of a cultural anthropology focusing on "local knowledge," and in a poststructuralist literary criticism influenced by Bakhtin and Foucault which turns from matters of the state, revolution and ideology, towards village festivity, carnival and the politics of the body. The fundamental and determining horizon for these diverse approaches is, I would argue, academic anti-Marxism. See my "Ranting at the New Historicism," *English Literary Renaissance*, 19:2 (1989), 189–225.
29. James G. Turner, *The Politics of Landscape: Rural Scenery and Society in English Poetry 1630–1660* (Cambridge: Harvard University Press, 1979), 155.
30. C.H. Firth, ed., *The Clarke Papers: Selections from the Papers of William Clarke*, 4 vols. (n.p.: Camden Society, 1891–94; reprinted New York and London: Johnson Reprint Co., 1965), 2: 2094–10.
31. Christopher Hill, "The Norman Yoke," *Puritanism and Revolution* (London: Secker and Warburg, 1958), 50–122.
32. Thirsk, *Agrarian History*, 255.
33. Holstun, *A Rational Millennium*, 58–9, 71, 102–65.
34. J.G.A. Pocock, ed., *The Political Works of James Harrington* (Cambridge: Cambridge University Press, 1977).

35. Christopher Hill, "James Harrington and the People," *Puritanism and Revolution*, 299–313, quotation from 312.
36. I quote Marvell from Frank Kermode and Keith Walker, eds., *Andrew Marvell* (New York: Oxford University Press, 1990), and all other country house poems from Hugh Maclean, ed., *Ben Jonson and the Cavalier Poets* (New York: Norton, 1974). James G. Turner's *The Politics of Landscape*, which is close in method to Williams's *The Country and the City*, is the most detailed and astute study of the seventeenth-century tradition of country house and topographical poetry.
37. Raymond Williams, *Politics and Letters: Interviews with New Left Review* (London: New Left Books, 1979), 312.
38. See, for instance, George Parfitt, *Ben Jonson: Public Poet and Private Man* (London: Dent, 1976), 161; William E. Cain, "The Place of the Poet in Jonson's 'To Penshurst' and 'To My Muse'," *Criticism*, 21 (1979), 34–48; Don E. Wayne, *Penshurst: The Semiotics of Place and the Poetics of History* (Madison: University of Wisconsin Press, 1984), 17; Jonathan Goldberg, *James I and the Politics of Literature* (Baltimore: Johns Hopkins University Press, 1983), 226.
39. For a critique of the new historicist and revisionist model of a deferential literary culture in early modern England, see my "Ehud's Dagger: Patronage, Tyrannicide, and *Killing No Murder*," forthcoming in *Cultural Critique* (1992).
40. Ernst Bloch, "Nonsynchronism and the Obligation to Its Dialectics," trans. Mark Ritter, *New German Critique*, 11 (1977), 22–38.
41. Generally speaking, time, intentionality and the prophetic tradition in English literature have received much better treatment from ostensibly "formalist" critics such as Northrop Frye, who read English Renaissance literature from the point of view of prophetic English romanticism. See also David Norbrook's argument that we should look at the prophetic and oppositional neo-Spenserian tradition in seventeenth-century poetry as well as the dominant and courtly tradition in *Poetry and Politics in the English Renaissance* (London: Routledge and Kegan Paul, 1984). See also Peter Kitson's critique in this volume of the new historicist focus on synchronic analysis.
42. See Sharon Achinstein's essay in this volume.
43. Kevin Sharpe, *Politics and Ideas in Early Stuart England* (London: Pinter, 1989), 306.
44. Richard T. Vann, "The Later Life of Gerrard Winstanley," *Journal of the History of Ideas*, 26:1 (1965), 136; James D. Alsop, "Ethics in the Marketplace: Gerrard Winstanley's London Bankruptcy, 1643," *Journal of British Studies*, 28 (1989), 97–119.
45. This argument is very common. For a few examples, see Winthrop S. Hudson, "Economic and Social Thought of Gerrard Winstanley: Was He a Seventeenth-Century Marxist?" *The Journal of Modern History*, 18:1 (1946), 1–21; Lotte Mulligan, John K. Graham and Judith Richards, "Winstanley: A Case for the Man as He Said He Was," *Past and Present*, 28:1 (1977), 57–75; and John R. Knott, Jr., *The Sword of the Spirit: Puritan Responses to the Bible* (Chicago: University of Chicago Press, 1980). The most telling response to this argument has been Hill's in "The Religion of Gerrard Winstanley."
46. J.C. Davis, *Utopia and the Ideal Society: A Study of English Utopian Writing, 1516–1700* (Cambridge: Cambridge University Press, 1981), 169–203.
47. E.P. Thompson, *Whigs and Hunters: The Origin of the Black Act* (Harmondsworth: Penguin, 1990).
48. Susanna Hecht and Alexander Cockburn, *The Fate of the Forest: Developers, Destroyers and Defenders of the Amazon* (New York: Harper, 1990), 271.
49. Ibid., 107, 142.
50. Chico Mendes and Tony Gross, *Fight for the Forest: Chico Mendes in His Own Words* (London: Latin American Bureau, 1989), 70.
51. Hecht and Cockburn, *The Fate of the Forest*, 261–4.

52. Ibid., 244.

53. Karl Marx, *Capital, Volume 1* (New York: International Publishers, 1967), 713–74.

54. A wide variety of critics (including poststructuralists, neo-Marxists and capitalist ideologists) have proclaimed post-industrial postmodernism the regnant mode of global cultural life. They extract the existence of agrarian and industrial labourers with a facility that the country house poets would envy, and their seemingly autochthonous VCRs and computers jump into their global information networks as magically as do carp into the nets of Penshurst. On the absurdity of the notion of "post-industrialism," see Alex Callinicos, *Against Postmodernism: A Marxist Critique* (New York: St Martin's, 1990).

55. Hecht and Cockburn, *The Fate of the Forest*, 1.

"Sages and patriots that being dead do yet speak to us": Readings of the English Revolution in the Late Eighteenth Century

PETER J. KITSON

I

It has become unfashionable in literary critical circles to develop historicist readings of literature which structure themselves upon the diachronic as opposed to the synchronic paradigm. This is largely the result of the challenges made to traditional literary historians by a wide range of critics whom it is now commonplace to group together as "new historicists": a term apparently introduced into Renaissance studies by Michael McCanles but often associated with the work of Stephen Greenblatt.[1] In the words of Louis A. Montrose, "this project reorients the axis of inter-textuality, substituting for the diachronic text of an autonomous literary history the synchronic text of a cultural system."[2] This new historicist concern with "the synchronic text of a cultural history" coupled with the concern for subjectification disallows the diachronic and effectively denies the role of oppositional praxis. In this article I wish to suggest that certain radical writers of the late eighteenth century used the diachronic text of a tradition of religious and political dissent to create an ideology of opposition to the established political and social structures of the time, and that although this tradition itself is inevitably a part of a synchronic cultural system, nevertheless it was formed from the awareness of a diachronic struggle, however mythologized and elaborated. It is in this way that I should like to question and modify the new historicist model, which, persuasive as it is, provides no real explanation for the processes of historical change.

New historicist writing, whether about the Renaissance or Romantic periods, has tended to neuter the radicalism of figures traditionally regarded as oppositional (at least during a period of their lives) by arguing that their discursive practices are determined by the dominant culture. Such a totalizing system and subject model fails to do justice to the diversity of thought and complexity of political ideology available to radical writers in the 1790s. The tendency to dismiss all oppositional proselytizing as implicated in the dominant episteme ignores the differing ways radicals in the 1790s and other times defined themselves and their dissent, not only against authoritarian ideologies but also within their own communities, where differing strengths of opposition resulted in different interpretations of the same radical precursors as well as other appeals to contrasting precedents.[3] Both Joseph Priestley and John Thelwall, for instance, opposed the repressive measures of Pitt's government and favoured reform, yet defined their opposition within different historical traditions: Priestley praising Cromwell and the Independents, while Thelwall, despising Cromwell, adopted instead a Leveller position. This notion of a unified synchronic cultural system accounts for the avoidance of discussion in recent historicist writing of key texts by which historical precedents were mediated to late eighteenth-century radicals, especially the histories or memoirs of Burnet, Clarendon, Whitelocke and Ludlow and the political tracts of Commonwealthsmen, such as James Burgh and the author of *An Historical Essay on the English Constitution*. All these works were immensely influential in transmitting readings of the events of the 1640s and 1650s to later generations.

Milton's and Harrington's prose were also readily available in John Toland's editions of their works, respectively published in 1678 and 1700.[4] A number of seventeenth-century works were also reprinted in new editions. The radical publisher Joseph Johnson republished Milton's *A Treatise of Civil Power in Ecclesiastical Causes* in 1790 and issued a new edition of Sidney's *Discourse on Government* in 1795.[5] Zera S. Fink claims that the English Jacobins who frequented Johnson's shop were "high on Sydney and Milton."[6] Several of Milton's works were republished during the 1790s; *Areopagitica* appeared in three different editions between 1791 and 1793, and *The Readie and Easie Way* was republished in 1791. Milton's *Tenure of Kings and Magistrates* was republished in 1784 in Dublin, contributing to the ideological justification for rebellion of the United Irishmen in 1798.[7] Indeed, it was the writings of the Commonwealthsmen, Harrington, Milton and Sidney, which inspired the French Revolutionaries as well as the English Jacobins.[8] The reappearance of these texts outside their specific synchronic systems and the recourse later writers make to them establishes a strong and clear diachronic, oppositional element in political pamphleteering. It is this kind of diachronic text which I believe has been avoided in recent writing and which I would like to explore in this essay. I argue that the late eighteenth-century radical writers – the anonymous author of the *Historical Essay*, James Burgh, Richard Price,

Joseph Priestley, John Thelwall and the young S.T. Coleridge – engage in the English political struggle by emplotting the 150-year-old English Revolution and the contemporary French Revolution in various ways to substantiate and differentiate their own dissent. The most radical and sustained engagement with the writers of the English Revolution is provided, perhaps surprisingly, by the young Coleridge. By presenting such a thesis, involving the temporal mediation of seventeenth-century republican thought to radicals of the late eighteenth century, I go some way in the direction of linking diachronically the Renaissance and Romantic periods: the two main areas of the "synchronic" new historicist focus.

II

Our own view of seventeenth-century Republicanism is perhaps some-what constricted, and constructed, in that, as literary critics, we have tended to foreground Milton. Of course, as political and intellectual historians of the period have shown, an understanding of what constitutes republican thought at this time must take into account a whole range of writers, including Marchamont Nedham, John Selden, James Harrington, Algernon Sidney, as well as Andrew Marvell.[9] When invoking the good old cause for their own benefits, the writers of the 1790s and beyond usually call on Milton first, but he is seldom alone. In 1802 Wordsworth wrote 14 "Sonnets dedicated to Liberty" which condemn contemporary Britain for its lethargy and sordid materialism. One of these begins "Milton! thou shouldst be living at this hour;/England hath need of thee" and invokes the elder poet and republican to provide us with "manners, virtue, freedom and power." Yet a further sonnet expands this range considerably:

> Great men have been among us; hands that penned
> And tongues that uttered wisdom – better none:
> The later Sidney, Marvel, Harrington,
> Young Vane, and others who called Milton friend.
> These moralists could act and comprehend.[10]

This formulaic invocation of the names of Milton, Harrington, Sidney, and sometimes Vane and Marvell, is fairly common among writers and politicians of the 1790s. Richard Price in his *Discourse on the Love of Our Country* ahistorically links the names of Milton, Locke, Sidney and Hoadly.[11] Coleridge, in 1795, lumps together the "Sages and patriots that being dead do yet speak to us, spirits of Milton, Locke, Sidney,

Harrington" (*LPR*, 290). In 1795 Coleridge had planned to give a series of six lectures in Bristol under the title "A Comparative View of the English Rebellion under Charles the First, and the French Revolution" which would ground his political and religious dissent on a more historical basis. The second of these lectures was to be concerned with the liberty of the press and was to involve a discussion of "MILTON. SYDNEY. HARRINGTON. BRISSOT. SEYEYES. MIRABEAU. THOMAS PAYNE." (*LPR*, 255).

Although the events of the 1640s and 1650s seem to be well known and the writings of Milton, Harrington and Sidney appear to have been read, none of the figures I discuss here shows any real understanding of the strong differences between these republican heroes. Milton and Harrington, for instance, were not close political allies and they differed in their respective political programmes: Milton eventually favouring a permanent council of "the better sort" as a government, whereas the Harringtonians argued for a rotating system of representation.[12] In giving common purpose to the Commonwealthsmen and ignoring their party differences, Coleridge and Wordsworth find what they are looking for in the precedents they adopt. They allow spurious unity and coherence of purpose and principle to the Commonwealthsmen and by so doing provide a clearer historical pedigree for their own political values. Indeed, both Coleridge and Wordsworth actually claim more than that they have read and been impressed by these writers. They assert that the writers themselves are in some ways not dead but a part of a community: they "live among us" or, despite being dead, they "do yet speak to us." It is easier to thus appropriate for our own political philosophies the writers who are in some sense a part of us and, as such, a part of each other. This notion of a conversation with Milton and the Commonwealthsmen resuscitates the classical republican philological ideal of reading as a conversation between men in time.[13]

The writers I discuss in this essay were either unwilling or unable to outline the differences and oppositional writings of seventeenth-century republicans. Given Wordsworth's abandonment of the democratic ideals of the French Revolution at the time of his writing of the poems, the sonnets imply that the poet is claiming Milton, Harrington, Sidney and Vane as Whigs rather than democrats, whereas Coleridge desires their spiritual support in his argument for a democratic and, implicitly, republican constitution. Because formulaic invocations of the Common-wealthsmen were often indiscriminate, a certain latitude in interpretation was thus permissible, allowing radicals of differing political positions to claim these Republican heroes as their own. In the 1790s both Wordsworth and Coleridge claimed Milton, Harrington and Sidney as fellow democrats. As both men later moved towards positions of conformity, they emphasized instead the more conservative and oligarchic elements in Commonwealthsman thought. This process was not swift nor abrupt and it allowed a gradual re-evaluation of Commonwealthsman definitions of what constituted "the people."[14] Seventeenth-century republican writers were thus capable of being interpreted from differing perspectives depending on the interpreters' own political agenda. More than this, the kind of writer appealed to differentiated varied oppositional positions. Wordsworth and Coleridge tend to prefer Milton, Harrington and Sidney, yet John Thelwall highlights the role of the more obviously radical and troublesome seventeenth-century Leveller, John Lilburne. Most radical of all, however, was Robert Southey's praise for the regicide Henry Marten in his *Poems* (1797). Commenting on Marten's incarceration, Southey asks his readers:

> . . . Dost thou ask his crime?
> He had rebell'd against the king, and sat
> In judgment on him; for his ardent mind
> Shaped goodliest plans of happiness on earth.
> And peace and liberty.

In condoning the execution of Charles I, Southey was also condoning that of Louis XVI and his republicanism did not go unnoticed by the Tory editors of *The Anti-Jacobin*, who pilloried his poetry in their journal during 1797.[15]

III

Events and figures from the English Revolution formed an important element of the rhetoric and substance of political writing of the 1790s. When he sought to discredit the ideas expressed by Richard Price in his famous *Discourse on the Love of our Country* (1789), Edmund Burke in his *Reflections on the Revolution in France* claimed that Price's sermon was of a strain which had not been heard in the country "since the year 1648, when a predecessor of Dr Price, the Rev. Hugh Peters, made the vault of the king's own chapel at St James's ring with the honour and privilege of the saints." Burke twice makes this comparison between Price and Hugh Peters, an Independent minister and propagandist for the Army during the Civil War and Commonwealth who became prominent chiefly for his sermons justifying the execution of Charles I. Burke strengthens the link between the two preachers by noting the similarity of their rhetoric, pointing out their fondness for Psalm 149 which was used by Milton and others to justify the destruction of earthly tyrants.[16] Burke attempts to distance his readers by placing Price's sermon in the context of the 1640s, where the "spirit of moderation" was also in short supply. Burke is, of course, doing much the same thing as Coleridge and Wordsworth but in a more ironic way. He is trying to construct a transhistorical community of dissent, the attitudes and ideas of which surface historically to disastrous effect.

What Burke seeks to bring out in his attack on Price and what he believes defines this community is religious radicalism, the conflation of religion with politics: "politics and the pulpit are terms that have little agreement," and Burke claims that "No sound ought to be heard in the church but the healing voice of christian charity." In some ways it is the style of Price's sermon that disturbs Burke almost as much as the matter; it is a "pulpit style" which has been "revived after so long a discontinuance." When Price talks as if he had made a discovery, he "only follows a precedent." Once again, Burke's point is textual and allusive. Peters, after the trial of Charles I, alluded to the same biblical text as Price in his sermon *On the Love of Country*. Given Peters' fate, Burke's comparison strikes Price as sinister:

> the same Dr Peters, concluding a long prayer at the Royal Chapel at Whitehall, (he had very triumphantly chosen his place), said, "I have prayed and preached these twenty years; and now I may say with old Simeon, *Lord, now lettest thou thy servant depart in peace, for mine eyes have seen thy salvation*." Peters had not the fruits of his prayer, for he neither departed so soon as he wished, nor in peace.

Burke complains that, like Peters, Price had profaned "the beautiful and prophetic ejaculation, commonly called *'nunc dimittis'*," by applying it to a political revolution.[17] In so doing he is attacking the whole tradition of the reading of prophecy in political terms.

In the 1790s, a wide range of people were using Scripture to give authenticity to their political beliefs and expectations, including Priestley, Coleridge, Blake, Richard Brothers, Joanna Southcott and a substantial number of plebeian and popular prophets to whom Iain MacCalman has recently drawn our attention.[18] For Price, Priestley, Coleridge and others, there could be no separation of the meaning of the words "religion" and "politics." These words were artificially sundered by the establishment in order to mystify its own usurped authority in *"jure divino"* claims. The point is a crucial one, and one which Coleridge makes in the second of his "Lectures on Revealed Religion" of 1795:

the very name (Priest) is no where applied to Christians in the new Testament except in one Text – and there it is said, Ye shall be all Priests – in the same sense as it is elsewhere – Ye shall be all Kings, and, I suppose, if we were all Priests and all kings, it would be all one as if there were no Priest and no King.[19] (*LPR*, 137–8)

Coleridge takes to an extreme the Lutheran notion of individual autonomy in matters of religion. In excluding religion from politics, Burke, however, is mystifying the Established Church in a way that disallows political scrutiny. Significantly, he sees the ancestry of this inability to separate religion and politics in the Commonwealth and the political destabilization which resulted. Coleridge and Price effectively deny the hierarchy of mystery by believing that in a true theocracy every person is a priest and thus social and political distinctions are invalid. Coleridge, as we shall see later, argued that this was the position of the Hebrew nation under the Mosaic dispensation, and it was a key idea underpinning his own radical dissent in the mid-1790s. Burke's point in comparing Price with Peters is thus not simply a rhetorical flourish, but an illustration of his central political philosophy. For Burke, beneath the novelty of reform lurks simply the revival of the Good Old Cause and the religious enthusiasm it spawned; in making this charge against the novelty of Price's position Burke hoped to indicate what the consequences of that position might be. Price might look forward and prophesy what the future would be like, but Burke could return to precedent and indicate the likelihood of the monstrous triumph of the French Revolution. Both prophets and ironists could use the events of the English Revolution for their own cause. Price was sufficiently rattled to single out this particular "horrid misrepresentation" for specific rebuttal in the Preface to the fourth edition of his *Sermon*.[20]

IV

Burke was not alone in making this charge against the religious radicals of the period. The Methodist minister Martin Madan, in his *Letters to J. Priestley* (1786), compared the opponents of George III to the executioners of Charles I, linking the Presbyterians of the 1640s with the Nonconformists of the 1780s and 1790s.[21] Priestley replied to this charge in his *Familiar Letters Addressed to the Inhabitants of Birmingham* (1790). Priestley argues that it is necessary to study history to gain an understanding of the workings of Divine Providence, and also essential to attempt to define the laws that govern the operation of history in order to display in narrative form the effects of those laws. For Priestley, it is important to point out that "a century and a half" separates the two groups of dissenters and that the Presbyterians of the 1640s, although they may be in some ways the ancestors of the dissenters of the 1790s, were radically different in their ideas from their descendants. Moreover, it was Cromwell's Independents who put Charles to death, not the Presbyterians who opposed the execution and were, in fact, the "last well-wishers of the King." In his attempts to demonstrate Madan's inept historical knowledge, Priestley argues that in the Long Parliament, which Charles called in 1642, the majority were Episcopalian, not Presbyterian, and that these were the men who prosecuted the war against the king. Priestley is, however, keen on one historical parallel. In comparing the times of George III and Charles I, he argues, Madan has confounded the characters of the two kings and implied that they were "governed by similar maxims, so that whoever could take it into their heads to rise against the one, and dethrone him, would do the same by the other if they could." Priestley considers that Madan mistakes the case: the king was put to death not because of the wickedness of his subjects but because he violated natural law. The death of the "*blessed martyr*" must be ascribed to his own treachery:

> But to *what* was he a martyr, but to his own tyranny and duplicity? He would have governed in an arbitrary manner, without any parliament, and actually raised taxes by his own authority . . . and would not such measures as these justify resistance to *any* king?

Priestley, unlike Coleridge and Wordsworth, argues for the complexity of the political issues involved, and, while he does not deny that the Presbyterians and Independents of the 1640s and 1650s are the ancestors of the dissenters of his own day, he does deny that there is any link of the kind that Burke and Madan have forged between the comparatively small number of Independent regicides and the reformers of his own time. In any case, it was the Presbyterians who supported the return of the Stuart monarchy to Britain in 1660. Priestley claims that the execution of Charles I was not due to religious motivation:

> Besides, the Independents of that day did not behead the king from any principles peculiar to their religious persuasion. *Cromwell*, and the rest who joined him in that action, would have cut off the king, whatever had been *their* religion or *his*. They consulted not their *religion*, but their *safety* and their *ambition*. And in all these measures the *Independents* were joined by the *Deists*, and men of no religion at all.[22]

It is not clear who Priestley means by "Deists." Presumably he is using the term as a synonym for scoffer or blasphemer and is possibly referring to the regicide Henry Marten who had a reputation for scandalous talk.[23] Priestley, here, is interested in denying traditions of influence for obvious reasons and, elsewhere, had already dissociated himself from the Levellers of the Civil War period, although his political beliefs were close to those of the movement.[24] Despite this, it is plain that in his various writings on the period he inclines towards Cromwell in his support of tolerance and the "free liberty . . . given to the professors of any form of the Christian religion."[25]

V

To a certain extent, all the writings discussed in this essay were dependent on six particular accounts of events during the 1640s. Four of these are written by actors or spectators of the times they describe and two are later discussions of the times. In his *Lectures on History and General Policy* (1785), Priestley rehearses the arguments in favour of the four contemporary histories of the Commonwealth. He praises Clarendon's *History of the Rebellion and Civil Wars in England* for its "full and pretty faithful history of the civil war in the reign of Charles I" but adds that Clarendon adheres "too much to the royal party," proclaiming the necessity of supplementing his history with those of Bulstrode Whitelocke and Edmund Ludlow – one a "zealous Presbyterian" and the other an Independent. The two latter figures, in Priestley's eyes, "had no less advantage than Clarendon of being well informed of what they wrote." Priestley admires Clarendon's attempt to write history with a "degree of dignity," although he finds the historian's long periods and frequent parentheses "very tiresome." Priestley's other chief source is the *History of His Own Times* by Bishop Burnet, who is well informed but "charged with great partiality" by those opposing his advocacy of the House of Orange.[26] Priestley is historically sophisticated enough to realize the partiality of these four accounts, and he attempts to balance the contrasting viewpoints of the narrators in constructing his own history. For those who were interested in the events of the Civil War period – such as Priestley, Price, Godwin, Coleridge and Thelwall – Burnet and Clarendon appear to have been the main authorities.[27]

These authorities were often mediated through other texts, chief among these being the anonymous *An Historical Essay on the English Constitution* (1771) and James Burgh's *Political Disquisitions* (1774–76). The *Historical Essay* is interesting mainly for its extended argument idealizing the Saxon constitution and denouncing the Norman Yoke of Kingship, itself one of the key themes of seventeenth-century radical thought.[28] The treatise had a very wide circulation and was heavily used by late eighteenth-century radical thinkers, such as James Burgh, John Cartwright and Coleridge.[29] The *Historical Essay*'s programme of reform calls for the restoration of annual parliaments, secret ballot and the elimination of rotten boroughs. It also, however, contains a fairly extensive discussion of the constitutional developments of the Civil War period. The essay is obviously hostile to Charles I, who was "of a very obstinate, inflexible temper," having "a design to render himself absolute master of the kingdom." Following Harringtonian and Leveller critiques of Charles, the *Historical Essay* argues that his fault was that he would not distinguish between "the executive power" of the crown and the "supreme power" lodged "in the law of the land, and no where else." Yet the essay criticizes most of all "the leading men of the house of commons" who subverted the mode of government from that of constitutional monarchy to "what they called, a COMMONWEALTH" but what was in reality "a standing aristocracy." The essay is hostile to the continuance of parliaments without annual or, at least, frequent elections, and the Long Parliament is thus an anathema to its author:

> There is no chief magistrate, no political body of men, call them by what name you please, whether the many, or the few, let them be ever so wise, ever so virtuous, ever so moderate, or high in your expectation, at the entrance upon their office, but what will (if you make them powerful, and fix them above your control) most certainly degenerate into tyrants and make you slaves. This doctrine was amply verified, in the conduct of this parliament. (*Essay*, 80, 108, 112)

To this intoxication with power the essay attributes the vengeful destruction of the king, to whom they never gave "one moment's respit, till they brought his head to the block, and made way, through his blood, to establish their own sovereign authority." For the essay, the Long Parliament was a tyranny of the few which attempted to destroy the elective power of the people. The Long Parliament continued in this state until "they were forced out of the house, by a file of musketeers, under the command of Oliver Cromwell" (*Essay*, 114–17).

The *Historical Essay* demonstrates an interesting feature of later readings of the events of the 1640s and 1650s. For supporters of the monarchy, Charles I appears as the "blessed martyr" of *Eikon Basilike*, for republicans and democrats he generally appears as a mean-spirited, arbitrary tyrant. Nevertheless, most writers on the period choose to define their position not *vis-à-vis* Charles but in terms of the Long Parliament, Cromwell or the Rump. James Burgh's equally influential

Political Disquisitions follows the broad ideological perspective of the *Historical Essay* in its demands for religious toleration, extension of the franchise, annual parliaments, secret ballots and the exclusion of placemen, and in its justification of the rights of resistance.[30] Burgh, however, inclines towards single-chamber government and is more sympathetic to the Long Parliament. J.C.D. Clark argues that Burgh's *Political Disquisitions* "stood at the end of a tradition and summed it up."[31] However, this ignores the influential nature of Burgh's work and its status as a mediating text for later writers. Certainly Burgh is heavily dependent on the writings and ideas of Sidney, Milton and Harrington, as well as on the histories and accounts of Burnet, Clarendon, Ludlow and Whitelocke. The debate, although ostensibly about what actually happened in the 1640s and 1650s, is contained within certain textual parameters, necessitating an engagement with shared issues.

Burgh repeats the usual Commonwealthsman invective against the "desperate Tyrant" Charles I, but he criticizes the author of the *Historical Essay* for his severity against the Long Parliament, which he wishes to rescue from the charge of tyranny: "They certainly meant honestly, having no byas to draw them from the public interest, though they stay too long, fearing, perhaps that their successors might not be as faithful as themselves" (*BPD*, 1: 89, 90). Burgh commends Harrington who laboured "to show that all well conducted states have avoided the error of suffering power to remain too long in the same hands" (*BPD*, 1: 112), yet he defends the Long Parliament on grounds of historical necessity. The length of that Parliament's sitting was justifiable only because of exceptionable circumstances, although Burgh admits it was a dilatory body. Burgh's ideal is the single-chamber government of the Rump Parliament, what he calls "the *English* republic" which was demolished by "the villainous *Cromwell*." This, Burgh argues, was one of "the most unmixed that ever was known" and one that was "a true government by representation" (*BPD*, 1: 9). Although Burgh presents the standard iconoclastic image of Charles as the tyrant, it is Oliver Cromwell who appears as the real villain of *Political Disquisitions* for his dismissal of the Rump (*BPD*, 2: 375–82). For Burgh and other Commonwealthsmen, the model of the Rump Parliament, which in 1649 abolished monarchy and declared England to be "a Commonwealth and a Free State," became a near ideal example of single-chamber government.

The notion that the Rump was composed of serious revolutionaries gained credit over the century. Although there were ardent republicans within it, such as the regicides Thomas Scot, Henry Marten and Thomas Chaloner, as well as the more famous Sidney and Vane, this reading of the Rump's status has not impressed modern historians.[32] Yet

eighteenth-century radicals and reformers wanted to emplot the history
of the period in a somewhat different way and to a substantial body of
them, who desired a sovereign, single-chamber parliament, the Rump
became a yardstick by which to measure contemporary corruption. In
Burgh, the myth of the betrayed republican parliament becomes fully
established and it is Cromwell who is its executioner.

It was the presence of a standing army that allowed Cromwell to purge
the Long Parliament and later to dismiss the Rump. Burgh gives a fairly
detailed, though confused, account of the events of 1647–48 (*BPD*,
2: 373–8) in which he pictures Cromwell as an ambitious dictator
who rules, without parliamentary or popular consent, simply by the
power of his army. Cromwell's usurpation is a tragic event, occurring
when England was on "her way to her highest pinnacle of glory."
Burgh's view of Cromwell is close to that of the seventeenth-century
Commonwealthsmen:

> He destroyed the liberties of his country, and with them ruined the
> happiness of his own life. Wretched ambition! To what dost thou
> bring thy votaries. See *Cromwell*, who might have lived peaceful
> and happy, had he, immediately after settling the commonwealth,
> disbanded his army, and returned to a private unenvied station, and
> who might have been to all ages celebrated among the illustrious
> founders of states, and patrons of liberty, and destroyers of tyrants
> – behold him, canting, sneaking and dissembling, to curry favour
> with those he despised; behold him tortured with guilt, and fear
> of assassination, and of damnation; scared at the sight of every
> stranger; terrified at pamphlets and paragraphs encouraging to
> destroy him; armed with a coat of mail under his clothes. (*BPD*,
> 2: 377–81)

Although Burgh does not refer to it, one of the pamphlets that so
terrified Cromwell was Edward Sexby's *Killing No Murder* (1657) which
was republished throughout the eighteenth century.[33] Burgh's picture of
Cromwell as a leader who failed to respond to the republican moment
recalls James Holstun's recent discussion of the figurings of Cromwell
in Harrington's *Oceana*, where the Lord Protector faces the choice of
becoming "either the architect of a new republic or the tyrant enslaving
his state."[34] This choice was also faced by Parliament after Cromwell's
death when they could have established a republican government on
the resignation of Richard Cromwell, had they "not been bullied out of
it by *Monck* and the army, who brought in against their country, the
curse of the *Stuarts*" (*BPD*, 2: 382). Thus Burgh emplots the events of
the Interregnum tragically, as a lost opportunity and as a polemic for

a popular militia rather than a standing army. Clearly, Burgh admires and sees himself in the line of the commonwealthsmen of the Rump, like Harrington, Milton, Sidney, Scot, Marten, Vane and others. The regicide itself did not disturb him. Had Charles "as many heads as the *Lernean hydra*," he writes, "he ought to have lost them all" (*BPD*, 1: 186).[35]

Both the *Historical Essay* and the *Political Disquisitions* discuss the nature of the Long Parliament and the Rump, utilizing the texts available to them. Clearly, both attempt to use events between 1640 and 1660 to support their own ideological position. The two works were extremely influential in radical and dissenting circles and their modes of configuration were adapted and transformed by later writers, two of whom, in the mid-1790s, were concerned to appropriate this diachronic text for their own ideological standpoint.

VI

John Thelwall was prominent as one of the leaders of the English Jacobins at the time of the French Revolution and as one of the defendants in the celebrated Treason Trials of 1794. Thelwall's political writings are substantial; while they are chiefly concerned with the immediate political context, they are firmly grounded in a historical awareness of opposition and struggle.[36] Thelwall specialized in political lecturing, delivering a series of lectures in support of parliamentary reform and opposing the repressive nature of William Pitt's government. Many of these lectures had a historical basis, including his lecture on "The History of Prosecution for Political Opinion" – a subject close to his own experience. Significantly, Thelwall traces this history back to the seventeenth century. He regards the Commonwealth as a period when "Democracy triumphed for a while over the tyranny of courts." Nevertheless, for Thelwall, all the prosecutions taking place at this time were not justifiable. He was attracted to the case of John Lilburne, whose virtue and energy he admired. Lilburne, like Thelwall himself, was a victim of the attempts of government to subdue the "rousing of the human faculties" which had resulted in a progressive illumination and a "wider diffusion of political truth." The Civil War period was thus a key moment in this general and progressive spread of truth:

> In the reign of Charles I, the light had diffused itself somewhat
> further; and a great majority of virtuous and intelligent gentlemen
> in the House of Commons were animated by a strong desire
> of liberty . . . though Cromwell's usurpation checked, in some
> degree, the progress of political illumination, these principles of

liberty still found to extend themselves through a wider and wider circle.[37]

In a later lecture, Thelwall traces the history of trial by jury from its alleged ancient origins to his own times. Again, the point is a polemical one: it had been an independent jury that had acquitted the reformers of the charge of high treason, despite expectations to the contrary. Once again, Lilburne's "persecution" serves as a useful model illustration for Thelwall's grand argument:

> In the time of *Cromwell*, we have an instance of a virtuous and gallant patriot, Col. *John Lilburne* who was four times tried for high treason, and died a natural death at last. We find in that instance, that juries could be found under all forms, and the prevalence of all factions, to resist tyrannical encroachments; and who disdained alike to be the instrument of the cruel malice of a *Stuart*, or the usurping tyranny of an Oliver Cromwell. (*Tribune*, 3: 226).

Thelwall does not appear to have much understanding of the details of Lilburne's political beliefs nor does he point out that the Leveller was on parole when he died "a natural death," although Thelwall, in a number of ways, is particularly close to the Leveller position. Thelwall's purpose in discussing the events of the 1640s is polemical rather than historical (in the limited sense of Priestley's attempt to uncover the laws of Providence). He is concerned to compare the events of 1649 with those of the revolution in France, with the aim of privileging the later revolution. In two lectures on the "Unfortunate Restoration" of the Stuarts delivered on 29 May and 3 June 1795, Thelwall discusses the Commonwealth and the Restoration. The point made in these lectures is that although the son of Charles I was restored in 1660, it does not follow that "the son of *Louis* the Sixteenth will be restored in France." The second lecture compares the two revolutions and stresses their difference rather than their similarity. Thelwall explains the causes of the English Revolution in simplistically causal terms, ascribing it to "the rising spirit" of liberty which had been suppressed since the Norman overthrow of Saxon freedoms. However, he is keen to point out the fanaticism of the people, distancing his own deistic or Paineite radicalism from that of the English sectaries, and thus, by implication, from that of Priestley and Price. Once again, it is Cromwell, rather than Charles I, who is the target of radical invective. For Thelwall, although he complains of Cromwell's ambition, it is the Lord Protector's fanaticism which provides his defining character trait: "*Oliver Cromwell*; who, though he set out perhaps, with as large a portion of the love of liberty as was possible for a hypocritical fanatic, yet undoubtedly in the end proved himself to be, not a reforming patriot, but an ambitious usurper" (*Tribune*, 3: 188, 183–9).

It soon becomes clear that Thelwall is describing Cromwell through the filter of his own times. His portrait of Cromwell would irresistibly remind his audience of a more unavoidable dictator, Robespierre, who was at the height of his power when Thelwall lectured:

> Thus the *Protectorate*, or, as it is called the Republic, continued as long as he lived, because the superior activity of his mind, the terror of his name, and that sort of fanatic eloquence which he possessed, kept all other persons in awe and, so long as the architect remained, the pillars of the revolution appeared to be secure, whatever change might take place in particular parts of the building. (*Tribune*, 3: 190)

Thelwall's view of Cromwell is close to Coleridge's contemporaneous portrayal of Robespierre in the *Conciones ad Populam* (1795), where the dictator's energy and activity are stressed along with an "enthusiasm . . . blended with gloom, and suspiciousness, and inordinate vanity" (*LPR*, 35). In denying that the English and French Revolutions have any similarity, Thelwall nevertheless approaches the earlier revolution through the rhetoric of the 1790s – the textual descriptions of both periods engaging in a kind dialogue with each other. In attempting to demonstrate that there is no real similarity between the two revolutions, and thus that there will be no restored monarchy in France, Thelwall is led to contrast the motivations of the "people" involved. The mass of people in the French Revolution were quickened by "the generous spirit of liberty" not "the active spirit of fanaticism." The revolution of 1649 was not the revolution of "the great body of an enlightened nation" but one that was produced by a few intelligent minds who stimulated the people to act on principles they did not understand (*Tribune*, 3: 188–90).

Presumably, Thelwall, although admitting that the spirit of liberty permeated seventeenth-century Britain, believed that the English Revolution came too early and drew its leadership from too limited and élitist a group (chiefly the "virtuous and intelligent" men in the House of Commons) to be successful and permanent. The French Revolution, however, he believes to have been a mass enlightenment. The distinction is broad and unclear and it results from Thelwall's wish to claim the 1640s as a revolutionary decade while, at the same time, protecting the contemporary revolution from historical pessimism. Behind this rudimentary historical analysis is his polemical attempt to rescue the

French Revolution from a reductive comparison with that of the English Revolution. There will be no French Cromwell or French Restoration. Thelwall vehemently asserts that "the same causes which produced the revolution in 1649, did not produce the revolution in *France*" and that "the causes which enabled *Oliver Cromwell* to usurp a tyranny over this country, and make himself Protector, do not exist, nor ever have existed, at any period of the French Revolution." Unlike the English Revolution that in France is "built upon the broad basis of public and almost universal opinion." Thelwall therefore concludes that his audience can have "no foundation whatever to expect a similar catastrophe to that which took place in this country" (*Tribune*, 3: 192).

Ironically, Thelwall pins his hopes on the separation of senatorial and military popularity, resulting from the wisdom of the French people, to prevent political and physical power being concentrated in one Cromwellian person. Thelwall writes this just before the rise of Bonaparte. He foresees the mechanism by which a Bonaparte might come to power, but he stubbornly refuses to apply this analysis to revolutionary France (*Tribune*, 3: 195). In so doing, he is taking issue with Burke's polemical point against the actions of the French revolutionaries that now,

> in the weakness of one kind of authority, and in the fluctuation of all, the officers of an army will remain for some time mutinous and full of faction, until some popular general, who understands the art of conciliating the soldiery, and who possesses the true spirit of command, shall draw the eyes of all men upon himself.[38]

Arguably, Thelwall's reading of the English Revolution is conditioned by his desire to discredit Burke's polemic against the French Revolution, and it is intertextually within this Burkeian critique of contemporary events that Thelwall must establish his own reading. Thelwall's account of the events of the 1640s is interesting and somewhat unusual in that he is keen to advance the religious enthusiasm of the time as a reason for the failure of the English Revolution. Although pillorying Cromwell, Thelwall avoids the usual formulaic appeals to the sages and patriots of the time, keen to prevent Burkeian readers from using 1653 or 1660 as a weapon against 1789.

VII

Finally, I should like to turn to the work of the early S.T. Coleridge who, more than most, grounded his dissent on a historical basis. He had planned to give a series of lectures comparing "the English Rebellion under Charles the First and the French Revolution" (*LPR*, 253–6), which would have compared Cromwell with Robespierre, and Milton, Sidney and Harrington with Paine, Sieyès, Mirabeau and others. By 1795, Coleridge certainly had a good knowledge of the works of Milton, Harrington, Clarendon, Burnet and Burgh, possibly as background reading for his lectures.[39] Although these lectures were probably not given, it is interesting that Coleridge, like Thelwall, felt that he had to place his understanding of the events in France against the backdrop of the English Revolution. More than this, as I have argued elsewhere, Coleridge's attack in *The Plot Discovered* on the British government's two Bills (1795) to restrict the rights of petitioning and of meeting to discuss political grievances appropriates the style and ideas of the Commonwealthsmen, functioning as a jeremiad in the tradition of Milton's *The Readie and Easie Way*. Coleridge had castigated the English people for allowing their liberties to be taken from them so easily and he presented a prophetic lament over the backsliding of the covenanted nation, looking back to a mythic past of "Sages and patriots" who are dead but "do yet speak to us" (*LPR*, 290).[40] Coleridge moved from a neo-Harringtonian utopian position in his "Lectures on Revealed Religion" to that of the Miltonic anti-utopian jeremiad in the slightly later *The Plot Discovered*.[41] His engagement with the Commonwealthsmen is thus much more complex than that of his immediate contemporaries, Price, Priestley or Thelwall, being more aware of the deep structure of the historical imagination. By this I mean that Coleridge was not just concerned with the polemical uses a writer or a series of events can be put to, but that he also realized that the form in which a series of events is emplotted or configured determines the kind of narrative which is told.[42]

Coleridge's engagement with the Commonwealthsmen is thus more sophisticated than that of his contemporaries for a number of reasons. First, Coleridge's own religious radicalism was much closer to that of Milton and his contemporaries than was Thelwall's deistic belief. Second, Coleridge was also a poet who consciously, in "Religious Musings" and elsewhere, attempted to appropriate the Miltonic role of the poet-prophet.[43] Third, and perhaps most importantly, the main focus of Coleridge's religious radicalism was on the relations between property and power. As such, his discourse engaged with that of Harrington's *Oceana* and its admirers.[44] By 1795, Coleridge had come to believe that the system of owning property was responsible for the problems confronting humanity. He and his fellow poet, Robert Southey, had originated a plan, known as Pantisocracy, in which a small familial-based community would emigrate to the banks of the Susquehanna

River in Pennsylvania and hold property in common, thus removing any temptation to evil. The sources of this experiment have been widely discussed but its similarity to the Puritan utopias discussed in James Holstun's *A Rational Millennium* argues for a longer history for Pantisocracy than has hitherto been given.[45] Certainly, the scheme recalls Winstanley's Digger cultivation of the common land of St George's Field in 1649.[46] In the second of his "Lectures on Revealed Religion," Coleridge outlines a theory of agrarian republicanism which, as Nigel Leask points out, is "pure Harrington, as transmitted through the medium of Moses Lowman's popular *Dissertation on the Civil Government of the Hebrews*."[47] In the "Lectures on Revealed Religion" Coleridge appropriated this version of the Harringtonian commonwealth, which he opposed to the materialism and commercialism of his own time. He identified the Mosaic Dispensation as the "republic of God's own making" analogous to the millenarian kingdom of Christ which he believed was being ushered in by the French Revolution.[48]

The Jewish constitution that Coleridge came across in Lowman's *Dissertation* contained a number of features similar to those found in Harrington's *Oceana*, including fixed laws, the rotation of office-holders, and the existence of a popular militia rather than a standing army.[49] Coleridge's treatment of the Jewish constitution was based upon an understanding of the relationship between property and power that was essentially Harringtonian. Harrington had argued in *Oceana* for an agrarian law by which all landholders whose property brought in an income of more than £2,000 a year must distribute it among their heirs so that no heir received an income greater than £2,000 a year, or so that any surplus was distributed among all heirs. Dowries were limited to £1,500. Primogeniture was to be ended and estates to be divided up among all children.[50] By this law, Harrington argued that the restoration of aristocracy and monarchy would be impossible. Thus, a free commonwealth would be created based upon an extensive body of independent freeholders.[51]

Whether directly or through Lowman, Coleridge discusses the Jewish constitution in Harringtonian terms.[52] He describes the Jewish constitution as being founded on an original contract between God and his chosen nation. The nation was a kind of federal republic of 12 tribes. Land was equally divided among the people. To prevent the accumulation and alienation of property, interest on loans was forbidden and all debts were abolished every sixth year. Every fiftieth year the Jewish Jubilee was appointed by which all lands were restored. Coleridge regards this law as "replete with practical Wisdom and Benevolence." By it, every Hebrew was the subject of God alone and equality prevailed.

Coleridge has accepted the Harringtonian equation between property and power:

> Property is Power and equal Property equal Power. A Poor Man is necessarily more or less a Slave. Poverty is the Death of public Freedom – it virtually enslaves Individuals, and generates those Vices, which make necessary a dangerous concentration of power in the executive branch. If we except the Spartan, the Jewish has been the only Republic that can consistently boast of Liberty and Equality. (*LPR*, 124–6)

Coleridge argues that it is the system of accumulation of property to which "we are indebted for nine-tenths of our Vices and Miseries." He denies that anyone can claim an absolute right to ownership of land and that "an abolition of all individual Property is perhaps the only infallible Preventative against accumulation" (*LPR*, 126–8). The Jews were, however, too ignorant at this stage in their history to be able to cope with the complete abolition of property, so the Divine Wisdom demanded its mere equalization.

The Mosaic constitution itself ensured a perfect balance between the power of equal property rights and the authority of a genuinely representative senate. The representative Congress of the Hebrew community of 24,000 men was composed of a rotated militia representing the entire Jewish nation, balanced by a Sanhedrin or Senate of 70 Elders who could deliberate on laws but not enact them; the Assembly would accept or reject these by ballot. The executive was, of course, divine as the "Laws of the Nation had proceeded miraculously from God" (*LPR*, 128–30). Self-rule by the people in the Senate and Assembly thus excluded the *jure divino* claims of monarchy and the priesthood. The Jewish constitution lasted until the days of Samuel when the Jews committed the foulest crime "of which human nature is capable" in petitioning for a king. Coleridge's treatment of the backsliding of the Jews recalls that of Milton in *The Readie & Easie Way*, where Milton warned how "God in much displeasure gave a king to the *Israelites*, and imputed it a sin to them that they sought one." Both Coleridge and Milton refer to the jeremiadic lament of the prophet Samuel on this occasion (*LPR*, 132–3).[53] Coleridge's strong sense of kinship with Milton and the Commonwealthsmen is nowhere more apparent than in the following republican sentiment:

> the Dispensations of God have always warned Man against the least Diminution of civil Freedom. The Israelites however listened not to Samuel and afterwards severely repented of it so that there was

among them this figurative Remark. A cockatrice is a Dragon with a Crown on his head, and hatched by a Viper on a Cock's Egg. The Viper was the symbol of Ingratitude among them and a Cock's Egg of Credulity.[54] (*LPR* 134)

Coleridge's radicalism as expressed through the "Lectures on Revealed Religion" and *The Plot Discovered* is thus a curious combination of Harringtonian utopianism and Miltonic jeremiad.[55] Although Coleridge at this time goes considerably beyond Harrington (and towards Winstanley) in desiring the abolition of property as an ideal, he is indebted to the analysis by the Commonwealthsman of the correspondence between property and political power, as his description of the Jewish constitution demonstrates. Believing that property rights were incompatible with liberty and equality, Coleridge rejected the notion of an equal commonwealth based on independent proprietors in favour of one based on the common ownership of property; as John Morrow puts it, "Christian egalitarianism necessitated the abandonment of the independent-property-holder myth that lay at the heart of Harringtonian discourse."[56] In many ways it was Coleridge's engagement with the Harringtonian discourse of property which led him to his fundamental understanding of the relationship between political power and property rights. Harringtonian discourse thus radicalized Coleridge's dissent far beyond that of his contemporaries, few of whom, with the exception of Thomas Spence, appear to have desired the abolition of property itself.

VIII

All the writers I have discussed were engaged in different ways in a synchronic debate about political and social structures. The radical thinkers among them were also attempting to appropriate a diachronic aspect to their dissent, enabling them to ground their politics on a historical basis. In their desire to provide an oppositional politics, these writers had to rewrite history in a way that allowed them to commune with certain Commonwealth figures and to distance themselves from others. Although the English Revolution is only one event in a pageant of tyranny, oppression and betrayal, it is a determining event that late eighteenth-century radical thinkers could not ignore and which they needed to engage with in order to construct their own positions. Although this historical perspective is clearly intertextual, dependent on previous written accounts and the ideologies which produced them, nevertheless it constitutes a diachronic text which allows later thinkers to define and construct their own oppositional positions within a dominant cultural system. The tendency of studies of "cultural poetics" to flatten ideological stances into a unified system is thus somewhat belied by the deeply fissured nature of English republican responses to the events and ideas of the English Revolution.

ABBREVIATIONS

BPD James Burgh, *The Political Disquisitions: or an Enquiry into Public Errors, Defects, and Abuses* (London: E. and C. Dilly, 1774–75), 3 vols.

Essay *An Historical Essay on the English Constitution; or an impartial Inquiry into the Elective Power of the People, from the first Establishment of the Saxons in this Kingdom* (London: E. and C. Dilly, 1771).

LPR S.T. Coleridge, *Lectures 1795: On Politics and Religion*, L. Patton and P. Mann, eds., Vol. I of *The Collected Works of Samuel Taylor Coleridge*, Bollingen Series 75 (London and Princeton: Routledge and Kegan Paul and Princeton University Press, 1969 –).

Tribune John Thelwall, *The Tribune, A Periodical Publication consisting chiefly of the Political Lectures of J. Thelwall*, 3 vols. (London, 1795–96).

NOTES

1. Michael McCanles, "The Authentic Discourse of the Renaissance," *Diacritics*, 10: 1 (Spring 1980), 77–87. The term seems to have gained currency from its use by Stephen Greenblatt in his introduction to "The Forms of Power and the Power of Forms in the Renaissance," *Genre*, 15: 1–2 (1982), 1–4. Earlier in his influential *Renaissance Self-Fashioning* (Chicago: University of Chicago Press, 1980), Greenblatt had called his project "cultural poetics." Greenblatt, "Towards a Poetics of Culture," in *The New Historicism*, H. Aram Veeser, ed. (New York and London: Routledge, 1989), 1–14.
2. Louis A. Montrose, "The Poetics and Politics of Culture," in *The New Historicism*, op. cit., 15–36 (quote on 17). The notes to Montrose's essay provide a useful bibliography of new historicist work in Renaissance studies.
3. See, for instance, Marjorie Levinson, "Back to the Future," in *Rethinking Historicism: Critical Readings in Romantic History*, M. Levinson, M. Butler, J. McGann and Paul Hamilton, eds. (Oxford: Blackwell, 1989), 18–63 (35–7); idem, *Wordsworth's Great Period Poems: Four Essays* (Cambridge: Cambridge University Press, 1986); and Alan Liu, *Wordsworth and the Sense of History* (Stanford: Stanford University Press, 1989).
4. *A Complete Collection of the historical, political and miscellaneous works of John Milton*, John Toland, ed., 3 vols. (Amsterdam (London), 1698); *The Oceana of James Harrington and his other works*, John Toland, ed. (London, 1700). Coleridge certainly

had access to Toland's *Milton*, and he may have owned the edition of Harrington's works by 1795, certainly he had acquired a copy by 1800, *The Notebooks of Samuel Taylor Coleridge*, Kathleen Coburn, ed. (Vol. 4 with Merton Christensen) (Princeton: Princeton University Press, 1957–), 4 vols., 1: 39n, 106–10, 113–15, 118–19, 639–41, 934 and nn. For Toland's influence on Coleridge, see Nigel Leask, *The Politics of the Imagination in Coleridge's Critical Thought* (London: Macmillan, 1988), 28–30.

5. John Milton, *A Treatise of Civil Power in Ecclesiastical causes, shewing that it is not lawfull for any power on earth to compell in matters of religion* (London: J. Johnson, 1790). The editor of Johnson's edition of Sidney praises Toland "who was not only the first to publish Sidney's inestimable Discourses on Government, but also to bless mankind with the prose of Milton, and the works of Harrington," *The Essence of Algernon Sidney's Work on Government to which is annexed his Essay on Love by a Student of the Inner Temple* (London: J. Johnson, 1795), viii.

6. *The Early Wordsworthian Milieu: A Notebook of Christopher Wordsworth with a Few Entries by William Wordsworth*, Zera S. Fink, ed. (Oxford: Clarendon Press, 1958), 110; Zera S. Fink, "Wordsworth and the English Republican Tradition," *Journal of English and Germanic Philology*, 4 (1948), 107–26 (111–2); David Erdman, "Milton! Thou shouldst Be Living," *The Wordsworth Circle*, 19: 1 (1988), 2–9; Nicholas Roe, "Wordsworth, Milton, and the Politics of Poetic Influence," *The Yearbook of English Studies*, 19 (1989), 112–26; Robin Jarvis, *Wordsworth, Milton and the Theory of Poetic Relations* (London: Macmillan, 1991), 77–83

7. See John T. Shawcross, "A Survey of Milton's Prose Works," *Achievements of the Left Hand: Essays on the Prose of John Milton*, Michael Lieb and John T. Sawcross, eds. (Amherst: University of Massachusetts Press, 1974), 292–391 (313, 319, 333, 336).

8. Milton's *Pro Populo Anglicano Defensio* was translated at least twice as *Théorie de la Royauté d'après la Doctrine de Milton*, 2 parts (Paris, 1789) and *Défense du peuple anglais sur le jugement et la condamnation de Charles Premier, roi d'Angleterre . . . Ouvrage propre à éclairer sur la circonstance actuelle où se trouve la France* (Valence: P. Aurel, 1792). *Areopagitica* was translated by Mirabeau as *Sur la liberté de la presse, imité de l'anglais, de Milton. Par le Comte de Mirabeaus* (Londres, Paris, 1788); reprinted 1789 (twice), 1792 (Paris: Le Jay). See Shawcross, "A Survey of Milton's Prose Works," op. cit., 305–6. A French version of Toland's edition of Harrington was published in 1795, *Oeuvres politiques . . . précédées de l'histoire de sa vie, écrite par J. Toland*, trans. P.F. Henry, 3 vols. (Paris, an III, 1795). S.B. Liljegren has argued that Harrington's ideas were important in the discussions leading to the French constitution of 1792, see S.B. Liljegren, ed., "A French Draft Constitution of 1792 Modelled on James Harrington's *Oceana*", *Skrifter utgivna av Kungl. Humanisticka Vetenskapssamfundet i Lund*, 17 (1932), 3–43. See also Iain Hampsher-Monk, "Civic Humanism and Parliamentary Reform: The Case of the Society of the Friends of the People," *Journal of British Studies*, 18 (1979), 70–89, which discusses the use of Harringtonian arguments by the Society of the Friends of Freedom. John Morrow provides a useful overview of these areas in *Coleridge's Political Thought: Property, Morality and the Limits of Traditional Discourse* (London: Macmillan, 1990), 27–42. See also Olivier Lutaud, *Des Révolutions d'Angleterre à la Révolution Française: Le Tyrannicide & Killing No Murder* (La Haye: Martinus Nijhoff, 1973), 117–254, which describes the reception of Edward Sexby's *Killing No Murder* during the revolutions of 1688 and 1789.

9. For the influential nature of these thinkers, see Caroline Robbins, *The Eighteenth-Century Commonwealthman: Studies in the Transmission, Development and Circumstance of English Liberal Thought from the Restoration of Charles II until the War with the Thirteen Colonies* (Cambridge, Mass.: Harvard University Press, 1959), 22–55; J.G.A. Pocock, *The Machiavellian Moment: Florentine Political Thought and the Atlantic Republican Tradition* (Princeton: Princeton University Press, 1975); idem, *Virtue, Commerce, and History: Essays on Political Thought and History,*

chiefly in the Eighteenth Century (Cambridge: Cambridge University Press, 1985). The identification of the ideas of the English Jacobins with the Radical Independents was made by E.P. Thompson in *The Making of the English Working Class* (Penguin: Harmondsworth, 1963), 19–206.

10. *The Poetical Works of William Wordsworth*, E. de Selincourt and H. Darbishire, eds. (Oxford: Clarendon Press, 1940–49), 5 vols., 3: 116.

11. Richard Price, *A Discourse on the Love of Our Country, delivered on Nov. 4, 1789, at the Meeting-House in the Old Jewry, to the Society for Commemorating the Revolution in Great Britain*, second edn. (London: T. Cadell, 1789), 14.

12. See James Holstun, *A Rational Millennium: Puritan Utopias of Seventeenth-Century England and America* (Oxford: Oxford University Press, 1987), 252, 260.

13. See Eugenio Garin, *Italian Humanism: Philosophy and Civic Life in the Renaissance*, trans. Peter Munz (New York: Harper, 1965).

14. The idea that the Commonwealthsmen mediated between the radical and conservative phases of Coleridge's political thought is a thesis convincingly developed by Nigel Leask in *The Politics of Imagination in Coleridge's Critical Thought*, op. cit., 9–45 (44–5). Leask argues that Coleridge and Wordsworth are much closer politically in their appeal to the Commonwealthsmen than my discussion would have it; however, Coleridge's theory of property does seem to me to change more drastically around 1798–99 than Leask suggests. For this debate, see Michael H. Friedman, *The Making of a Tory Humanist: William Wordsworth and the Idea of Community* (New York: Columbia University Press, 1979); James K. Chandler, *Wordsworth's Second Nature: A Study in Poetry and Politics* (Chicago: University of Chicago Press, 1984); Alan Liu, *Wordsworth: The Sense of History*, op. cit.; David Erdman, "Milton Thou Shouldst be Living," *The Wordsworth Circle*, op. cit.; Peter J. Kitson, "The electric fluid of truth," in *Coleridge and the Armoury of the Human Mind*, Peter J. Kitson and Thomas N. Corns, eds. (London: Frank Cass, 1991), 36–62; John Morrow, *Coleridge's Political Thought: Property, Morality and the Limits of Traditional Discourse*, op. cit.

15. Robert Southey, *Poems 1797* (Bristol: J. Cottle, 1796), reprinted (Oxford: Woodstock Books, 1989), 59–60.

16. Edmund Burke, *Reflections on the Revolution in France and of the Proceedings in Certain Societies in London relative to that Event in a Letter intended to have been sent to a Gentleman in Paris* (London, 1790), C.C. O'Brien, ed. (Harmondsworth: Penguin, 1970), 94–5.

17. Burke, *Reflections*, op. cit., 156–9; Price, *Discourse on the Love of our Country*, op. cit., 48–51.

18. Iain MacCalman, *Radical Underworld: Prophets, Revolutionaries and Pornographers in London, 1795–1840* (Cambridge: Cambridge University Press, 1988); see also E.P. Thompson, *The Making of the English Working Class*, op. cit., 385–440; W.H. Oliver, *Prophets and Millennialists* (Auckland: Auckland University Press 1978); Clarke Garret, *Respectable Folly: Millenarianism and the French Revolution in France and England* (Baltimore and London: Johns Hopkins University Press, 1975); J.F.C. Harrison, *The Second Coming: Popular Millenarianism 1780–1850* (London: Routledge and Kegan Paul, 1979); Morton Paley, "William Blake, The Prince of the Hebrews, and the Woman Clothed with the Sun," in *William Blake: Essays in Honour of Sir Geoffrey Keynes* (Oxford: Clarendon Press, 1973), 260–93; Peter J. Kitson, "Coleridge, Milton and the Millennium," *The Wordsworth Circle*, 17: 2 (1987), 61–6; idem, "Coleridge, Southey, and Richard Brothers: An Incident from Charles Lloyd's *Edmund Oliver*," *Notes and Queries*, 37: 4 (1990), 405–7.

19. For Priestley and Price, see Jack Fruchtman, *The Apocalyptic Politics of Richard Price and Joseph Priestley*, Transactions of the American Philosophical Society, 73: 4 (Philadelphia: American Philosophical Society, 1983).

20. Price, *Discourse on the Love of our Country*, op. cit., (fourth edn.), iii–vi.

21. Martin Madan, *Letters to J. Priestley . . . occasioned by his late controversial writings* (London: J. Dodsley, 1786); Joseph Priestley, *Theological and Miscellaneous Works*,

J.T. Rutt, ed., 25 vols. (London, 1817–32), 14. Samuel Horsley, Bishop of Rochester, also makes this kind of historical appeal similar to that of Burke when attacking the English Jacobins in his *A Sermon Preached . . . on Wednesday, January 30, 1793: Being the Anniversary of the Martyrdom of King Charles the First* (London, 1793). John Reeves, the founder of the Association for Preserving Liberty and Property Against Republicans and Levellers, makes a similar point in his *Thoughts on the English Government* (London: J. Owen, 1795), 36.

22. Priestley, *Works*, 15: 144–8.

23. See Keith Thomas, *Religion and the Decline of Magic: Studies in Popular Belief in Sixteenth- and Seventeenth-Century England* (Harmondsworth: Penguin, 1971), 233; G.E. Aylmer, "Unbelief in Seventeenth-Century England," in *Puritans and Revolutionaries: Essays in Seventeenth-Century History presented to Christopher Hill*, Donald Pennington and Keith Thomas, eds., (Oxford: Clarendon Press, 1978), 22–46.

24. Joseph Priestley, *Essay on the First Principles of Government* (1771), *Works*, 22: 57.

25. Joseph Priestley, *An History of the Christian Church* (1803), *Works*, 10: 401–10 (410).

26. Joseph Priestley, *Lectures on History and General Policy* (1785), *Works*, 24: 173–4.

27. Histories of the English Revolution proliferated in the nineteenth century, the fir substantial account being that of William Godwin's *History of the Commonweal:* (London: Henry Colburn, 1824–28), 4 vols. Godwin's main praise is for the Rump of 1649–53. For later nineteenth-century accounts of the Civil War period and Interregnum see John Burrow, *A Liberal Descent* (Cambridge: Cambridge University Press, 1981); idem, "Coleridge and the English Revolution," *Political Science*, 40 (1988), 128–41; Peter Karsten, *Patriot Heroes in England and America* (Madison, 1978); Biancamaria Fontana, *Rethinking the Politics of Commercial Society* (Cambridge: Cambridge University Press, 1985).

28. This essay has been attributed to both Obadiah Hulme and the younger Allan Ramsay. For its place in Norman Yoke theory, see Christopher Hill, *Puritanism and Revolution: Studies in Interpretation of the English Revolution of the 17th Century* (London: Secker and Warburg, 1958), 50–122 (95–6).

29. See Kitson, "The electric fluid of truth," op. cit., 42–4, 60.

30. For Burgh, see Gilbert Cahill, "James Burgh," in *Biographical Dictionary of British Radicals Since 1770*, Vol. 1: 1770–1832, J.O. Baylen and N.J. Gossman, eds. (Brighton: Harvester Press, 1979), 72–4; Caroline Robbins, *The Eighteenth-Century Commonwealthman*, op. cit., 364–8; Albert Goodwin, *The Friends of Liberty: The English Democratic Movement in the Age of the French Revolution* (London: Hutchinson, 1979), 53–5; Oscar and Mary Handlin, "James Burgh and American Revolutionary Theory," *Proceedings of the Massachusetts Historical Society*, 73 (1961), 38–57; Carla H. Hay, "The Making of a Radical: The Case of James Burgh," *The Journal of British Studies*, 28 (1979), 90–117; Kitson, "The electric fluid of truth," op. cit., 44–6.

31. J.C.D. Clarke, *English Society 1688–1832* (Cambridge: Cambridge University Press, 1985), 322–3.

32. See Blair Worden, *The Rump Parliament 1648–1653* (Cambridge: Cambridge University Press, 1974), 40, 33–60, 172–7; David Underdown, *Pride's Purge: Politics in the Puritan Revolution* (Oxford: Clarendon Press, 1971), 281–3.

33. Lutaud, *Des Révolutions d'Angleterre à la Revolution Française*, op. cit.

34. James Holstun, *A Rational Millennium* op. cit., 220–32 (222).

35. Burgh also wishes that the nation had "unheaded" Henry VIII, Mary I, James II as well as Charles I, "tyrants and murderers all" (*BPD*, 3: 166).

36. For Thelwall, see Charles Cestre, *John Thelwall: A Pioneer of Democracy and Social Reform* (London, 1906); Albert Goodwin, *The Friends of Liberty*, op. cit.; Nicholas Roe, *Wordsworth and Coleridge: The Radical Years* (Oxford: Clarendon Press, 1988).

37. John Thelwall, *Political Lectures. Volume the First* (London, 1795), 39, 51–4.

38. Burke, *Reflections*, op. cit., 342. Although horrified by the regicide, Burke's view of Cromwell was not surprisingly more positive than that of the radicals: "Cromwell had delivered England from an anarchy. His government, though military and despotic, had been regular and orderly. Under the iron, and under the yoke, the soil yielded its produce" (Burke, *Letter to a member of the National Assembly* (London, 1791), cited in *Reflections*, op. cit., 382n).

39. See notes 7 and 4; George Whalley, "The Bristol Library Borrowings of Southey and Coleridge 1793–98," *Library: Transactions of the Bibliographical Society*, fifth series, 4 (1949), 114–31; Kitson, "The electric fluid of truth," op. cit., 44–50.

40. See Kitson, "The electric fluid of truth," op. cit., 50–6.

41. I am indebted to James Holstun's treatment of these issues in chapters 4 and 5 of *A Rational Millennium*, op. cit.

42. For discussions of the deep structure of the historical imagination and related ideas, see Hayden White, *Metahistory: The Historical Imagination in Nineteenth-Century Europe* (Baltimore: Johns Hopkins University Press, 1973); idem, *The Content of the Form: Narrative Discourse and Historical Representation* (Baltimore: Johns Hopkins University Press, 1987); David Lowenstein, *Milton and the Drama of History: Historical Vision, Iconoclasm, and the Literary Imagination* (Cambridge: Cambridge University Press, 1990).

43. See Ian Wylie, *Young Coleridge and the Philosophers of Nature* (Oxford: Clarendon Press, 1989); H.W. Piper, *The Singing of Mount Abora: Coleridge's Use of Biblical Imagery and Natural Symbolism* (London: Associated University Press, 1987); Peter J. Kitson, "Coleridge, Milton and the Millennium," *The Wordsworth Circle*, 17 (1987), 61–6.

44. Scholars disagree about the extent of Coleridge's first-hand knowledge of Harrington before 1800. The editors of *LPR* believe it unlikely that he had read *Oceana* before this date (126n). Leask thinks it probable that Coleridge knew Harrington at first-hand by 1795 (and I would tend to agree), *Politics of Imagination*, op. cit., 223n. In any case, Coleridge was aware of the summaries of Harrington's thought in *BPD* and Moses Lowman's *A Dissertation on the Civil Government of the Hebrews* (London, 1740), see *LPR*, 122, and Morrow, *Coleridge's Political Thought*, op. cit., 29–31.

45. Holstun also points out that the Dutch Mennonite, Pieter Cornelisz Plockhoy, established a communist colony based on his utopian principles in New Netherland (Delaware), *A Rational Millennium*, op. cit., 60. The Manuels have pointed out that the communistic features of Pantisocracy were not common in this period, Frank E. and Fritzie P. Manuel, *Utopian Thought in the Western World* (Oxford: Blackwell, 1979), 736. For Pantisocracy, see J.R. MacGillivray, "The Pantisocratic Scheme and its Immediate Background," in M.W. Wallace, ed., *Studies in English* (Toronto, 1931), 131–69.

46. It is unlikely that Coleridge or Southey knew of Winstanley. Of the radicals of this time only Godwin appears to have first-hand knowledge of Digger writing. Godwin notes that the Digger's principle belief was that "God gave all things in common, and that every man has a right to the fruits of the earth," but remarks that the Diggers actions were "scarcely indeed worthy to be recorded." William Godwin, *History of the Commonwealth*, op. cit., 3: 81–2.

47. Leask, *Politics of the Imagination*, op. cit., 29.

48. See Kitson, "Coleridge, Milton and the Millennium," op. cit.; Wylie, *Young Coleridge and the Philosophers of Nature*, op. cit.

49. *The Political Works of James Harrington*, J.G.A. Pocock, ed. (Cambridge: Cambridge University Press, 1977), 181–5, 213.

50. Holstun, *A Rational Millenniun*, op. cit., 171.

51. See Christopher Hill, "James Harrington and the People," in *Puritanism and Revolution*, op. cit., 299–313; Holstun, *Rational Millennium*, op. cit., 166–245.

52. Caroline Robbins argues that Lowman had confused Harrington's *Oceana* with the theocratic republic of the Jewish constitution, *Eighteenth-Century Commonwealthman*, op. cit., 242. However, as Nigel Leask points out, "Lowman's work is

closely based on another of Harrington's treatises republished in the Toland edition, the second book of the *Art of Lawgiving* (1659) which located the ideal of *Oceana* within the narrative of Christian eschatology"; Leask, *The Politics of Imagination*, op. cit., 34–5.

53. *Complete Prose Works of John Milton*, op. cit., 7: 424, 450. See Holstun, *A Rational Millennium*, op. cit., 246–65; Kitson, "The electric fluid," op. cit., 54–6.

54. In a letter to Southey, Coleridge takes his allegory of the cockatrice much further, "The Cockatrice is emblematic of Monarchy – a *monster* generated by *Ingratitude* on *Absurdity*. When Serpents *sting*, the only Remedy is – to *kill* the *Serpent*, and *besmear* the *Wound* with the *Fat*. Would you desire better *Sympathy*?" *The Collected Letters of Samuel Taylor Coleridge*, E.L. Griggs, ed. (Oxford: Clarendon Press, 1956–71), 6 vols., 1: 84.

55. In addition to James Holstun's discussion of these terms in *A Rational Millennium*, I am also indebted to Laura Lunger Knoppers, "Milton's *The Readie and Easie Way* and the English jeremiad," in *Politics, Poetics and Hermeneutics in Milton's Prose*, David Lowenstein and James Grantham Turner, eds. (Cambridge: Cambridge University Press, 1990), 213–25; T.N. Corns, *Uncloistered Virtue: English Political Literature, 1640–60*, forthcoming.

56. Morrow, *Coleridge's Political Thought*, op. cit., 31.